The Practical Guide to
SUCCESSFUL
GARDENING

In collaboration with
The Royal Horticultural Society

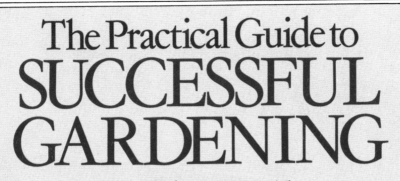

The Practical Guide to
SUCCESSFUL
GARDENING

In collaboration with
The Royal Horticultural Society

Alec Bristow

Foreword by Chris Brickell
Director of the RHS Garden at Wisley

Photography by Paul Roberts

A MERMAID BOOK

The Practical Guide to
Successful Gardening
was conceived, edited
and designed by
Holland & Clark Limited, London

Consultant
Elspeth Napier
(Editor, the Royal Horticultural Society)

Photographer
Paul Roberts

Artists
Nicolas Hall
Martin Smillie
Roger Twinn

Designer
Julian Holland

Editor
Philip Clark

Additional text by Ann Bonar

First published in Great Britain in 1985 by
Webb & Bower (Publishers) Ltd
9 Colleton Crescent, Exeter,
Devon, EX2 4BY

This paperback edition first published in
Great Britain in 1987 by
Mermaid Books
27 Wrights Lane, London
with Webb & Bower (Publishers) Ltd

Copyright © 1985 by Holland & Clark Ltd

British Library Cataloguing in Publication Data

Bristow, Alec
 The practical guide to successful
 gardening.
 1. Gardening
 I. Title   II. Royal Horticultural Society
 635   SB450.97

 ISBN 0-7181-2840-0

Contents

Foreword

by Chris Brickell

Director of the Royal Horticultural Society's Garden at Wisley, Surrey

In an era when every year sees a plethora of books on all aspects of gardening, it is a great pleasure to be asked to write the foreword to an eminently practical and stimulating book based on the author's own wide experience and knowledge. Many recent horticultural publications carry the clear imprint of the professional researcher, whose first-hand knowledge of the subject matter is scanty. However thoroughly research is carried out, such a book is unlikely to possess that indefinable spark of quality necessary to ensure that it becomes a standard work in its field.

Alec Bristow's background knowledge and expertise in a very wide range of horticultural topics from orchids to vegetables fits him extremely well for the difficult task of preparing what is virtually a year-long *vade-mecum* for the gardener. *The Practical Guide to Successful Gardening* is not only a month-by-month gardening calendar of work to be carried out in the flower, fruit or vegetable sections, or in the glasshouse. It also covers a wide range of gardening techniques and the author places considerable emphasis on the importance of choosing and growing the right plants in the right places. Ideas are given of suitable plants to grow for particular conditions and periods of the year as well as suggestions on improving cultivation techniques, maintenance and garden planning.

Mr Bristow has used the Royal Horticultural Society's Garden at Wisley to illustrate many of the ideas put forward and the plants he recommends should be more widely grown. The Society's purpose has always been to stimulate, encourage and improve horticulture in all its branches and Alec Bristow's authoritative and practical guide to successful gardening admirably complements these aims and ideals.

Chris Brickell

Garden Design and Planning

Few garden sites are exactly alike; even plots of the same size differ in such important matters as type of soil, aspect, exposure, locality and whether the ground is level or sloping. In addition, few gardeners are likely to share exactly the same tastes and needs.

It is therefore quite impossible to provide ready-made plans for the purpose of producing gardens to standard designs. Each garden has a character of its own; in that lies a great deal of its attraction.

All the same, the making of a garden need not be, and should not be, a haphazard affair. There are certain guiding principles to help the gardener achieve a successful result, and these are illustrated in the pages that follow.

The most practical help towards the creation of a satisfying design is the example of others. Visiting gardens and noting down pleasing features of design and construction, together with the names of particularly appealing plants, both individually and in association, will suggest many ideas that, with any necessary modifications, can be applied to the home plot.

The model gardens at Wisley, designed to show what can be achieved with some typical small sites, provide a constant source of planning ideas throughout the seasons. Hundreds of thousands of people visit them during the year, not only to admire their beauty but to examine the practical ways in which they provide answers to design problems that often arise.

Among the commonest of such problems at the present time is what to do with the typical narrow, oblong strips belonging to houses in densely built up areas, where very little space has been left for gardens. The first model design demonstrates some of the ways in which such an unpromising shape and limited area can be put to best advantage. The other model gardens planned for different purposes demonstrate many more of the principles of successful design in action.

The small town garden

If, like so many gardeners nowadays, you live in a town, it is likely that the plot of ground you will be faced with for the garden will be a rectangular strip. If the house is semi-detached or part of a terrace, that strip is likely to be narrow in relation to its length, forming a kind of corridor enclosed by a boundary fence. How can such a site be made into an attractive garden? That was the question which the first of the Wisley model gardens has been designed to answer in a practical way.

Though fences can to some extent be softened in appearance, if not completely disguised, by covering them with climbers, the result of a narrow field of vision bounded by straight lines on either side is to draw the eye to the back fence, and so exaggerate the corridor-like effect.

To overcome this, the eye must be stopped, guided in direction and helped to rest upon other things. Several ways of doing so are demonstrated in this typical town plot, laid out with the needs of a young couple in mind, both of them working and with a limited amount of time to give to gardening.

The four main methods used here to arrest the eye are: dividing the plot, using curves, creating focal points and constantly changing the picture.

One of the principles of good planning is that a garden should not show all its attractions at once. Here, dividing the plot into sections has ensured that fresh viewpoints will be discovered during a walk through the garden. The section with the lawn, linked to the house by a patio in the foreground, is the largest. The distant part is hidden from view by a hedge planted at right angles to the side boundary. This hedge does not extend the whole width of the plot; the reason is both to allow access through the path along the left-hand side and also to give a promising glimpse of what lies beyond without revealing too much.

The second element in the design is its use of curves. Their value lies largely in the fact that there are few if any straight lines in nature. Even the most regular of plots can be made more attractive and less box-like by a curve in the right place. It is important, however, not to overdo the use of curves.

Too many of them are likely to produce a result that looks fussy, restless and contrived. In the model garden shown here, the single bold curve where lawn meets flower-bed is balanced in appearance by the more formal straight line of the paved walk at the left-hand side of the plot.

The third element of the design is the provision of focal points. Wherever a person stands or sits in a garden, there should always be some feature to attract the eye and hold the attention. In this example, viewed from where the house is assumed to stand, the curve of the lawn draws the eye along the border towards the hedge and from there to the walk leading beyond. As each season progresses, the growth and coming into flower of more and more plants in the border will catch the eye on its journey. Many things besides plants can provide focal points: a well placed statue, a sundial, a bird-bath, a stone urn or other ornamental container. The table and chairs in the sitting-out area beyond the end of the walk give the far section visual interest, and may provide a resting place for the eye as well as the body.

The fourth element in keeping up the visual interest is to present a constantly changing picture. By careful choice of plants a garden can be made to provide something that will give pleasure all the year round: not only beautiful flowers but attractive foliage and fruits, coloured and patterned bark, even graceful branches sparkling with frost on cold winter days. A plan of the model town garden is given overleaf on page 12, followed by an examination of the constructional features, together with a selection of the plants that were chosen to make it a place to enjoy all the year round.

Right Photographed at the Royal Horticultural Society's garden at Wisley in early summer, the model town garden has been designed for a typical small rectangular plot. The design demonstrates several ways of overcoming the tendency of such a site to have a hard, geometrical look. The garden is assumed to be viewed from a paved terrace at the highest point of the site and immediately next to the house.

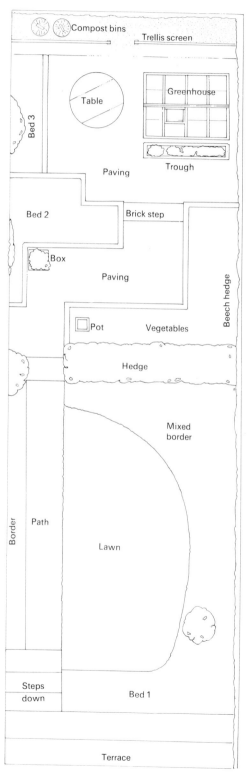

Left A model town garden for a typical narrow rectangular site, measuring seventy-two by twenty-four feet (22 × 7.3 m), with a gentle downward slope from a paved terrace adjoining the house. To avoid a corridor-like effect, the plot has been divided into sections, each of them level and linked by formal flagged paving and steps, as shown on the plan.

To balance the formality of the lawn's straight edge on its west side where it adjoins the pathway, it meets the border to its north and east in a bold curve.

Beyond a dividing hedge is a vegetable bed with a brickwork surround beside a paved area, on the opposite side of which is a bed displaying a mixed collection of flowering plants.

A brick step leads to a further paved area where a table and chairs may be set out during the summer. A greenhouse occupies one side and a flower bed the other. Beyond that is a trellis screen, with compost bins behind it.

A selection of plants used in the design of this model town garden will be found in the next column.

The main border skirting the lawn, backed by a beech hedge to the east, contains a mixed collection of shrubs and herbaceous plants, designed to be attractive throughout the year. Starting from the house end, shrubs include *Mahonia* 'Charity', *Potentilla* 'Elizabeth', *Deutzia* 'Rosealind', *Fuchsia magellanica* 'Versicolor', *Elaeagnus pungens* 'Maculata' and *Acer palmatum* 'Bloodgood'; at the front are patches of *Erica × darleyensis* 'Silberschmelze' and *E. carnea* (now *herbacea*) 'Vivellii'. Herbaceous plants include *Achillea* 'Coronation Gold', *Centaurea* 'John Coutts', *Helleborus kochii* 'Bowles' Yellow', *Lythrum salicaria* 'Zigeunerblut', *Alchemilla mollis*, *Agapanthus* Headbourne Hybrids, *Hosta undulata*, *Aster dumosus* 'Rosenwichtel', *Inula ensifolia* 'Compacta' and *Stachys olympica* (*byzantina*). Bulbs include *Lilium* 'Enchantment' and *Narcissus* 'Bawn Boy'.

Bed 1, photographed in spring with a display of tulips and wallflowers, will later contain summer bedding plants.

The dividing hedge at the north of the border is the golden-foliaged conifer *Chamaecyparis lawsoniana* 'Mason's Orange'. Opposite, across the path, is the narrowly conical *Chamaecyparis lawsoniana* 'Allumii', with soft blue-grey foliage.

The fence on the west boundary is clothed with climbers and wall-plants. In sequence from the house end these include *Rosa* 'Golden Showers', *Hedera colchica* 'Dentata Variegata', *Clematis viticella* 'Abundance' and *Pyracantha* 'Mohave'. Ground cover plants along the narrow bed include *Pachysandra terminalis* and *Pulmonaria* 'Mrs Moon'.

Beds 2 and 3 contain an assortment of herbaceous perennials interplanted with annuals and biennials, backed by *Chaenomeles speciosus* and *Lonicera periclymenum* against the wall. Trained on the trellis at the far end are *Ceanothus* 'Delight' at one side and *Weigela florida* at the other.

The containers standing at the corners of the paved area and the trough beside the greenhouse are used for colourful summer bedding plants such as french marigolds and pelargoniums.

The vegetable plot produces salad crops, carrots, beans and marrows, together with tomatoes and peppers from the greenhouse.

The Established Garden

In a large number of cases a town garden will be attached to an old house – very likely part of a terrace – and will have been inherited from previous owners or tenants who designed it to suit their own preferences and needs. Along with more permanent features such as steps and paths, it will probably contain a collection of established plants, which may or may not be to the liking of the new occupier.

In such circumstances the first question to be answered is how far alterations should be made. Where the present layout is acceptable there is little point in making changes merely for changes' sake; on the other hand, the new occupier does not want to be forced to live with the tastes of the previous one.

Where constructional features are concerned it is often best to leave them alone, so long as they are not unsightly and are in a satisfactory condition. If not, they should be repaired or replaced as soon as possible. A wobbly step or unsteady paving stone which predecessors had learned to avoid can cause a nasty accident to an unwary newcomer. (For step-by-step details of construction work, see pages 186–187.)

Though plant material is usually much easier to shift around and replace, it is a good idea to consider first whether any of the existing plants should be retained. An established tree or shrub that is healthy and thriving might be thought worth keeping so long as it is attractive. A new one might not find the conditions quite as suitable, and even if it did it would most likely take several years to reach a similar size.

Herbaceous plants are in a different category. They are usually modest in price, and most of them take no more than a year or two to reach a good size; indeed, many of them give their best display within two or three seasons from the time of planting. After that they may need to be split up and replanted (see page 197) to prevent them from becoming overcrowded.

It is possible that herbaceous plants left behind by previous occupiers may be first-class. The chances are, however, that they could be replaced by better ones; for comparison, see what nurserymen have to offer, and study the lists in this book.

The New Garden

Consider next the case of a completely new garden, attached to a house that has just been built, perhaps as part of a newly developed housing estate on the outskirts of a town. Most likely the house will be semi-detached, and the site, though probably somewhat broader than that of the small town garden, will once again be oblong and bounded on three sides by a fence. The ground, until recently part of a field, is bare except perhaps for coarse grass, and maybe weeds that have grown up during building operations. There are also likely to be a few heaps of builder's rubble left lying around.

It will save a considerable amount of labour later on if as a first step a scale plan is made of the site before any design work is started. Mistakes made on paper can easily be rubbed out and corrected, but mistakes made in the garden itself may need a great deal of hard work to put them right, and may even remain for ever, causing much continuous and unnecessary labour. So never skimp the number of hours spent on the plan to begin with; it may save many times that number of hours afterwards. A good general rule in starting to make a new garden is this: never do any work on the site till it has been worked out on paper first.

With a new property there may be a copy available of the site drawing required by the local planning authority before permission to build was given. Unfortunately that drawing may be on too small a scale to be of much use. It is best to make the plan as large in scale as possible, so that there is plenty of room to mark in every detail. A great help is a large sheet of graph-paper, which will save much time and effort.

Start by measuring not only the length and width of the site but the diagonals to the angles of the boundary fences from each corner of the house; this is because plots of ground are often not quite as straight as they might seem. When the boundaries have been drawn on the graph-paper, ink them in, together with the positions of such things as drains and the covers of inspection chambers. The reason for using ink is that these items are fixed. The design can be added in soft pencil, to allow for alterations.

The family garden

The design of the second model garden at Wisley demonstrates what can be done with an average-sized plot to suit the needs of a family consisting of a young couple with small children.

The first problem to be solved is how to create a garden that will satisfy different and in some ways opposing requirements. Though it will have to stand a good deal of rough treatment as a playground, there is no reason why, with skilful planning, it should not present an attractive and colourful picture throughout the year. At the same time it should be designed to need as little work as possible to maintain it. The demands of a young family tend to take up a large part of their parents' time and energy, at weekends as well as during the week, leaving little over for attending to the garden.

The plot shown here has been divided basically into two sections. The dominant feature of the near section is the lawn, fully visible from the house (from which the scene is assumed to be viewed), so that adults can watch small children playing on it, and help is at hand in case of accidents. It will be noticed that there is also a garden seat beside the lawn at the left of the picture against the boundary fence, so that the supervising adult can sometimes sit outside to watch, perhaps to join in the game, or to provide a comforting lap for a tired child.

It is important to make sure that the grass used is suitable for its purpose. The finer lawns, much admired for their velvet-like texture, are unfortunately not able to withstand constant heavy wear; so if the lawn is intended for games a grass mixture designed for that purpose should be used. Most seedsmen and garden centres sell suitable hardwearing mixtures – which usually have the additional practical advantage that they are cheaper than the finer ones.

To revert from the type of grass to the design, the illustration shows how a short lawn has been given an appearance of depth. The eye is drawn diagonally across it from front right to back left, guided by the curves of the adjoining beds. The tree standing just beyond the far left boundary of the lawn provides a focal point for the eye to rest upon at the end of its journey.

Nothing has been placed on the lawn in the demonstration plot, but on the lawns of real family gardens there may be climbing frames, slides or swings. A wide range is available from many garden centres, sports shops and department stores. Several models are designed to be erected easily for use during the milder part of the year and quickly dismantled for storing in a shed or garage during the winter. Be careful to buy only those makes that conform to recognized safety standards; they may cost more, but they are likely to last longer and still have a resale value when the children grow out of them.

It is not only the lawn that needs to be able to stand some rough treatment from a young family. Plants in beds and borders are likely to receive an occasional direct hit from a ball as the result of a wild kick, a smash by bat or racquet, or a missed catch. The most sensible precaution is to grow only plants that are tough enough to survive such incidents without too much harm. There are several robust shrubs and other sturdy plants well suited to such conditions. After the removal of damaged portions many of them rapidly replace what has been lost with vigorous new growth. Above all, it is unwise to attempt to grow rare, delicate and expensive plants while the children are young; even if no disasters occur, the fear that they might can lead to friction, and even to attempts – usually futile, as well as deeply resented – to declare parts of the garden out of bounds.

The best way to help children to develop an interest in gardening is to give them little patches of ground of their own, to grow what they like. To avoid disappointment, it is a good idea to give the children something very easy to start with, such as some hardy annuals or a few carrots or radishes.

Right A model garden designed for a family with young children. The central feature is the lawn, intended to be used as a play area and therefore composed of a mixture of grasses that will stand up to a considerable amount of wear. The border plants have also been chosen for their resistance to damage. Half the garden has been designed to supply the family with plenty of fresh fruit and vegetables.

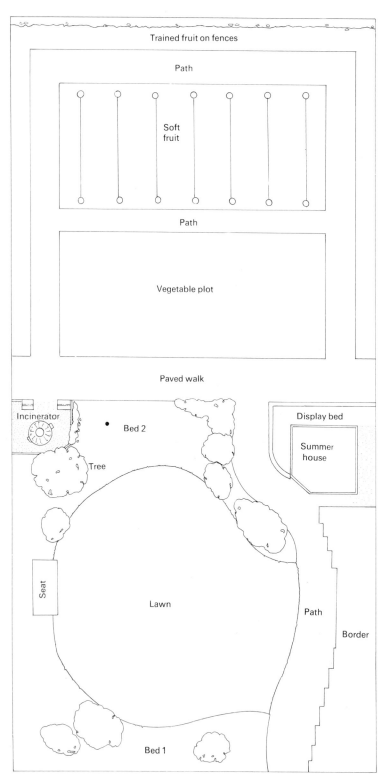

Trained fruit on fences

Path

Soft
fruit

Path

Vegetable plot

Paved walk

Incinerator

Bed 2

Display bed

Tree

Summer
house

Seat

Lawn

Path

Border

Bed 1

Left This plan of the model garden illustrated on the previous page demonstrates how a typical rectangular site, measuring seventy-three by thirty-eight feet (approximately twenty-two by twelve metres), has been adapted to suit the needs of a family with young children.

The plot, which is level and almost exactly twice as long as it is wide, has been divided across the middle into two nearly square sections, separated by a paved walk. The section adjoining the house has been designed as a pleasure garden, and the other section has in its turn been divided into two halves, the first to form a vegetable plot and the second a fruit garden.

This particular site runs almost due north from the house, so that in fine weather it receives sun for most of the day, with the east-facing boundary on the left of the plan getting more of the morning light and the west-facing boundary on the right getting more of the afternoon and evening sun.

To avoid the hard, angular effect that can all too easily result from a square plot flanked by boundary fences, the lawn, which is the dominant feature of the pleasure garden, has been given a boldly curved outline, and its axis has been turned diagonally to give it an appearance of greater length. Another effect of the curves has been to vary the width of the beds bordering the lawn.

To continue the informal treatment of this section of the design, the flagged path on the right leading to the summer-house and beyond has also been given a curve. As a result, the border between it and the boundary fence on the right broadens at each end and narrows in the middle, giving the opportunity for a varied mixture of plants.

The distant section of the plot, divided off by a paved walk and framed on one side by the summer-house and on the other by a fencing screen, has been made entirely formal, with straight paths and rectangular beds, both to make its management easier and to emphasize its utilitarian nature.

Bed 1 starts at the junction of path and house terrace with a group of heathers, including *Calluna vulgaris* 'Sunset' and two cultivars of *Erica cinerea*, 'Atrorubens' and 'Hookstone White'. Other plants include *Berberis thunbergii* 'Atropurpurea Nana', *Potentilla* 'Woodbridge Gold', *Dianthus* 'Swan Lake', *Salvia nemorosa* 'Superba' and *Helleborus niger*. Several daffodils have been included in the planting for spring colour. The dense, rounded bush seen in the photograph at the apex of the bed is *Hebe rakaiensis*. Next to the fence is *Rosa rugosa* 'Nyveldt's White', and against the fence are *Garrya × thuretii* and *Jasminum beesianum*.

On each side of the seat are dwarf rhododendrons. Beyond the seat are *Centaurea* 'John Coutts' and a group of *Agapanthus* Headbourne Hybrids, with several bulbs and corms in front, including *Anemone* De Caen.

The tree at the angle of the fence and the screen is the ornamental crab *Malus tschonoskii*, with the large, handsome leaves of *Crambe cordifolia* making a spreading mound of green beside it.

Bed 2, curving round beyond the tree, contains a mixture of herbaceous plants, including *Aster acris, A. thomsonii* 'Nanus', *Chrysanthemum maximum* 'Bishopstone', *Anaphalis triplinervis, Salvia nemorosa* 'Mainacht' and *Bergenia purpurascens*. A planting of shrubs where the bed reaches the curved path includes *Fuchsia magellanica* 'Thompsonii', *Hibiscus syriacus* 'Woodbridge' and a group of *Calluna vulgaris* 'Sunrise'.

The border to the east of the path gives a colourful display of spring bulbs followed by summer bedding plants. The small bed beside the summerhouse is planted during the summer with vivid subjects such as carnations and pelargoniums.

The vegetable plot provides the family with a succession of crops throughout the season, including beetroot, cabbages, carrots, cucumbers, lettuces, leeks, onions and beans (french and runner).

The soft fruit plot, enclosed in netting against birds, includes raspberries, black and red currants and gooseberries. Trained against the fence and also protected by netting, are cordon apples and pears, fan-trained peaches, morello cherry and a grape.

Children's Gardens

If children are to be given plots of their own, it is important that these should be in the most favourable positions possible to produce rapid and satisfactory results. All too often children have to make do with the least promising places, frequently in deep shade, where during warm weather the ground tends to become parched because insufficient rain reaches it, and in cold, wet weather constant drips from buildings or trees, together with stagnant air, create dank conditions which promote disease. In such discouraging circumstances it is natural that children lose interest.

Sites for children's gardens should be as open as possible, and the soil should be well cultivated and fertile. An important point is that such plots should be easily reached by a hard path; this will not only make gardening easier and more inviting for the children but should considerably reduce the amount of earth that is apt to be brought into the house on the boots of young gardeners. A suitable site on the plan opposite might be a small patch at the end of the vegetable garden. This would have the advantage that during routine cultivation the adults would be able to keep an eye on progress, and perhaps lend a helping hand on the quiet by removing weed seedlings before the young plants are smothered.

Where two or more children are to be given gardens, it is wise to have these clearly separated from each other; otherwise there are likely to be endless boundary disputes about who owns what.

Where the garden will be used by very young children, a warning is needed against including potentially harmful plants. Laburnum seeds are well known to be poisonous; other dangerous seeds and fruits that can prove fatally attractive include those of the holly, spindle-tree, cherry laurel, ivy, lily-of-the-valley and lupin.

Though the choice of plants for the garden must be determined by personal preference and by such factors as nature of soil, position and aspect, the principles on which the planting scheme for the model family garden have been based may be applied with advantage to the planning of other gardens with similar requirements.

The enthusiast's garden

Although this is one of the largest of the model layouts at Wisley, it is still quite a small garden, such as might well be found attached to a house in one of the outer suburbs. However, to quote the RHS Garden Adviser who was responsible for its design, 'The size of a garden has little to do with its quality; it is probably easier to maintain conditions of good cultivation in a small garden than in a larger one'.

However true that may be, there is a problem in designing a small garden for the enthusiast who wishes to grow a wide range of plants and has both sufficient interest and sufficient time to enjoy them and to give them the attention that they need. How is it possible in a limited space to provide the variety of conditions that plants of widely different habits and habitats require if they are to thrive and repay the care and devotion that they will require?

To establish the right conditions, several gardens-within-a-garden have been constructed, giving different types of plant the special situations, aspects, soil conditions and micro-climates that they prefer. To hold these separate units together in a coherent whole, vistas have been created, with points of interest for the eye to focus on in every direction.

Full advantage has been taken of the downhill slope of the site from its highest point in the foreground of the picture. The lower level has been used for a water garden, and the upper levels for the construction of a rock garden overlooking the pool. By means of these two linked features the right conditions have been created for two types of plant with opposite demands. The water plants below must have constantly wet roots, and the alpines above need rapid and efficient drainage.

To extend the range of these attractive plants so as to include many that are unable to survive severe cold, and others which, though completely hardy, are likely to be killed by the wet conditions commonly experienced in the open during winter, a greenhouse, including a rear shed section, and a cold frame have been included in the plan. These are unobtrusively sited in a paved area at the far right-hand corner.

The original slope of the ground, which was gradual and continuous for the whole length of the plot, has been considerably modified during the construction of the garden. The wide planting area in the left foreground of the picture has been built up with soil excavated from other parts of the site, so that its far side forms a bank immediately above the winding pathway, surfaced with crazy paving, which can be seen just beyond it and which curves round in a horseshoe to continue on both sides.

On the far side of the path the gradient continues, with a rock garden and a broadly curving bed sloping downhill towards the pool and its surroundings.

The lawn, which occupies the largest area in the centre of the garden, has been made level, as have the paved walks that flank it on either side. That on the left, approached from the upper levels by a flight of stone steps, is straight and formal, its formality emphasized by the wall bounding it on the left-hand side and the regularly spaced posts, on which climbers have been trained, along the other side.

This formality is offset by the flowing curves and counter-curves where the lawn meets the borders at its far end and along its right-hand edge. The irregular outline of the pool, and the outcrops of stone jutting out over the rim in places so as to break the line of the margin, help to create a natural appearance and provide a link between the less formal treatment of the areas in the foreground of the picture and the more formal treatment of those in the background. Note the focal point introduced by a decorative plant container on a plinth placed beside the path at the apex of the large bed bordering the lawn.

Right The model garden pictured here has been designed for the gardening enthusiast who has not only a deep interest in plants but plenty of time to give to studying and attending to their requirements. The sloping site has been turned into a series of gardens within a garden, providing the necessary conditions for groups of plants coming from widely varying habitats and having very different requirements.

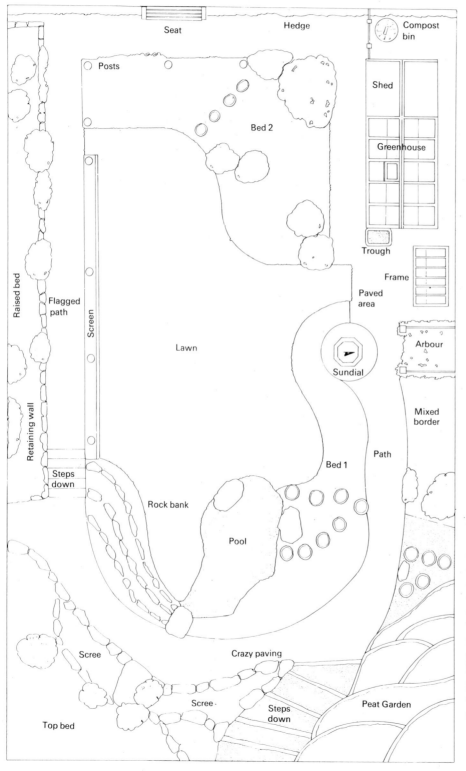

Seat   Hedge   Compost bin

Posts

Shed

Bed 2

Greenhouse

Trough

Frame

Paved area

Raised bed

Flagged path

Screen

Arbour

Lawn

Sundial

Mixed border

Retaining wall

Path

Bed 1

Steps down

Rock bank

Pool

Scree

Crazy paving

Scree

Steps down

Peat Garden

Top bed

Left The plan shows how a comparatively small site, measuring eighty-two by fifty-four feet (twenty-five by sixteen metres) has been used to construct a garden for the enthusiast who wishes to grow several different types of plant, many of which have widely divergent needs in such matters as nature of soil, drainage and aspect.

The original continuous slope of the ground has been considerably altered to create different levels. The beds shown at the base of the plan have been banked up and the soil texture changed to produce scree conditions on the left of the entrance steps and a terraced peat bed on the right.

A further slope beyond the cross-path of crazy paving, forming a rock bank on one side and a sloping bed on the other, leads to an informal pool and beyond that to a level lawn flanked by curving beds containing a selection of herbaceous plants and shrubs.

A straight path at the left of the plan, reached by a flight of steps, is flanked on the boundary side by a raised bed enclosed by a retaining wall and on the lawn side by a screen of posts and rails, covered with roses and other climbers.

The lines of circles beyond the peat bed, between the pool and the path and across bed 2 represent stepping places made of sawn lengths of branch embedded in the ground.

The following is a brief selection from the wide range of plants included in the design. The top bed on the left of the plan, composed of sandy loam, is planted with a wide range of spring bulbs and corms, including species and cultivars of *Chionodoxa, Crocus, Muscari* and *Narcissus*, with several compact flowering shrubs, including *Rhododendron* 'Elizabeth', *Hypericum* 'Hidcote' and the excellent berrying shrub *Viburnum dilitatum*.

Sloping downhill beyond a line of rocks is a scree, occupied by plants that thrive in the conditions of free drainage and full sun which it provides. Among them are species of *Androsace, Anthemis, Calceolaria, Campanula, Dianthus, Diascia, Epilobium, Gypsophila, Leontopodium, Lewisia, Nierembergia, Oxalis, Penstemon, Papaver, Phlox, Ptilotrichum, Ranunculus, Saxifraga* and *Sempervivum*. At points along the edge of the path and steps are low-growing and prostrate shrubs, such as *Sorbus reducta* and *Cytisus procumbens*, and dwarf conifers, including *Chamaecyparis obtusa* 'Juniperoides', *Juniperus communis* 'Compressa' and *J.* 'Silver Lining'.

Across the steps is a peat garden of terraced construction on a north-facing slope, suitable for plants that enjoy cool, moist, lime-free conditions. Among the herbaceous subjects are species of *Primula* from Asia. Others include species of *Corydalis, Cyananthus, Dodecatheon, Gentiana, Haberlea, Jeffersonia, Meconopsis, Ourisia, Ramonda, Saxifraga* and *Soldanella*. Low-growing shrubs include many species of *Arctostaphylos, Cassiope, Gaultheria, Pernettya* and *Vaccinium*, together with several dwarf rhododendrons and the prostrate willow *Salix serpyllifolia*.

The mixed border beyond the peat garden contains an assortment of shrubs, including *Azara serrata, Deutzia longifolia, Fuchsia magellanica* 'Variegata', *Lonicera × purpusii*, *Potentilla* 'Red Ace' and the dwarf almond *Prunus tenella* 'Fire Hill'. Among the herbaceous plants are *Doronicum austriacum, Liriope* 'Majestic' and *Sedum* 'Ruby Glow'. Bulbs include cultivars of *Narcissus* for spring flowering and *Nerine bowdenii* for late summer and autumn. At the end of the border an abour has been constructed which is festooned with the golden-leaved hop *Humulus lupulus* 'Aureus'.

The rock bank, across the path that curves past the scree, descends in tiers to the lawn, giving a mainly east-facing slope. It is planted with a collection of choice alpines, including species of *Aethionema, Antennaria, Aquilegia, Arabis, Armeria, Campanula, Dianthus, Draba, Gentiana, Myosotis, Phlox, Saxifraga* and *Wahlenbergia*. Bulbs and corms include *Iris danfordiae, I. reticulata, Crocus minimus* and *Tulipa tarda*.

The pool contains a selection of water lilies and other aquatics, including water-hawthorn, *Aponogeton distachyus*, and golden club, *Orontium aquaticum*. Plants for the shallows and around the margins include candelabra primulas, astilbes and hostas, *Acorus calamus, Caltha palustris, Geum rivale* and *Tiarella cordifolia*.

Bed 1, sloping down to the pool and continuing between the lawn and the path, contains mixed herbaceous plants and shrubs, starting at the rock bank end with the popular dwarf golden conifer *Chamaecyparis obtusa* 'Nana Aurea'. Shrubs include dwarf rhododendrons and the hummock-forming *Genista lydia*, with slender shoots smothered in early summer with bright yellow flowers. Herbaceous plants include species of *Alchemilla, Baptisia, Bergenia, Delphinium, Dicentra, Geranium, Heuchera, Ranunculus, Veronica* and *Valeriana*.

Bed 2 contains a selection of herbaceous plants. These include many similar to those in bed 1, with the addition of species of *Agapanthus, Aquilegia, Aster, Anchusa, Brunnera, Cephalaria, Echinops, Geum, Kniphofia, Lysimachia, Paeonia, Pulmonaria, Solidago* and *Symphytum*.

At the far end of the bed and along the straight edge of the lawn, dividing it from the path, are screens of posts and rails covered with climbers, including roses, clematis and *Akebia × pentaphylla*.

Between the path and the western boundary of the garden a retaining wall has been built of stones, enclosing a raised bed. This provides ideal conditions for a number of rock-garden plants, both herbaceous and shrubby. The wall accommodates and displays to perfection many crevice plants and trailers, both growing between the stones and cascading down from the bed above.

The disabled person's garden

Many of those who find great pleasure in gardening are disabled people, whose range of activity is restricted by physical handicaps. Their numbers are increased by the elderly, who form an ever larger proportion of the population and who, even if not handicapped, are not as active as they were.

It was with the special needs of these people in mind that the Royal Horticultural Society, in conjunction with the Disabled Living Foundation, created the fourth of the model gardens at Wisley, pictured here.

Though the garden is on different levels, steps have been entirely excluded from the design. Gentle slopes, wide enough for unimpeded passage, have been constructed instead, to meet the needs of those whose disability confines them to a wheelchair. It will be noticed that all paths from one part of the garden to another have been paved right up to the walled beds, in order to allow wheelchairs to be drawn in close beside them, so that the occupant can enjoy the flowers and plants in comfort, and can attend to such jobs as weeding and dead-heading without having to strain forward.

Wheelchair cases, however, probably represent no more than one in thirty of all people suffering from some form of physical disability which can make gardening difficult, or at least rob it of some of its enjoyment. There are dozens of different degrees of disability, ranging from the occasional twinge of rheumatism to chronic arthritis. If the infirmities of old age are included, it has been estimated that perhaps one person in seven has enough of a handicap to interfere with gardening to some extent; and with life expectancy increasing, that proportion is rising.

The needs of disabled people confined to wheelchairs are very similar to those of the larger number who are able to walk – even if only slowly, with the help of sticks, frames or crutches – and the model garden caters for both categories.

The wall-to-wall paving between the raised beds not only facilitates movement, on foot or on wheels, but has eliminated all weeds at ground level, and so has also eliminated the need for stooping and bending, the most taxing of operations for disabled people.

The paving which can be seen clearly in the foreground of the picture is made of identical, precision-made units cast in a mould and laid to a pattern that gives the impression of having been woven. The texture of the surface has been designed not only to be pleasing to the eye but to avoid the risk of skidding and falling over – a very important consideration, especially with infirm and elderly people, who can only too easily lose their footing.

All the beds are raised, the sides being built of brick or stone, mostly to a height of about eighteen inches (forty-six cm), which is approximately the same distance above the ground as that at which the occupant of a wheelchair sits, and involves very little stooping by those people who are able to walk.

One very important point to note is that these beds must not be too wide for the disabled gardener's reach; otherwise it will not be possible to cultivate the beds from the sides without having to strain. The beds in the model garden are mostly about four feet (120 cm) wide and accessible from both sides, so that it is possible to tend every part in comfort.

After completion of the building of the outer walls, the beds are filled with soil or a compost mixture, and when this has fully settled the chosen plants may be put in place. One advantage of this method of gardening in artificially constructed beds is that, as with growing in smaller containers, different compost mixtures can be used according to the needs of different kinds of plant. For example, species that cannot tolerate lime, such as rhododendrons and most heathers, can be grown in lime-free compost even where the soil is unsuitable.

Right A model garden specially designed to cater for the needs of disabled and elderly people. The raised beds, enclosed within walls of brick and stone, allow the disabled gardener to enjoy and tend a wide variety of plants at a comfortable level without stooping or stretching. Non-slip paving and gentle slopes instead of steps assist both those who walk with difficulty and those who are confined to wheelchairs.

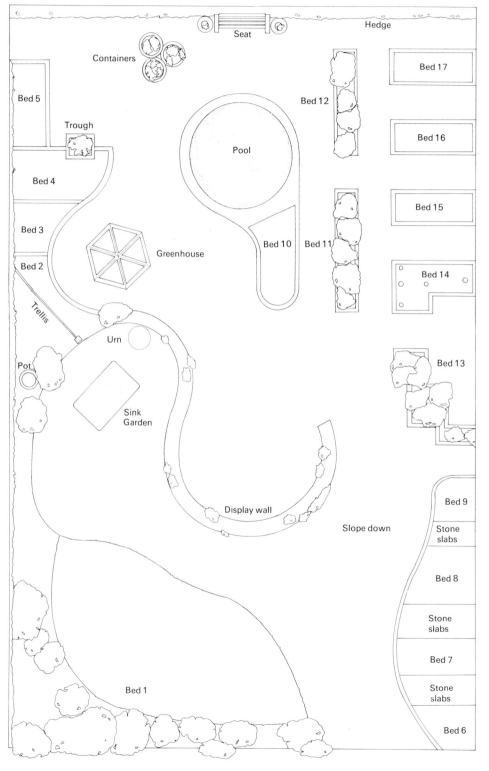

Seat

Hedge

Containers

Bed 17

Bed 5

Bed 12

Bed 16

Trough

Pool

Bed 15

Bed 4

Bed 3

Greenhouse

Bed 10 Bed 11

Bed 14

Bed 2

Trellis

Urn

Bed 13

Pot

Sink
Garden

Display wall

Slope down

Bed 9

Stone
slabs

Bed 8

Stone
slabs

Bed 7

Stone
slabs

Bed 1

Bed 6

Left Plan of the garden illustrated on the previous page. It was designed in association with the Disabled Living Foundation for the pleasure, convenience and safety of disabled and elderly gardeners.

The site, a typical rectangular plot, eighty-four feet long by fifty-four feet wide (twenty-six by sixteen metres) runs downhill from the entrance as indicated. Instead of steps, however, a gentle slope has been constructed, paved with a non-slip surface, easily negotiated by wheelchairs. To assist gardeners who have difficulty in walking, a handrail has been fixed to the display wall, surmounted by a flower bed, which is a central feature of the plan.

All beds, including that containing the pool, are raised so that they may be enjoyed and tended in comfort, even from a wheelchair. Much use has been made of plants growing in a variety of containers at a height that does not require stooping.

The following is a selection from the many plants chosen for their suitability.

Bed 1, starting from the garden entrance, features many trailers and compact shrubs, including *Hedera colchica* 'Dentata Variegata', *Hypericum × moserianum* 'Tricolor', *Lonicera* 'Baggesen's Gold', *Viburnum tinus* 'Eve Price', *Rhodendron kiusianum*, *Choisya ternata* and *Spiraea nipponica* 'Snow Mound', with some ground-cover plants and bulbs. At the narrowest part the compact conifer *Juniperus × media* 'Old Gold' provides a focal point; beyond it is a trellis over which a clematis has been trained.

Beds 2–5 contain small shrubs and sub-shrubs, including *Ribes sanguineum* 'Brockle-bank', *Daphne × burkwoodii*, *Hebe recurva*, *Potentilla fruticosa* 'Red Ace' and *Santolina chamaecyparissus*, interplanted with some herbaceous subjects and bulbs.

Beds 6–9, separated by stone slabs, contain mainly herbaceous perennials, planned to provide a succession of flowers throughout the season. A single conifer in the first bed, *Thuya occidentalis* 'Rheingold' adds contrast of form and a touch of brilliance.

A central feature is the display wall, curving gently down the slope in an inverted 'S'. The hollow top filled with soil provides a bed suitable for a wide range of alpines and plants that need similar culture. A strong handrail runs the length of the wall.

On the other side of the central paved area is a raised pool planted with an assortment of aquatics. Bed 10, projecting from the pool, contains a selection of rock plants grouped around *Chamaecyparis lawsoniana*.

Beds 11 and 12 are used for a display of half-hardy plants, such as french and african marigolds, petunias and begonias.

Troughs, sinks and ornamental pots, held high enough to avoid stooping, are used for a wide variety of plants (see pages 218–9).

Edible crops have not been forgotten. Bed 13 grows strawberries, gooseberries and currants. Bed 14 is planted with cucumbers and tomatoes. Beds 15–17 produce lettuces, carrots, french beans, cabbages, brussels sprouts, beetroot and leeks. Culinary herbs are grown in the two containers at the ends of the seat and in the nearby group of three made from lengths of piping stood on end.

Though there are several of the heavier gardening tasks that many disabled people cannot manage, or would be unwise to attempt, a new range of tools and other devices has been developed during recent years that enable physically handicapped people to do certain jobs that would have been difficult, if not impossible, before such things were invented.

Even in a conventional type of garden without raised beds, chairbound people who cannot use an ordinary garden fork or spade may be able, with the help of one of the long-handled small forks or cultivators, light in weight but extremely strong, to cultivate the ground to a sufficient depth to allow the successful raising of flowers and vegetables from seed and the growing of bedding plants for summer display. Since force exerted in a forward direction may lead to loss of balance, and tends to be more tiring and wasteful of effort, most people confined to wheelchairs prefer the sort of implement that is pulled rather than pushed through the soil. Hoes used with a pulling rather than a pushing action are also often preferred as being more effective with less effort. There are also kinds that use a broad blade with a zigzag edge at the back and front which can be both pushed and pulled.

Many people who find difficulty in gripping the handles of such tools as trowels and hand forks are changing over to patterns with larger and more bulbous handles which are more easily grasped by hands suffering from muscular weakness.

An excellent tool that can be used in one hand for the dual purpose of snipping off flowers and gathering them, either for use in room decoration or to remove faded blooms, is the cut-and-hold device, which severs and holds the flower-stem at one and the same time.

For those nearing retirement age and still in good shape, it might be a good idea to consider whether some of the features of the model garden for the disabled, such as a gently sloping ramp instead of or in addition to steps, and perhaps a raised bed, might be incorporated in the garden now, or at any rate in the not too distant future, to prepare for less active days.

The vegetable garden

In addition to the sections devoted to vegetables in some of the other model gardens at Wisley, there is a separate model vegetable garden, illustrated here. This demonstrates what crops may be grown, and how to grow them successfully. It has been designed for the benefit not only of people with gardens but also of these who have no gardens but still wish to be able to enjoy vegetables that they have grown themselves.

Many people have small plots of ground that are used solely as ornamental gardens. Others, in ever-increasing numbers over recent years, live in apartment buildings, where the only home gardening possible is the cultivation of house plants in pots, perhaps with the addition of a window-box or two. In spite of such limitations, enthusiasts for home-grown produce can find pleasure and profit in joining the allotment-gardening movement.

Allotment gardens, provided by local councils, are usually rented for a modest sum and are likely to pay for themselves many times over in the value of the produce they yield, quite apart from its greater freshness and better flavour than much that is offered for sale. Few other leisure activities are able not only to provide an enjoyable hobby but at the same time save a considerable amount of money.

The provision of allotments is subject to certain statutory requirements, as well as local regulations. People who wish to apply for one may be able to obtain information and help from their local allotments association, horticultural society or gardening club, membership of which brings benefits not only in sharing the company, knowledge and experience of other members but often in the savings that can be made by the joint purchase of seeds and other gardening materials.

An allotment garden is defined in law as a plot not exceeding a quarter of an acre (about 1012 sq m), but most are considerably smaller. The largest plot in the model vegetable garden at Wisley is a quarter of that size, measuring ninety feet (nine metres) by thirty feet (three metres), and may be expected if properly managed to supply most of the vegetables needed by an average family for most of the year.

For those whose family requirements are more modest, there is a plot about half the size of the largest one, measuring forty-eight by sixteen and a half feet (14.5 by five metres). This is used for demonstrating how to produce a useful quantity of green crops, salads and root vegetables, but it does not include maincrop potatoes, which take up too much space in a small plot and are usually obtainable when needed at a reasonable price and of good quality.

Another plot is devoted to vegetables grown with the protection of various types of glass and plastic cloches, tunnels and frames (described and illustrated on pages 226–7). On the far left of the picture can be seen two unheated greenhouses, at the north end of the model vegetable garden, in which may be grown tomatoes, sweet peppers, cucumbers and melons, together with other crops that respond well to similar growing conditions. A six-feet wide border along the eastern side of the model garden is used for growing a variety of crops, including several of the less commonly grown vegetables such as Florence fennel which as they gain in popularity are being introduced by seedsmen into their lists.

Vegetables that occupy the same ground for several years, such as asparagus, globe artichokes, rhubarb and seakale, are planted in a separate area, since they cannot be fitted into the normal rotation of crops (see pages 220–1).

Different methods of cultivation are explored in the model garden, in order to establish whether they are likely to give better results. In addition Wisley trials are regularly held to compare the quality and performance of cultivars submitted and to give awards to those of proved worth.

Right Part of the model vegetable garden at Wisley, pictured in late spring and demonstrating a variety of crops and cultivation methods. In the central plot the crops in the foreground, from left to right, are hardy peas and broad beans, sown during the previous autumn, and overwintering onions sown during the summer. The plot has been divided into beds cultivated from footways between.

The fruit garden

When designing a garden for the average small modern plot, many people decide for reasons of space to give up the idea of growing fruit altogether or to limit it to a small section containing soft fruit, with perhaps the addition of top fruits such as apples and pears grown in restricted forms such as fans, cordons or espaliers, on walls or fences, as in the model family garden shown on pages 14–17.

Where space permits, however, the choice may be widened to include free-standing fruit trees of several kinds. Apart from the crop they produce – a pleasing picture in itself as it swells and ripens – they can form extremely attractive elements in the garden design; few sights are lovelier than that of a fruit tree's branches laden with blossom on a sunny day in the spring.

From a more practical point of view the free-standing forms, which are mostly pruned in the winter, need considerably less attention than the restricted forms, which must also be pruned in the summer, when there are many other tasks demanding the gardener's attention.

In planning a fruit garden, one of the most important questions to be considered is that of pollination. Unless the flowers are fertilized, as the result of the right pollen reaching the stigma at the right time, there will be no crop.

Several fruit trees, including apricots, peaches, nectarines and some plums and gages, are self-fertile, which means that they can be fertilized by their own pollen, so that a single tree will produce a crop. Most apples and pears, however, are self-sterile and need to be fertilized by pollen from a different cultivar. It is best, therefore, to plant apples and pears in groups of two or more cultivars which blossom at the same time. (Note, however, that apples and pears are unable to fertilize each other.) The different cultivars need not be grown in the same form, but they should be planted within easy flying distance for bees and other pollinating insects.

Since certain cultivars will not pollinate each other satisfactorily even if they are in flower at the same time it is best to make sure before buying that those you choose make a suitable combination.

It should be pointed out that in areas where neighbours grow apples and pears, a good crop may often be produced by a solitary tree in a garden. Also many of the ornamental crabs that blossom at the same time may be excellent pollinators for apple trees.

All cherry-plums are self-fertile, as are most of the morello and other acid cherries and several plums, damsons and gages. Many, however, are not, so they need to be planted near compatible cultivars.

Until recently all sweet cherries were self-sterile and would not produce a crop unless pollinated by a cultivar within its compatibility group; pollen from a member of another group would produce no results. Now, with the introduction of the cultivar 'Stella', a self-fertile sweet cherry is available to the gardener, so that one tree will produce a crop without needing another cultivar to pollinate it. In addition, the semi-dwarfing rootstock 'Colt' now enables it to be grown in a limited space, even in a large tub or a similar container.

One of the most important modern advances for those who wish to include fruit trees in the garden design is the development of the dwarfing and semi-dwarfing rootstocks that enable them to be grown in a small space. For apples there is the very dwarfing M27, the dwarfing M9 and the semi-dwarfing M26 and MM106. For pears there is Quince A, which gives trees of moderate size, and Quince C, which makes smaller trees that start to crop within a shorter time.

For plums and damsons, St Julien A produces a more compact tree than the more vigorous rootstocks of the past, and the newer rootstock 'Pixy' is more dwarfing still.

To ensure the right size of tree, never buy without knowing what the rootstock is.

Right Apple 'May Queen', notable for its compact habit of growth, which makes it particularly well suited to small gardens, and for the long-lasting nature of its handsome fruit, which may remain crisp and juicy till the spring if carefully stored. It is one of the many established cultivars grown at Wisley together with newer introductions, in order to compare them for performance and quality.

Month-by-Month in the Garden

The twelve chapters in this section of the book are designed to show what may be enjoyed in the garden month by month, illustrated with photographs taken throughout the year at the Royal Horticultural Society's world-famous garden at Wisley in Surrey.

The selection of plants given in each month's notes is based on what may be expected in an average season at Wisley. The same plants may be earlier in the warmer south-west and later in the colder north. At Wisley itself unusual weather conditions may advance or delay the season. It should also be pointed out that many garden favourites, especially among summer-flowering plants, may be continuously in bloom for several months on end. To avoid duplication and allow room for as many names and descriptions as possible, such plants are usually listed once only, in the month when they may be expected to come into flower.

The botanical names under which the plants appear are intended to be of as much use to the amateur gardener as possible. Generally the name used is the one accepted as correct according to current botanical opinion. In some cases this is followed by a second name in brackets if that is the name under which it is commonly grown and sold. In those cases where the currently accepted botanical name is at present used by few if any nurserymen, it has been thought more helpful to place the generally known name first, followed in brackets with the correct name preceded by 'now': for example *Erica carnea* (now *herbacea*) and *Acidanthera bicolor* (now *Gladiolus callianthus*).

At the end of each month's notes will be found timely reminders of what to do, grouped under identical headings to those on the preceding pages dealing with what to enjoy that month. For details of how to carry out the various tasks listed, these reminders include references to the step-by-step instructions given in the later section on Practical Gardening Techniques.

January

January brings the snow,
Makes our feet and fingers glow.

Sara Coleridge (1802–1852)

Although weather conditions vary from year to year, Britain is more likely to have snow in January than in December. While the shortest day is now behind us, the combined effect of the diminished hours of light and the declining power of the sun has been to cool down the earth and the atmosphere above it. Though the days are now beginning to grow longer again, it will take several weeks for the effects to become apparent, so January remains on average the coldest month, with the cold often continuing into February.

When the sky is overcast, the sun may not be able to struggle through, and in such conditions the temperature may remain at around freezing-point both by day and by night. It is, however, when the sky is clear and the sun's rays bring a touch of warmth during the day that night temperatures are likely to plunge below freezing point, and that is when garden plants on the borderline of hardiness suffer most.

The damage is done by what is known as radiation frost, caused by the fact that there is no cloud to act as a blanket and so prevent warmth from being lost straight up into the sky.

The danger is at its worst in the open ground, where there is no protection between the vulnerable plant and the cloudless sky. In such a situation a covering of straw or bracken, some bushy pea sticks or a piece of sacking rigged up before nightfall could make the difference between life and death for the plants.

A covering of snow may provide just the right blanket if left intact until it melts naturally when the weather turns milder. It is, however, wise to shake snow off the branches of trees and shrubs; if allowed to build up, its weight may cause them to break.

Left *Erica carnea* (now *herbacea*), the winter-flowering heath, is seen here on a clear January day reflected in the water, against a background of mixed dwarf conifers.

What to see and enjoy in January

Trees and Shrubs

A notable feature of the limited number of trees and shrubs in bloom this month is that their flowers, though often borne in profusion and forming large clusters, tend to be individually small, perhaps because larger ones would run more risk of being torn and damaged by winter gales. What they lack in size, however, many of them – such as those of the wintersweet, the witch hazels, the bush honeysuckles and the viburnums – make up for in their delightful scent, often powerful enough to carry some distance and waft into the house.

To these plants may be added, towards the end of the month in mild or sheltered places and a week or two later in less favourable conditions, the sweet-scented, purplish red flowers of *Daphne mezereum*. This easily grown deciduous shrub, which thrives on chalky soils, bears its blooms in clusters of two or three on the previous year's shoots, to be followed by scarlet fruits.

Many of the flowering trees and shrubs dealt with in the December notes (see list on page 170) will continue to bloom well into the new year. Two welcome additions to the shrubs this month are the first camellias to come into flower, of which an excellent example is pictured opposite, and the earliest rhododendrons, a beautiful specimen of which may be seen overleaf on page 36.

Colourful bark continues to attract the eye, as do berries that have not been taken by birds (see selection on page 162) and variegated evergreens (page 170).

Climbers and Wall-plants

The lovely winter jasmine, *Jasminum nudiflorum*, from China, continues to open its bright yellow flowers. The silver wattle, *Acacia dealbata*, though not reliably hardy in the open, may produce its fragrant golden flowers (the mimosa of florists) against a sheltered wall in the latter half of this month or early in February.

Right *Hamamelis* x *intermedia* 'Diane', an outstanding witch hazel hybrid raised in Belgium, has won the Royal Horticultural Society's prized Award of Merit.

Below *Pieris japonica* 'Daisen', introduced from Mount Daisen in Japan, is a choice form of one of the most ornamental of evergreen shrubs for lime-free soil, with coral red flower buds which provide an attractive display throughout the winter before they eventually open during the spring.

There are many hardy border plants besides hellebores with foliage that remains handsome when most herbaceous perennials are leafless. Among the most striking are bergenias, whose large, rounded, leathery foliage makes an effective ground cover, and several pulmonarias, or lungworts, whose leaves are marbled with silvery grey.

Many dwarf junipers and other conifers also help to give the border interest, with their decorative foliage in many different tones, from golden to steely blue-grey.

Evergreen ferns have their own beauty of form. Among hardy species some of the most decorative are to be found in the genera *Phyllitis* (hart's-tongue fern), *Blechnum* (hard fern), *Dryopteris* (buckler fern), *Polypodium* and *Polystichum* (shield fern).

Below *Camellia* 'Sea Foam' is a fine cultivar of the early-flowering species *Camellia sasanqua*, bearing many slightly fragrant, waxy blooms of shining white.

Roses

Even without flowers, some of the shrub roses have very attractive stems in various shades of red, brown and green, ornamented with thorns and hairs. They look particularly striking in the morning sunshine when glistening with frost after a cold night, giving interest and beauty to an otherwise bleak scene.

Decorative hips (often called heps) of different shapes, sizes and colours may still be found on several species; a list of some of these, selected for the attractiveness of their fruits, will be found on page 155.

Borders and Beds

Christmas roses, *Helleborus niger*, and other hellebores (see page 172) are perhaps the most striking border plants of the winter, with their bowl-shaped flowers carried on stout stems above their handsome, saw-toothed, evergreen foliage, which also provides pleasing and contrasting background for early flowering bulbs at the front of the border.

Several plants that retain their foliage can, with their different textures and varying shades of green, prevent the border from looking bare and ugly during the winter.

Above *Rhododendron dauricum* 'Midwinter' is an outstanding cultivar of one of the most reliably hardy of all early-flowering rhododendron species, introduced into cultivation from regions of intense cold, including northern China and eastern Siberia. It gained the Award of Merit of the Royal Horticultural Society in 1963, followed six years later by the highest distinction the Society can confer upon a plant, its much sought-after First Class Certificate.

Bulbs and Corms

Many delightful winter crocuses will now be coming into flower. Two extra-early species worth trying, which may even start flowering in December, are *Crocus imperati* and *C. laevigatus*, with their beautiful and delicately veined lilac flowers.

Others due to bloom now are *C. ancyrensis*, with brilliant orange flowers, *C. flavus (aureus)*, from which the well-known 'Dutch Yellow' has been derived, and the deservedly popular *C. tommasinianus*, of which there are several garden forms, with flowers ranging in colour from the mauvish blue of the species to deep reddish purple.

Winter aconites, which though tuberous are generally included among bulbs, are among the brightest of early flowering plants with their shining, buttercup-yellow petals. Perhaps the hardiest of all is the common but very attractive species *Eranthis hyemalis*, but unfortunately the short-stemmed flowers are apt to become splashed with dirt. There are, however, garden cultivars with longer stems; 'Guinea Gold', with deeper yellow flowers, is particularly good.

The last blooms of the increasingly popular autumn snowdrop, *Galanthus reginae-olgae*, will now have faded, but the snowdrop season may be continued with little interruption by the coming into bloom of those kinds which open their flowers early in the new year. Of these, one of the finest is *G. byzantinus*, a robust, broad-leaved species from Turkey, whose flowers are distinguished by the deep green blotch at the base as well as the apex of the inner segments.

Another excellent early species is *G. caucasicus*, from Russia, happy in sun or shade and distinguished by the absence of green markings at the base of its flowers. The common snowdrop, *G. nivalis*, most widely grown of all, is a very variable species, of which many different cultivars may be found in gardens, with flowering dates between early January and late March.

Several bulbous iris species may begin to flower late in the month. They are dealt with in the notes for February (page 44).

Rock Gardens and Pools

Among the earliest and most attractive of wild flowers are those of the celandine, *Ranunculus ficaria*, with the satiny golden sheen of buttercups, but somewhat deeper in colour. They are not to be trusted in the border, where they can propagate themselves with alarming speed.

There are, however, some more restrained cultivars, with flowers of different colours, including white, which are suitable for the rock garden, where they blend well with the few other early flowers, such as those of some species of *Primula* and *Viola*.

Waterside plants with bold foliage, including moisture-loving ferns, provide the pool's main interest this month.

Lawns

Grass in good condition is best admired without being trodden on during winter; better keep to paths or stepping-stones.

Fruit

There are probably few, if any, apples or pears still in store, but if carefully kept in wraps or plastic bags, some of the choicest varieties are now at their best.

Left *Galanthus nivalis*, the common snowdrop, is pictured here as its flowers are starting to open. It is among the best-loved early bulbs with many named cultivars and hybrids, a choice of which can extend the flowering period till April.

Below *Euphorbia pulcherrima*, the poinsettia, here displays its vivid colours against other greenhouse plants. In the background can be seen the magnificent flowers of the orchid Showgirl, a fine example of a hybrid *Cymbidium*.

Vegetables

From a fair-sized vegetable garden that has been well planned and intensively cropped (see pages 220–223) it should still be possible to provide from store at least some of the average family's requirements in such staple items as onions, carrots and potatoes.

Other vegetables that may be gathered from the open are detailed in the notes for December (see page 173).

Greenhouse and Frame

Most of the plants that can be brought into flower in the cool or intermediate house during January are of the same kinds as those listed for November and December (see pages 165 and 173). To these may be added some with decorative foliage; a selection is given on page 45.

House Plants

Flowers on house plants given as Christmas presents (see page 173) will last longest and give most enjoyment if the rooms in which they are kept are neither stuffy nor subject to cold draughts.

What to do in January

Trees and Shrubs

Though planting of deciduous trees and shrubs may still be carried out (see page 198 for step-by-step instructions), it is important not to do so unless the ground is in suitable condition. If it is either frozen hard or wet and sticky, wait till things improve.

If the young plant is to have a good start in its new home, the soil should provide a welcoming environment for its roots (see page 183 for methods of improving the soil). So if trees and shrubs should arrive when conditions are unfavourable, stand the package in a cool but frostproof place till conditions are right for planting.

Only if the unfavourable spell is likely to be prolonged will it be necessary to heel the plants in temporarily (see page 199).

Since severe frosts and icy winds are at their most likely during January, it is good practice to give some protection at the time of planting (see page 174) and to provide firm support (page 200). With established plants too it is wise to examine stakes and ties and to renew them if necessary.

After freezing nights, go round and see whether newly planted trees and shrubs have been lifted by the action of frost. If so, firm the soil round them, and then apply a good surface mulch (page 191) to prevent the same thing from happening again.

Dead, damaged, badly placed or diseased branches should be removed as soon as possible. Be careful to cut them off flush, leaving no snags (see page 210).

Climbers and Wall-plants

In severe weather some protection may be needed (see page 174). Cut out overcrowded shoots, and train the remaining growths in securely. Renew ties as necessary.

Roses

Start the year with tidy rose beds by removing all fallen leaves. Put them on the compost heap (see page 183) unless they show signs of disease (page 235), in which case they are better burnt. Next remove all weeds, which may harbour pests and diseases. If possible, finish by spreading a mulch of garden compost or similar material over the surface (see page 191) to protect it from being beaten down by heavy rain. A dressing of fertilizer (see page 183) is best applied to the ground before the mulch is laid on the surface.

Planting may still be done if the ground is in the right condition, neither frozen nor sticky; full details are given on page 198.

Pruning at this time is usually confined to cutting out any dead, weakly or inward-pointing shoots, and shortening long stems to help reduce wind resistance and so prevent the plant from being torn or rocked in the ground during squally weather. The majority of gardeners prefer to complete the main pruning during early spring, when the buds begin to swell (see page 213 for step-by-step details).

There is still time to dig ground in preparation for new rose beds, but this operation should be completed as soon as possible if the soil is to benefit fully from exposure to winter weather.

Borders and Beds

Here also digging in preparation for new planting should be completed as soon as possible. Exposure to frost can do much more to bring a heavy soil into good condition for planting and sowing than any amount of human effort at a later date.

Annual weeds (see page 241) may be buried beneath the surface during digging or removed to the compost heap (page 183). Perennial weeds should be dug out and burnt.

Christmas roses are joined by other species of *Helleborus* in producing magnificent January blooms when there are few other flowers out in the border. Their blooms can be protected against battering and splashing with mud and rain by means of some sort of shield, as explained on page 174.

Many successful gardeners leave at least some dead foliage on herbaceous perennials for their protection, and do not remove it till the winter is over. Even so, it is best to cut off withered tops to just above knee height to prevent strong winds from tugging at them and loosening the plants or even tearing them from the ground.

Biennials and those perennials whose leaves remain green through the winter should have any debris such as dead leaves that may have fallen on them regularly removed. If left, it will interfere with the proper functioning of the foliage, and may lead not only to poor growth during the following season but to disease through conditions of constant dampness and lack of air.

Bulbs and Corms

As the earliest bulbs appear through the ground, the surface of the soil may with advantage be given a light stirring, to a depth of an inch or so, with a small fork, so as to break up any hard cap which may have formed and let in some air. It will also enable you to rid the surface of any green film that may have grown over it, together with any moss or weeds. A dressing of fertilizer (see page 183) will help to stimulate growth.

Usually the first of the bulbous irises to bloom in the open is *Iris histrioides*. Its royal blue flowers, which may be expected about the middle of the month, should be protected well in advance from slugs (see page 234).

The ever popular *Iris reticulata* does not normally flower in the open till February in most parts of Britain. It may, however, be brought into flower in January, to provide some early blooms for cutting, similar to those displayed in many florists' windows, by placing cloches (see page 227) over one or two selected plants.

Potted hyacinths and narcissi may be brought in from the plunge bed when the flower buds are well up out of the necks of the bulbs. If brought in too soon, the flowers – if they open at all – will remain short stemmed and stay half hidden among the leaves. Be careful not to bring the plants into too high a temperature; they need cool conditions if they are to produce sturdy, long-lasting flowers of good colour.

Rock Gardens and Pools

There is very little to be done in the rock garden now, except for clearing away fallen leaves which may have accumulated, covering the newly-emerging bulbs and spoiling their flowers. They also provide a perfect hiding place and breeding ground for diseases and pests – particularly snails and slugs, which during mild spells may stir from their winter torpor and begin to nibble holes in tender flower-buds and juicy young leaves.

It is also wise to keep garden pools free of dead leaves and other debris. If they are allowed to remain in the water they will decay and cause pollution, giving rise in the process to noxious gases, which will be trapped under the surface if the pool becomes iced over. An accumulation of such gases can be lethal, not only to plant life but to fish.

During very severe frost, shallow pools are liable to become frozen solid, and if this is likely to happen many people take the precaution of putting goldfish in a bucket of water in a shed or garage till the ice melts.

Lawns

Although it is best to keep off the grass as much as possible at this time of year, there are occasions when the lawn can do with a little attention even if that does mean a certain amount of trampling on the surface.

Worms can be a great nuisance during mild spells, coming up near the surface and defacing it with their casts. These are not only unsightly but harmful, causing uneven patches, caking after heavy rain and drying winds, and so stifling the finer grasses and encouraging the coarser ones, as well as providing a perfect seedbed for invading weeds.

These wormcasts may be dealt with as they appear, by distributing them over the surface with a broom or a flexible rake. At the same time moss may be raked out, and any remaining fallen leaves removed and placed on the compost heap.

If puddles or wet patches persist after rain, the faulty drainage responsible for them may be dealt with by spiking the surface with a fork (see page 208) if that has not already been done. A dressing of grit or sharp sand may also improve matters.

Fruit

Pruning and spraying are the main operations to be carried out now. If the work has not already been done, it should be completed as soon as the weather permits, while the trees and bushes are still dormant and before buds start to swell.

Pruning is basically of two kinds: renewal pruning, of which raspberries are an example, where young canes carry the fruit and older ones are removed, and spur pruning, as with apples, where older wood produces the fruit. Full details are given on pages 214 and 215.

As soon as the pruning is completed, spray with winter wash to destroy pests and their eggs.

Vegetables

The most urgent task in the vegetable garden is to complete the digging of vacant ground as soon as possible; an illustrated guide will be found on pages 184 and 185. At the same time, the soil may be improved and enriched by the methods shown on pages 182 and 183. In deciding where to use manures, compost and fertilizers, the requirements of the different crops must be taken into account.

For good results a plan should always be worked out to give the best rotation of crops for your plot and the kinds of vegetables that you wish to grow. This may be done by consulting pages 220 to 223, where detailed information and advice are given.

If you have not ordered your seeds yet, do so now, before the varieties you want are sold out. Supplies of the best kinds are always limited.

Greenhouse and Frame

Chrysanthemums and carnations can be propagated from cuttings as these become available; full details are shown on page 193.

If your greenhouse is warm enough, with a minimum temperature of 55–60°F (13–15°C), tuberous begonias and gloxinias may be started into growth in boxes of moist (but not soaking) peat.

Sweet peas in frames should not be coddled. Give free ventilation except on the coldest nights.

House Plants

Plants in the home, particularly flowering ones, need all the light they can get during these short days; on the other hand, they should be kept out of draughts. Be careful not to over-water them while growth is at its minimum; if the room atmosphere seems dry, a bowl of water stood nearby may help to moisten the air.

February

February, fill the dyke
With what thou dost like.

Thomas Tusser (1524–1580)

February's reputation of being the wettest month of the year is not usually supported by the rainfall figures; in fact the amount of rain in February is often well below the average. All the same, it is true that generally speaking the ground is too cold to dry out readily. It tends – at least in the first half of the month – to be either sticky or frozen hard. Much depends on the wind. In Britain, an east or north-east wind is likely to prolong the winter by bringing severe frost when the sky is clear, or snow when the sky is overcast. If the wind is from the west or south-west the weather will be milder, but there is a strong probability of rain, which may be heavy. If the wind is from the south, a spell of sunshine may occur, and the temperature may become quite warm. Do not, however, make the mistake of assuming that winter is over; cold weather is only too likely to come back. Severe frosts may be expected many more times yet, even in the south.

More and more hardy plants will now be coming into flower. With the exception of some hellebores, among the most beautiful of plants to bloom early, very few of these flowers will be found on border perennials, since most of them manage to survive the winter only by remaining dormant under the ground. Such flowers as do appear so early in the year were all formed during the previous season. They have spent the winter in the form of buds, carried either above ground on the woody stems of trees and shrubs or below ground on storage organs such as bulbs, corms and tubers. The chemical and physical changes that have taken place inside those buds have brought them to the stage where, under the influence of lengthening days and increasing warmth, they are now ready to open.

Left *Galanthus* 'Magnet', an old favourite among garden snowdrops, is distinguished by the very long, graceful stalks from which the flowers hang.

What to see and enjoy in February

Above *Erica carnea*
(now *herbacea*)
cultivars 'Springwood
White' and the pink-
flowered 'King George'
have both received the
Award of Garden Merit
from the Royal
Horticultural Society.
Immediately behind
them is the small,
spreading conifer
Chamaecyparis obtusa
'Pygmaea', which was
introduced from Japan
in 1861 and has proved
ideal for the small
garden, its bronze-
green foliage becoming
flushed with red during
the winter.

Trees and Shrubs

Most of the brightly-coloured berries which
provide so much enjoyment during the winter will now have fallen, or been carried off by
birds. An exception is the butcher's broom,
Ruscus aculeatus, a shade-tolerant shrub of the
lily family. Its cherry-like fruits of sealing-
wax red, borne in abundance when male and
female plants are grown together, are rarely
taken but remain till the spring.

The winter scene continues to be brightened by the many evergreens with variegated
foliage (see the list of selected kinds on page
170) and by the trees and shrubs with
coloured bark (listed on page 162). Among
the most striking are the dogwoods, whose
stems are at their most vivid at this time of
year, particularly if they are pruned back hard
each spring. They are ideal for moist
situations.

Many wind-pollinated species will be producing beautiful catkins, notably alders,
hazels, poplars and willows. As the days
lengthen, others will be coming into flower
besides those already listed on page 162, many
of which may be still in bloom. A selection is
given in the next column.

SELECTED TREES AND SHRUBS

In flower

Several early-flowering cultivars of
Camellia japonica, *C. sasanqua* and *C.
x williamsii*; *Cornus mas* and *C.
officinalis*; *Daphne mezereum* and *D.
odora*; many cultivars of *Erica carnea*
(now *herbacea*), *E. x darleyensis* and *E.
mediterranea* (now *erigena*); *Garrya
elliptica*; many cultivars of *Hamamelis
x intermedia*, *H. japonica*, *H. mollis* and
H. vernalis (witch hazels); *Lonicera
fragrantissima*, *L. standishii* and *L. x
purpusii*; *Mahonia japonica* and *M. x
media* varieties; early-flowering
japanese cherry *Prunus incisa*
'Praecox' and chinese peach *Prunus
davidiana*; *Rhododendron arboreum*,
R. dauricum and *R. mucronulatum*;
Sarcococca confusa; *Sorbus
megalocarpa*; *Stachyurus praecox*;
Viburnum x bodnantense and *V.
farreri*.

Beautiful bark

For a selection of species with
colourful winter bark see page 162.

Left *Rhododendron* 'Olive', a hardy hybrid between *R. dauricum* and *R. moupinense*, forms a small shrub of neat habit, bearing early flowers in profusion.

Roses

Against a wintry background and lit by a shaft of sunlight, the prickly and bristly stems of many shrub roses can still look very attractive. So can the colourful hips (also known as heps) that some of them still carry. For a selected list of these turn to page 155.

Borders and Beds

Hellebores continue to give interest and beauty to the border. Many of the species and varieties that have already been in bloom for some time (see page 172) will go on flowering into February. In this way they overlap with other species opening their blooms during winter and early spring, including the lenten rose, *Helleborus orientalis*, and its variants with flowers ranging from creamy white through shades of pink to ruby red, spotted with purple, also the native species *H. foetidus* and *H. viridis*, with long-lasting flowers of brilliant green.

Other border plants that may be in flower now include species of adonis, with buttercup-like flowers of yellow, white or red, *Iris unguicularis*, polyanthus, primroses and pulmonarias.

Climbers and Wall-plants

Wintersweet, *Chimonanthus praecox*, though perfectly hardy, is at its best against a sunny wall. Here its bare branches, well ripened by last year's sun, produce throughout the winter their pale yellow, waxen flowers, intensely scented with a mixture of sweetness and spice. The type, with the centre of its blooms stained purple, may now be reaching the end of its flowering period, but the variety *luteus*, without the purple blotch, will now be at its best. A stem or two, cut when the flower buds are beginning to open and brought indoors, will scent a room for days.

Winter jasmine, *Jasminum nudiflorum*, continues to produce its bright yellow flowers in abundance, even against a north or east facing wall. Ivies too – in particular the variegated ones – do much to brighten dull walls and unsightly sheds on winter days.

The popular large-flowered varieties of clematis will not be in bloom for some months yet. However, the evergreen fern-leaved *Clematis cirrhosa* var. *balearica* continues through the winter to open its small but attractive pale yellow flowers spotted with purple, to be followed by silky seed-heads.

Below *Helleborus orientalis*, the lenten rose, from the Eastern Mediterranean, opens its long-lasting blooms from winter to early spring.

Above *Eranthis hyemalis*, winter aconite, is among the most welcome of all garden plants, opening its bright, yellow-gold cups early in the year when little else is in flower. It is very easy to naturalize, readily increasing by means of self-sown seedlings, and will thrive in part shade, under deciduous trees or between shrubs.

Bulbs, Corms and Tubers

Several of the winter-flowering crocuses mentioned in the notes for January (see page 36) will still be in bloom this month. Depending on district and season, they will soon be joined by the earliest of the spring-flowering species and their varieties and hybrids. Out of a large number to choose from, a selection of the best must include *Crocus angustifolius*, the aptly named cloth of gold crocus commonly known as *C. susianus*, with brilliant orange-yellow flowers marked with mahogany in the centre and on the outside.

Others include the pale lilac-grey *C. versicolor*, feathered with violet, the very early *C. fleischeri*, with white flowers striped indigo at the base, as well as the beautiful *C. sieberi* and its many cultivars, with flowers of purple, violet and white, all distinguished by an orange-yellow throat.

Perhaps the most popular of all among early garden flowers is *C. chrysanthus*, to-gether with the very large number of its excellent offspring. Their colours range from white through cream and yellow to soft blue and rich purple, with feathery markings, and mostly with a delicate silvery sheen.

Of the hardy *Cyclamen* species flowering now, the most widely grown in gardens is *Cyclamen coum*, with a large number of variants in shades and combinations of pink, carmine, magenta and white.

Winter aconites and snowdrops are now joined in flower by early scillas. In favourable locations and seasons, some of the charming small-flowered early species of *Narcissus* may be coming into bloom during the latter part of the month.

Iris reticulata and its many forms, with gold-marked flowers of blue, mauve and purple, join the slight *I. bakeriana* and more robust *I. histrioides* in braving the cold, together with the related, yellow-flowered *I. danfordiae*.

Rock Gardens and Pools

Many welcome flowers in the rock garden are those of the bulbs and corms mentioned on the opposite page. Some early-flowering species of corydalis are coming into bloom, including *Corydalis solida*, with short, dense racemes of purplish pink or white flowers.

Early primulas will be starting to flower, including that garden favourite *Primula juliae*, with bright purple blooms, and the many hybrids such as 'Wanda' of which it is a parent, known as Juliana primroses (*P.* × *pruhoniciana*). Several saxifrages will be in flower, as will some violas (winter pansies).

Foliage plants and ferns round the pool's edge continue to provide interest.

Lawns

The same advice applies as in last month's notes: however inviting the lawn may look, try to avoid treading on the surface. Keep to paths and stepping-stones.

Fruit

Besides soft fruit bottled or frozen from last season's crop, there may still be late-keeping apples and pears to enjoy.

Vegetables

From the open ground it should be possible to enjoy some of the vegetables detailed on page 173. From store there may still be supplies of onions, potatoes, beetroot and other root crops.

Greenhouse and Frame

For plants in flower now, turn to pages 165 and 173. Foliage plants for the cool house include those with coloured leaves such as coleus varieties and *Hypoestes phyllostachya* (*H. sanguinolenta* of gardens); grey-leaved kinds such as *Senecio cineraria*; pelargoniums with decorative leaves; feathery asparagus fern and many true ferns; and small palms such as *Chamaedorea elegans* (*Neanthe bella*), *Cocos* (now *Microcoelum*) *weddeliana* and *Phoenix roebelenii*.

House Plants

Pot plants for the home in flower this month include many of those dealt with elsewhere in the book (see pages 59 and 173).

Left *Iris reticulata* 'Joyce', one of many cultivars of a lovely bulbous species, is suitable for a sunny, well drained spot in a rock garden or the front of a border. It is also an excellent pot plant for the alpine house or cool greenhouse.

Below *Scilla bifolia*, pictured here in the alpine house, is also hardy and will flower outdoors next month. There are blue, pink and white forms.

What to do in February

Trees and Shrubs

There is still time to plant trees and shrubs if this task has not already been completed. Full instructions will be found on page 199. Any necessary staking (see page 200) should be done at the time of planting, to protect the plants against being rocked, or even blown over, by strong winds before enough new roots have grown to anchor them into the ground. Do not attempt any planting if the soil is sticky or frozen hard. It is better to wait till conditions are right.

Meanwhile the plants should either be kept in a cool but frostproof place or heeled in (see page 199). If freezing weather should occur after planting, go round and examine whether the frost has lifted or loosened newly-planted trees and shrubs; if so, it will be necessary to firm the soil round them again.

A start may be made, if conditions are favourable, with the pruning of shrubs that flower on the current season's growth (see page 213 for full details). In most cases, however, the majority of experienced gardeners prefer to leave this operation till next month, or even April, when the buds can be clearly seen as they start to swell.

Climbers and Wall-plants

Species and cultivars of clematis that flower during the summer and autumn on new shoots made in the current season will benefit from hard pruning now. This will prevent them from becoming bare and leggy at the base and producing their flowers only at the top. Cut the stems back to the lowest pair of buds, or even right down to the ground if new shoots appear from below the surface. Full details are given on page 215.

Wisteria tends to make excessive growth for the amount of wall space usually available if it is not kept under control. The lateral shoots, which were cut back in the summer

to within six of seven leaves from the branches forming the main framework, should now be shortened still further to no more than two or three buds, so as to form flowering spurs. (For full details see page 215.)

Roses

Any planting that still remains to be done should be completed as soon as possible (see page 199 for details), but not if the ground is frozen hard or in a wet and sticky condition.

The main pruning of bush and standard roses should be carried out between the middle of the month and late March, according to the mildness or otherwise of the district and the season. Follow the instructions given on page 216.

Borders and Beds

Many herbaceous perennials, including such favourites as oriental poppies, anchusa, Japanese anemones and phlox, can be propagated from root cuttings taken early in the month, while the plants are still dormant. The process is very simple, and particularly suitable for those choice garden varieties which will not come true from seed. Full details of how to take and strike root cuttings are given on page 194.

Signs of waterlogging after rain should be dealt with promptly. Methods of draining are shown on page 182. As a temporary measure plants in danger of drowning may be rescued by spiking the soil round them with a garden fork pushed in to its full depth.

If soil conditions are favourable, lilies may be moved if this task was not carried out at the best time in the autumn. Since they will be showing signs of growth, they must not be damaged or allowed to dry out in the course of being transplanted. Lift them with great care, keeping a good ball of soil round them, and replant them without delay. Should there be

a drying wind, cover them with a piece of sacking or polythene while they are out of the ground to save them from desiccation.

During mild spells weeds will start into growth. Deal with them as soon as they appear, while they are easy to remove. Annual weeds may be put on the compost heap (see page 183), or simply turned under the surface if there is still digging to be done. Perennials, however, should have every last piece of root carefully dug out and burnt. Their roots are very brittle and even small portions left behind will quickly become new plants.

Established borders will benefit from a dressing of fertilizer (see page 182), which will become available to the plants in a few weeks' time when they are starting into spring growth.

If you have a supply of well-rotted manure, garden compost or similar organic material, now is the time to apply it as a surface mulch (see page 183), after digging and dressing with fertilizer have been completed. There is nothing better than a good mulch for preventing bare soil from being beaten down into an impervious surface by heavy rain.

Ground in which sweet peas are to be grown needs thorough preparation to ensure the best results. Few annuals are called upon to make so much growth in such a short time, and also to produce such a succession of flowers, both to brighten the garden and to provide a supply of cut blooms for the home. To keep up the vigour of the plants the soil needs to be in good physical condition and to contain an adequate supply of nutrients. If the ground has not already been dug, do so now, incorporating plenty of organic matter if available. It will then have settled down when the time comes for sowing the seeds or for transferring plants raised under glass to the open (see page 77).

Bulbs, Corms and Tubers

Dahlia tubers in store for the winter should be inspected to make sure that they are healthy and plump. Any that show signs of rotting should have the bad patches cut clean away with a sharp knife till only healthy tissue is left. Sometimes this will mean sacrificing whole tubers to prevent the trouble from spreading. Dust the cut surfaces with sulphur or a suitable fungicide (see page 236) as a precaution against infection.

A certain amount of shrivelling of tubers is no cause for concern, but any that appear to be excessively shrivelled may be stood in water which has had the chill taken off it until they have plumped up again. Dry them before replacing them in store, if necessary renewing the peat or other material in which they are being stored.

Further pots and bowls of bulbs may be brought in as they reach the right stage (see page 39) and placed in a cool greenhouse or room to flower. Those that have finished flowering can be planted out in suitable places in the garden to flower again next year.

If the soil is in suitable condition, now is a good time to plant anemones of the St Brigid and De Caen types. By early summer they will produce flowers which are ideal for cutting.

Rock Gardens and Pools

Even brief mild spells may bring two unwelcome visitors: weeds and slugs. Remove the weeds and sprinkle slug bait (see page 235) among the plants.

Primulas for the pool-side and other damp places may be sown now in boxes of seed compost (see page 219), and exposed to the cold, which assists germination.

Lawns

There is still time to lay turf, either to make a new lawn or to repair an old one. Full details will be found on page 207. Do not attempt the task if the ground is frostbound or muddy. On the other hand, the work should be finished as soon as possible, so that the newly laid turves have time to settle down and become established before the growing season gets under way.

If you intend to raise a new lawn, or renovate bare patches in an existing one, from a spring sowing (see instructions on page 208), every favourable opportunity should be taken to break down the surface of the soil in readiness (see page 206). This will encourage weed seeds to germinate early, and the seedlings can be hoed off and removed when the time comes for sowing the grass seed.

Fruit

There is still time, in suitable conditions, both for planting (see page 198) and for pruning (see pages 214 and 215), but try to complete both these operations as soon as possible, before new growth starts.

If apple and pear trees have not yet been sprayed with a winter wash, this job must not be attempted later than the beginning of the month, and must in any case be completed before the buds begin to swell. After that, they may be severely damaged by the very powerful ingredients of the wash.

Where destructive birds peck out blossom buds from fruit trees, it may be possible to limit the damage with a repellant spray. Other methods include stringing black cotton between branches or swathing them with a web made of fine synthetic threads.

Vegetables

Seed potatoes should be removed from their bags and set to sprout in trays or shallow boxes. Stand the tubers upright, with the end carrying the eyes (dormant buds) at the top, and place them in a light, cool but frost-proof place such as a shed or a spare room. By planting time the buds will have developed into plump, green, sturdy sprouts.

When the ground is workable, new rhubarb plants may be put in or old ones split up and replanted. Established plants may be forced, in order to produce early, tender stalks. Place large, inverted pots or boxes over them, and cover with a thick layer of strawy manure, compost or similar material.

In mild districts early sowings of peas and broad beans may be made (see page 190). Shallots, onion sets and garlic may be planted at the first favourable opportunity, to give them a long period of growth before harvest.

Greenhouse and Frame

Chrysanthemums and carnations may still be propagated from cuttings (see page 193 for details).

Dahlias may also be increased by cuttings. Stand the tubers in boxes of moist peat in a minimum temperature of $53°F$ ($12°C$) to make shoots which will provide cuttings in a few weeks' time.

Dormant fuchsias, hydrangeas and pelargoniums may be pruned and sprayed late in the month to encourage new growth.

Ventilate frames on sunny days to prevent them from overheating.

To give a protected start in cold districts, a seed bed may be prepared in a cold frame and sowings made of brussels sprouts and of early maturing cultivars of cabbages, cauliflowers and round lettuces, for transplanting later into the open ground.

House Plants

The air in heated rooms tends to become too dry for plant health. A good way to counteract this is to stand pots in saucers half filled with moist gravel.

March

March dust to be sold
Worth ransom of gold.

Thomas Tusser (1524–1580)

For the gardener the year really begins in March, with many sights and scents to be enjoyed and many things to be done. The strong winds which so often usher it in, and which have given it the reputation of being the month that comes in like a lion and goes out like a lamb, are among the gardener's best friends. They may test the strength or weakness of stakes and ties, and sometimes do considerable damage to inadequately protected plants, but it is upon those March winds that the earliness or lateness of the sowing season largely depends.

Though with the lengthening days the sun is gaining power, it is often hidden by clouds and does not yet have sufficient warmth to dry out the surface of the ground and so produce that precious dust a peck of which, according to an old saying by gardeners, is worth a king's ransom. That task is much more effectively performed at this time of year by drying winds, particularly those coming from the east and north; those from the south and west tend to bring rain with them. Though cold north and east winds may seem to prolong the winter, they are in reality hastening the day when the ground will readily crumble under the fork and rake to produce the perfect seed-bed.

In Britain, spring usually starts in the south-west at the beginning of the month, but it may take the rest of the month to reach most of the country. On northern hills winter may last into April. A very early spring may be a curse in disguise instead of a blessing, since a run of mild days may result in the premature unfolding of flowers and leaves, which are all too vulnerable to damage by a subsequent cold spell. Unfortunately for the gardener there is little that can be done to prevent such unduly early growth.

Left *Camellia japonica* 'Fred Sander', a crimson-flowered sport from 'Tricolor', whose flowers are white streaked with carmine, has received the Royal Horticultural Society's Award of Merit.

What to see and enjoy in March

Trees and Shrubs

During winter months, though several trees and shrubs brighten the garden with their fruits, bark and foliage, very few do so with their blossoms. Such flowers as do appear are largely pollinated by the wind and tend to be borne in catkins, which many species continue to produce until well into the spring.

Now, however, with lengthening days and bursts of sunshine, insects are beginning to emerge, and species that rely on them for pollination are opening a different type of flower, which uses colour, form and often scent to attract them. Listed below is a selection of some of the best of both kinds flowering at this time of year.

SELECTED TREES AND SHRUBS

In flower

Acer negundo (box elder), *A. opalus* (italian maple), *A. rubrum* (red maple); alders *Alnus orientalis* and *A. serrulata*; *Berberis linearifolia*; many cultivars of *Camellia japonica, C. sasanqua* and *C.* x *williamsii*; *Cornus mas*; *Corylus avellana* and many other hazels; *Corylopsis pauciflora*; *Daphne laureola, D. mezereum* and *D. odora*; *Erica arborea* (tree heath) and its variety *alpina*, and cultivars of *E. carnea* (now *herbacea*), *E.* x *darleyensis, E. lusitanica* (Portugal heath) and *E. mediterranea* (now *erigena*); several forsythias; the late-flowering cultivar of witch hazel *Hamamelis japonica* 'Zuccariniana'; shrubby honeysuckle *Lonicera fragrantissima* with sweet-scented blooms; *Magnolia stellata*; *Mahonia aquifolium* and *M. japonica*; *Osmanthus delavayi*; *Osmaronia cerasiformis*; many early-flowering ornamental cherries, including *Prunus* 'Accolade', cultivars of *P. cerasifera* (cherry-plum), *P. incisa* (Fuji cherry), *P. sargentii*, perhaps loveliest of all, and a large number of Japanese garden cultivars; the early almond *P. dulcis* 'Praecox', the Chinese peach *P. davidiana* and the Japanese apricot *P. mume*; many early rhododendrons; *Stachyurus praecox*; *Ulex europaeus* (gorse); *Viburnum* x *burkwoodii* and *V. tinus*.

Most of the other garden plants that flower in March grow close to the ground, many of them early-flowering bulbs, corms and tubers (see page 54).

The herbaceous plants which will carry their blooms on tall or moderately tall stems later in the season are barely starting to appear above the ground. Trees and shrubs in blossom are therefore doubly welcome at this time of year, not only as a sign that spring is on the way but also to give the dimension of height to the flowering scene.

On a cold, clear night, such as often occurs in March, flowers on trees and shrubs are particularly vulnerable to air frosts. They may all too easily be nipped in the bud, especially if low temperatures are combined with cutting winds. (Flowers near the ground may gain warmth from the earth, or even receive some protection from a blanket of snow.) It is then that those with delicately textured flowers may escape damage if they have been planted so as to take advantage of the shelter provided by light woodland conditions or the protection given by a wall (see opposite page).

Above *Ilex* x *altaclerensis* 'Lawsoniana' is a golden variegated form of a group of holly hybrids. One of the parents is the common holly but the hybrids are all more vigorous, with larger leaves. This one was raised in Edinburgh over a century ago, but it is liable to produce green-leaved shoots, and these need to be cut out so that they do not take over from the variegated ones.

Many spring-flowering shrubs that are perfectly hardy in the open ground are commonly grown against a wall. This is usually done in order to induce them to flower earlier, but in many cases also to protect vulnerable blooms from the damage that cold and wind can inflict on them in the open, and to give some support to species which tend to produce weak growth.

Among the most beautiful of wall-shrubs flowering this month are the camellias, of which a favourite cultivar is pictured on the left. Given lime-free soil, they thrive against any wall except one facing east, where early morning sun striking on flowers after a freezing night may ruin them. Many different camellias will now be starting to come into bloom in nurseries and garden centres, with flowers in a wide range of colours and forms set off by their shining evergreen foliage.

Another early-flowering hardy shrub which makes a first class wall-plant is the Japanese quince, *Chaenomeles speciosa*, with many fine cultivars, one of which is pictured below.

Above *Camellia japonica* 'Lady Clare' has received the Award of Garden Merit of the Royal Horticultural Society.

Right *Chaenomeles speciosa* 'Umbilicata', a fine cultivar of the japanese quince, has been granted an Award of Merit.

Climbers and Wall-plants

Among self-supporting climbers, clinging by means of aerial roots, the many different varieties of ivy will have proved to be of the greatest value during the winter, coming unharmed through the harshest weather.

The foliage of the common ivy, *Hedera helix*, as well as its golden and variegated forms, remains more or less unchanged by the cold. On the other hand, that of the popular Canary Islands species *H. canariensis* may have turned deep bronze during the winter, making an attractive contrast with the fresh colours of the new growths now beginning to appear.

Of climbers needing support, the evergreen *Clematis armandii* may, on a sunny wall, start to open its creamy white flowers towards the end of the month.

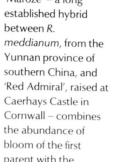

Left *Rhododendron* 'Maroze' – a long established hybrid between *R. meddianum*, from the Yunnan province of southern China, and 'Red Admiral', raised at Caerhays Castle in Cornwall – combines the abundance of bloom of the first parent with the earliness, greater hardiness and larger and brighter flowers of the second.

Left *Rhododendron* 'Bo-peep', a small Exbury hybrid of slender growth, the result of a cross between *R. lutescens* and *R. moupinense*, bears an abundance of early, primrose-yellow flowers and has been granted an Award of Merit by the Royal Horticultural Society.

Left *Rhododendron* x *cilpinense*, a free-flowering hybrid between *R. ciliatum* and *R. moupinense*, is one of the most dependable as well as beautiful rhododendrons to bloom in March, and has gained both a First Class Certificate and an Award of Garden Merit from the Royal Horticultural Society.

Forsythias, though completely hardy, are particularly good against a wall, where the extra protection can bring them into bloom several weeks ahead of those grown in the open. Their profuse golden-yellow flowers come at a time when those of the winter jasmine have reached the end of their season.

Among the best is *Forsythia suspensa*, whose slender, graceful stems are ideal for training against a wall, where they can reach a considerable height. They make an unforgettable sight when in full bloom. In addition to the species there are several excellent named cultivars available from nurseries.

Of those shrubs that must have wall protection because they are too tender to survive the winter in the open, except in very mild districts, species of *Azara* are at their most attractive. These evergreens from Chile bear conspicuous clusters of fragrant flowers, which appear early in the month. Most suitable for a wall is the tall-growing *Azara integrifolia*, with sweetly scented chrome-yellow blooms; its variety *browneae* has larger foliage, and the cultivar 'Variegata' has leaves beautifully marbled with pink and cream.

There is also the taller species *A. microphylla*, whose vanilla-scented flowers appear on the underside of the branches over several weeks during the late winter and early spring. This species may, however, become too big for the available wall space unless kept under control by regular pruning. In its native Chile it reaches the size of a small tree.

Roses

There may still be a few fruits on some of the shrub roses (see page 155 for a selected list). The buds will be reddening and swelling along the shoots as they burst into growth.

Borders and Beds

At this time of year, when there are as yet very few herbaceous plants in bloom, the mixed border with a few flowering shrubs shows its advantages for the average garden. Of special value are the magnificent early rhododendrons. The most widely grown of these, particularly useful where space is limited, are the small and medium-sized hybrids, of which three fine examples are pictured on this page.

An invaluable feature of the mixed border during March is a display of early-flowering hardy bulbs and corms. A selection is given overleaf, on page 54.

Some of the smaller-flowered species may be more suitable for the rock garden, or for naturalizing in grass, but several of the larger-flowered species are ideally suited to the front of the border. So are the large number of garden hybrids now beginning to come into bloom, such as the crocuses pictured here, many of which look overpowering among the alpines.

True, when the flowers are over the leaves must be allowed to die down naturally if there are to be flowers again next year. They are, however, not too obtrusive while they last, and in their dying stages the growing foliage of the herbaceous plants will be there to hide them, or at least to draw attention from them. It is also worth considering that bulb leaves in the border do not present the same problems as those in grass when the time comes to start mowing.

Of herbaceous plants, several hellebores will still be in flower, particularly *Helleborus orientalis* and its forms, joined by the green-flowered natives *H. foetidus* and *H. viridis*, whose long-lived blooms may last unblemished well into the summer.

Adonis species may continue to flower, as may *Iris unguicularis* and the pulmonarias, or lungworts, with pink or blue flowers and white-spotted leaves, together with polyanthus and primroses.

The large, round, leathery leaves of bergenias, handsome throughout the winter, are now surmounted by red stems with dense heads of pink, white and magenta flowers.

Among the first herbaceous perennials to flower is *Doronicum plantagineum*, known as leopard's bane, with cheerful yellow daisy flowers well displayed against bright green heart-shaped leaves. These vanish during the summer when the plants become dormant. Favourite garden cultivars are the single-flowered 'Harpur Crewe' and the double-flowered 'Spring Beauty'.

Below *Crocus* 'Pickwick', a cultivar with large flowers of palest mauve feathered with violet, was developed from the species *C. vernus*. It associates well with another old garden favourite *C.* 'Dutch Yellow', a richly-coloured cross between the two species *C. flavus* and *C. angustifolius*, which has been cultivated since as far back as the seventeenth century.

A very welcome plant that can be expected to come into bloom during March is *Primula denticulata*, a relative of our own native primrose and its many-coloured descendant the polyanthus. Coming as it does from the Himalayas and mountainous regions of western China, *P. denticulata* is one of the most reliable of all spring-flowering plants, its blooms opening at about the same time every year, regardless of the weather. As the days lengthen, so does the strong stem, surmounted by a tightly packed head of flower-buds, which at the appointed time open to form an almost spherical mass of crowded and very colourful blooms.

Though the original type, still widely grown both in borders and in rock-gardens, has flowers of pale lavender with an attractive yellow centre, breeders have now produced a range of colours, including purple, deep carmine and white. The drumstick primrose, as it is popularly known, may be easily raised from seed, and will flower the second year after sowing.

Above *Narcissus* 'Charity May' is one of the first hybrid daffodils to bloom. It derives its swept-back outer petals, its brilliance of colour and its earliness of flowering from its parent *N. cyclamineus*, which was crossed with a garden daffodil to produce this popular cultivar.

Left *Narcissus bulbocodium*, known as the hoop petticoat daffodil from the crinoline-like shape of its trumpet, is a favourite species for naturalizing in grass. On its left can be seen the flower of a dog's-tooth violet (*Erythronium denscanis*).

Bulbs, Corms and Tubers

For beauty, variety and quantity of flowers, the bulbs, corms and tubers are at their most valuable this month in almost every part of the garden, when there are so few other types of plant in bloom. The flower-buds, which were formed during the previous season, have been waiting underground, protected against frost by the insulating layer of soil above them, till the time is right for them to emerge above the surface and open.

Many of the early-flowering kinds already mentioned in the notes for February (see page 44) will still be in bloom. Others may perhaps only now be coming into flower for the first time if they are growing in less favoured areas or if the winter has been a long and hard one.

In addition, there are a great many that do not start to bloom till the length of daylight approaches that of darkness, and these will be opening their flowers in the latter half of this month. Favourites among them for brightening the garden are the many different kinds of narcissus, popularly known as daffodils. Few bulbous plants are so useful for many different purposes, from beds and borders to rock gardens and naturalizing in grass.

The daffodil season starts this month in many gardens with the small-flowered *Narcissus cyclamineus*, a native of Spain and Portugal. This species is valued not only for the earliness of its blooms, which often start to open in February, but for the unsurpassed richness of their colour and for their distinctive shape.

The trumpet, which is long, tubular and slightly frilled, is surmounted by narrow outer segments which stand upright like the petals of a cyclamen, from which it takes the second part of its name. It spreads freely, flowers punctually and reliably each year, tolerates shady conditions and seems to prefer damp places.

Several miniature hybrids between *N. cyclamineus* and other species are also now in bloom, one of the loveliest being the deep golden 'Minicycla', resulting from a cross with another small-flowered native of Spain and Portugal, *N. asturiensis*.

There are also many larger-flowered hybrids with garden daffodils, such as 'Charity May' (pictured opposite), which owe their earliness, their bright colour and the shape of their flowers to *N. cyclamineus*.

Right *Arabis caucasica*, from the eastern Mediterranean, is a favourite species of rock-cress, widely grown in rock gardens and on walls for its attractive grey-green downy leaves and its abundance of fragrant flowers from early spring.

Below *Petasites japonicus* makes a handsome waterside plant when its large leaves reach full size later in the year: its greenish flowers open very early, like those of the related winter heliotrope, *Petasites fragrans*, noted for their vanilla-like scent.

Above *Tulipa kaufmanniana* 'Shakespeare', with its striking salmon-pink and apricot blooms, is among the best and most popular of several excellent cultivars of the water-lily tulip, one of the first to flower and easiest to grow of all the many different species introduced to our gardens from central Asia.

A March-flowering narcissus species of great charm is *Narcissus bulbocodium*, known as the hoop petticoat daffodil because its flowers are shaped like miniature crinolines (see the photograph on page 54). It is native to several countries bordering the western Mediterranean, including Algeria, Morocco, Spain and France, and many different forms have been introduced to gardens, with flowers varying in colour from palest lemon to rich gold.

N. bulbocodium soon forms large clumps if it is happy with its growing conditions. It is excellent for naturalizing in grass, where it associates particularly well with *N. cyclamineus*.

If planted together, the two will provide continuous bloom for several weeks, starting with the first flowers of *N. cyclamineus*, following with a combined display by both species as their flowering times coincide, and ending with the last blooms to open of *N. bulbocodium*.

Other hoop petticoat daffodils include *Narcissus cantabricus*, of which the subspecies *monophyllus*, with a single long, narrow leaf, is best known to gardeners. Its flowers are snow-white, daintily pleated and almost transparent when the early spring sun shines through them.

Coming from the north of Africa, it needs plenty of sun and is best grown in a well-drained part of the rock-garden or under glass in an alpine house or frame, where it is safer and will flower a week or two earlier than if grown in the open.

A few of the large-flowered garden daffodils may be opening an early bud or two, but generally their flowering season starts next month, and they are mentioned on page 70. There are, however, several double-flowered cultivars which regularly come into full bloom early in March, including the well-named 'Butter and Eggs' (known also by many other names, such as Incomparable and Golden Phoenix) as well as the old faithful 'Telamonius Plenus' (also called Van Sion), which some say was brought over from Italy more than three centuries ago and has been cheering up our gardens with its rumpled golden blooms at the beginning of March every year since. Daffodils have few rivals for bringing spring colour.

Of the many other bulbs, corms and tubers now coming into flower, the crocuses are still prominent in beds and borders, rock gardens and grass. In addition to those already mentioned in the notes for January and February (see pages 36 and 44), many of which may still be producing flowers, several other species are now coming into bloom. One is *Crocus vernus*, which is native to a very wide area, from mountainous regions of Poland and Russia southwards through Yugoslavia as far as Sicily. Like all widespread species it is very variable, with subspecies and varieties ranging from the common white crocus of alpine meadows to the dark-flowered kind from which has come the popular large 'Dutch Purple'.

There are also several magnificent cultivars, developed over many years, such as the plum-coloured 'Remembrance', the dazzling 'King of the Whites' and the beautifully feathered 'Pickwick', pictured on page 53.

A *Crocus* species of great charm is *C. biflorus*, native to a wide area from southern Italy and Sicily eastwards as far as Turkey and along the Black Sea coast to the south of Russia and Iran. In its natural habitat the flowering time varies from as early as January in the warmer lowlands to as late as May in the chillier mountainous regions.

In British gardens the flowers usually open during March. They are mostly an attractive dusty lilac, but there are cultivars of different colours, such as subspecies *weldenii* 'Fairy', whose flowers are white inside and grey outside.

The species *C. etruscus*, with violet-blue flowers, is now rare in its native Italy, but the cultivar 'Zwanenburg' which has been developed from it, and which has larger, more shapely flowers of a more intense colour, has become a popular favourite and is to be found in flower at this time of year in gardens throughout Britain.

The miniature species *C. minimus*, which is little more than two inches (5 cm) high, produces its lavender flowers, with deep purple feathering, over a period of several weeks, starting early in the month, and is well suited to the rock garden, as are many of the other small *Crocus* species.

Some of the bulbous irises mentioned as flowering in February (see page 44) may still be in bloom, and they are likely to be joined by others this month. One of the most attractive is *Iris aucheri*, best under glass, with fragrant flowers of the palest blue clustered together on a stout stem above thick leaves arranged in opposite rows like those of a leek.

Another bulbous species coming into bloom now is the taller *I. bucharica*, the usual garden form of which has flowers the colour of clotted cream above handsome, shiny leaves. Its flowering time coincides with that of *I. persica*, best grown under glass, which has flowers in cool shades of green, fawn and grey.

All these irises need plenty of sun, both to show their flowers off to perfection and to ensure their well-being. They come from stony, arid places where the ground in which they grow is baked dry during the summer, so as well as exposure to full sun they need a well drained soil.

Left *Fritillaria imperialis*, otherwise known as crown imperial, is an Asian relative of the European native snake's head, *Fritillaria meleagris*. It produces its magnificent flowers in early spring under glass, or several weeks later in a warm border outside. Several named cultivars exist, with flowers ranging from lemon yellow to orange and tawny red.

Below *Saxifraga* x *jenkinsae* is an early-blooming, cushion-forming saxifrage, with silvery leaves and flowers of the palest pink, hardy in the rock garden and excellent under unheated glass.

Above *Cymbidium* Tyrian Cascade is one of the modern miniature hybrids which have been created by crossing some of the large standard varieties with smaller species. Such hybrids have brought the growing of these lovely orchids within the reach of owners of small greenhouses with a limited amount of space available.

Most of the many forms and varieties of the common snowdrop, *Galanthus nivalis*, will in a normal season have been in bloom for some weeks. Its flowers have the ability to remain undamaged under a layer of snow and emerge looking none the worse when it melts. Unfortunately this is not always the case with some of the taller-stemmed cultivars and hybrids, whose flowers may face severe air frost while those of the ordinary kind enjoy warmth from the earth as well as the protective covering of snow, which acts as a blanket against heat loss.

Most snowdrops will be past their best by the middle of March, but the late-flowering cultivar 'Scharlockii' may last longer. The related spring snowflake, *Leucojum vernum*, usually produces its clusters of green-tipped, creamy-white flowers at the ends of long stems just as most of the snowdrops are finishing.

The azure flowers of *Scilla bifolia* may have already started to open last month in sunny spots, or in the light shade of shrubs or small trees. Equally early is its close relative *S. mischtschenkoana*, generally known as *S. tubergeniana*, with larger flowers of the palest blue or nearly white. Both are in bloom for many weeks, during which they may be joined by *S. sibirica*, with prussian blue flowers, and its cultivars, notably the deep blue 'Spring Beauty'.

Many of the related chionodoxas may also be producing their first flowers this month. The most popular and easily grown species is *Chionodoxa gigantea* (*C. luciliae* of gardens), the glory of the snow, which produces a succession of mauvish blue flowers with a conspicuous white centre. The variant known as 'Rosea' has flowers of clear pink.

There is also a hybrid between the scillas and the chionodoxas called × *Chionoscilla allenii*, which often occurs naturally where the two are grown together and which is slightly variable. Some of the best forms have been given separate cultivar names.

The first of the spring anemones to come into flower is usually *Anemone blanda*, which was introduced into gardens from Greece and neighbouring lands a long time ago. In mild parts it may have begun last month to open its narrow-petalled flowers in shades of blue and white. Its many cultivars include 'White Splendour', the deep blue 'Atrocaerulea' and the vivid 'Radar', with flowers of rich pink with white centres.

Later in the month *Anemone nemorosa*, the native wood anemone, opens its pink-tinged white flowers. It has cultivars ranging from pale to dark blue.

Rock Garden and Pool

Many of the best March flowers in the rock garden come from the smaller bulbs, corms and tubers described in the previous section. Other plants now in bloom may include some listed on page 45, as well as early-flowering arabis, pictured on page 55.

By the pool the sweet-scented flowers of winter heliotrope, *Petasites fragrans*, and of the related *P. japonicus* (also pictured on page 55) open while the leaves, which will grow very large, are still small.

Right Cineraria 'Sky Blue' is an example of the many fine cultivars developed by breeders of one of the most popular of all plants for the greenhouse, with flowers in a great variety of different colours.

Fruit

If carefully gathered, free from bruises and blemishes, properly wrapped and kept in a cool place, some late-keeping dessert apples such as 'Sturmer Pippin' or 'Tydeman's Late Orange', and cookers such as 'Newton Wonder' or 'Wellington', may still provide excellent fruit from store.

Vegetables

Brussels sprouts may still be gathered from late varieties, and kales and savoy cabbages will be at their most useful.

The first sticks of forced rhubarb (see page 47) should be ready during the month.

In early districts the first spring cabbages may be ready for cutting, and sprouting broccoli may yield some early pickings.

Carrots, celeriac, onions, parsnips and potatoes may be used from store.

Below *Clivia miniata* is a handsome bulbous plant from South Africa, suitable for the cool greenhouse, with a long flowering period from March well into the summer.

Greenhouse and Frame

Many of the most appealing plants that can be brought into flower this month under unheated glass are the smaller species and varieties of bulbs, corms and tubers just covered on pages 54–8. Not only will they come into bloom earlier under glass but the flowers may be enjoyed, undamaged by adverse weather conditions outside, at a comfortable height for viewing them on the bench or staging.

Larger and more imposing bulbous plants which flower now, suitable for a greenhouse heated sufficiently to keep the night temperature from falling below 50°F (10°C), are the clivias, with showy flowers and glossy evergreen leaves, a beautiful example of which is pictured on the left.

Orchids gaining popularity as early-flowering plants for cool greenhouses of average size are the miniature cymbidiums, which take up much less space than the standard kinds. Pictured on the opposite page is an excellent example, and breeders are constantly making new crosses.

Cinerarias continue to make a decorative display, as do many of the other plants mentioned on pages 45, 165 and 173.

House Plants

With the days lengthening, several windowsill plants will be opening new flowers, including cultivars of begonia, cyclamen, impatiens and saintpaulia.

What to do in March

Trees and Shrubs

We are now coming to one of the busiest times of the year for two very important operations: pruning and propagating. But first any planting of deciduous trees and shrubs that still remains to be done must be completed just as soon as weather permits, before they start into growth. This is particularly urgent where those dug from the ground are concerned. With container-grown plants timing is not so vital, since they suffer little root damage from being transplanted. For full details of how to plant, see page 199.

Stake trees and tall shrubs (see page 200) to prevent them from being blown over during the gales that so often occur in March.

In exposed places a windbreak will protect newly planted subjects until they become established. Anything that reduces the force of the wind will do, such as sacking or wire-netting fixed between stakes, wattle screens, or even a row of bushy pea-sticks.

The planting of evergreens is best left for a month or two, till the days are growing longer and the weather warmer.

Those shrubs that flower on the current year's growth should be pruned now, to give the new shoots a long growing season. Shrubs in this group include *Buddleja davidii*, deciduous ceanothus, ceratostigma, fuchsia, *Hydrangea paniculata*, *Prunus glandulosa* and *P. triloba*, romneya, *Spiraea* × *bumalda*, *S. douglasii* and *S. japonica*.

Others, pruned to produce coloured stems for winter effect, include *Cornus alba*, *C. stolonifera*, *Rubus cockburnianus* and several willows. How to prune them is shown on pages 210–17.

A start may be made with propagation by various methods. The first of these is layering, a simple way to produce new plants,

especially of those shrubs which are difficult to strike from cuttings. Suitable subjects are several species of amelanchier, chimonanthus and rhus, and the method is shown in detail on page 196. Some shrubs which send up suckers from below ground level, such as the popular *Kerria japonica*, may most easily be propagated by digging up these suckers and planting them either in their permanent quarters or in a nursery bed to be transplanted at the end of the growing season.

Some shrubs and sub-shrubs such as the tree poppies *Romneya coulteri*, *R. trichocalyx* and their hybrid *R.* × *hybrida*, also the stag's-horn sumach *Rhus typhina*, may be propagated from root cuttings taken now, as explained on page 194.

Many shrubs are easily raised from seed sown now in pots or boxes, as described on page 219, and placed in a cold frame or greenhouse to germinate. Among those that may be raised in this way are the brooms (cytisus and genista), cotoneaster, laburnum, the shrubby mallow *Lavatera olbia* and wisteria. Garden varieties will not come true from seed, but there is always the possibility of an exciting new seedling.

Climbers and Wall-plants

There is still time to plant clematis and other deciduous climbers. Give them a good mulch after planting and never let them flag for lack of water. Clematis species and hybrids that flower only on current year's growth must be pruned now if they have not already been attended to. See page 215 for full details.

Roses

March is the month when experienced growers prune roses of the hybrid tea and floribunda types, as well as of the increasingly popular miniature varieties. They all bear

their flowers on wood of the current year's growth.

To produce blooms as early in the season as possible, it is necessary to prune them at the earliest opportunity, which in most seasons is at the beginning of this month in the south and towards the end of the month in the colder parts of the north.

Pruning done too soon runs the risk of stimulating premature growth which may be damaged by freezing weather. Pruning too late will waste the energy that the plant has put into the young shoots that must then be cut off, and will also delay flowering.

The right time to prune is when the buds can be seen starting to swell along the strongest stems.

Very hard pruning, almost to ground level, is nowadays only practised by those who want to produce a limited number of large blooms for exhibition purposes.

For roses that are not intended to carry off prizes but just to produce plenty of flowers to brighten the garden and provide some to cut for home decoration, less severe pruning is now usual, and is explained in step-by-step detail on page 216.

When the job has been completed, collect all the prunings and put them on the bonfire, together with any fallen leaves. These are better burnt than composted since they may carry disease. Remove weeds while they are still young, give the bed a dressing of fertilizer (see page 183) and if possible finish with a good mulch.

Borders and Beds

Herbaceous perennials may now be planted if the soil is in the right condition. Many kinds do better, especially on heavy clay, with this early spring planting, when the ground is beginning to warm up and encourage rooting, rather than with autumn planting, when the soil is becoming colder and less welcoming. Overgrown clumps may be split up and replanted, as shown on page 197. Discard the worn-out middle part and use only strong outside pieces for replanting.

Dead tops of herbaceous plants which were left on as protection during the winter may be removed as the weather improves. This clears the way for new growth and enables tidying up to be done.

Dead, decaying and brown-spotted leaves of bearded irises should be taken off, and diseased parts of rhizomes cut out. Dust the cuts with fungicide.

Remove weeds, by hand or hoe, while they are still small and easy to deal with. A dressing of fertilizer (see page 183) will help feed the plants as they start into growth, and a good mulch with garden compost or other organic material (see page 183) will not only conserve moisture but help suppress weeds.

Most hardy annuals are not usually sown till April, but if the ground is in a suitable state there is no reason why some of the hardiest should not be sown in the latter half of this month in order to gain time. (For detailed instructions on sowing, see page 191.)

Among the hardiest of hardy annuals are calendulas, annual candytuft and chrysanthemums, cornflowers, nigellas and Shirley poppies. Protect the newly sown seed from birds, as shown on page 191.

Bulbs, Corms and Tubers
Snowdrops establish themselves best if they are moved while still in leaf, so now is the time to plant new ones or to split up and replant overcrowded clumps. Crocuses and winter aconites may also be moved. Cut off faded flower-heads, to prevent energy from going into seed production.

If conditions allow, a first planting of gladiolus corms may be made towards the end of the month. In heavy soil put a layer of sand under each corm to assist drainage (see page 198). Do not plant all the corms at once. Two or three more plantings at two-weekly intervals will extend the flowering season.

Rock Gardens and Pools
Alpines may still be planted. If any have been loosened by frost, firm them down again. Remove weeds before they get a hold.

When pools are ice-free, half the old water can be removed and replaced with fresh clean water. If fish are becoming active, a little food may be given.

Lawns
Prepare for the mowing season by brushing with a stiff broom to distribute worm-casts and remove rubbish. Give a thorough raking with a springy steel rake, to make the grass – and the weeds – stand up, so that the mower cuts them instead of flattening them.

Give a first mowing when the grass is about three inches (eight cm) long. Set the mower blades high, so as to top the grass, not shave it.

Fruit
Any necessary pruning of stone fruits may be carried out as the sap starts to rise and the risk of infection is lessened. Cover the cuts with wound paint.

Give fruit trees and bushes a first spring spray at bud-burst and repeat at further stages, to protect against disease and pests.

Peaches, nectarines and apricots trained on walls and fences come into blossom early in the year, and their flowers are vulnerable to damage by spring frosts. It is therefore a sensible precaution as soon as the flower buds are showing pink to protect them during frosty periods by covering the trees with a double thickness of garden netting, or even a length of old net curtain. Be careful not to let the covering damage the flowers, and remove it as soon as the frosty weather is over.

Vegetables
The busiest time of the year is now beginning as the ground, after exposure to winter weather, becomes ready for surface cultivation in preparation for sowing (see page 190). Among the crops that benefit from early sowing, to give a long season for growth and ripening, are onions. Many people grow these from sets, which if not already planted should be put in as soon as possible, together with shallots.

Among crops which may be sown in the open as conditions allow are beet, broad beans, broccoli, brussels sprouts, cabbages, carrots, lettuces, leeks, parsnips, peas and radishes.

Early potatoes may be planted from mid-month, according to conditions and district.

Greenhouse and Frame
Rooted cuttings of chrysanthemums and carnations should be potted on as necessary. Further cuttings may be taken from dahlias and fuchsias. Pelargoniums can be started into growth if this has not already been done.

Half-hardy annuals may now be sown, also tomatoes, aubergines and sweet peppers, if a minimum of 68°F (20°C) can be maintained during germination. Celery may be sown in a cool house or frame.

House Plants
Repotting may now be started for plants which have outgrown their pots. Knock the plant out of its pot and carefully remove some soil. Cut back a few old roots and repot in fresh compost. Overpotting should be avoided; a pot one size larger is quite big enough.

April

April, April,
Laugh thy girlish laughter;
Then, the moment after,
Weep thy girlish tears.

Sir William Watson (1858–1936)

April is generally the most uncertain month in the garden, with bursts of sunshine and downpours of rain. Often there is hail or sleet, with occasional flurries of snow – sometimes within minutes of each other, and sometimes even at the same time. The days are now longer than the nights and the sun is higher in the sky, with the result that the ground is beginning to warm up. This encourages root growth of established plants and stimulates the germination of seeds.

Experienced gardeners welcome the mixture of different types of weather and are glad when the occasional shower interrupts a period of sunshine, even if it does drive them indoors and put a stop to gardening while it lasts. They know that a long, unbroken spell of sunny weather at this time of year can be very dangerous, for two different but related reasons.

First, the same clear sky that gives many hours of sunshine during the day may bring about a rapid fall in temperature during the night to freezing point or below, when there is no layer of cloud to act like a blanket and protect tender young growth and open blossoms from frost damage.

Secondly, a dry spell can cause excessive loss of moisture from the top layer of soil, with the result that roots of newly emerging seedlings may shrivel before they have grown sufficiently to penetrate to the lower levels where they can find enough moisture for their needs. In such circumstances it is usually the seedlings of cultivated plants that suffer most. Weeds, unless they are removed in their early stages, are likely to win the competition for moisture.

Left *Rhododendron* 'President Roosevelt', one of the very few variegated rhododendrons, remains brilliant, even when flowering is over, with its gold-splashed foliage.

What to see and enjoy in April

Above *Prunus subhirtella* 'Pendula', a weeping form of the spring cherry from Japan, makes a small, wide spreading tree, with slender, drooping branches wreathed in tiny, single, blush-pink flowers opening from deeper pink buds. It has received the Royal Horticultural Society's Award of Merit.

Trees and Shrubs

As spring progresses and the days continue to lengthen, many more trees and shrubs come into bloom to attract pollinating insects which are becoming increasingly active and eager for the nectar and pollen that the flowers provide. Many of their blooms are individually small – the gusty winds still to be expected might damage large ones – but they make up in profusion of flowering what they lack in size.

Some of the most spectacular April displays are provided by ornamental fruit trees and bushes. Among the earliest are many *Prunus* species and cultivars, including ornamental cherries, peaches, apricots and almonds. As the month proceeds they are joined by ornamental pears, foaming with clustered white flowers, and many different crab apples, with flowers ranging from palest pink to deep crimson.

The ornamental quinces, commonly called japonica and belonging to the genus *Chaenomeles*, may in mild places and against walls have started to flower last month, but it is mainly in April that they produce their clusters of brilliant blossoms in shades of orange, salmon and red. There are also white-flowered cultivars.

Flowering currants (*Ribes*) make a vivid display with their racemes of intense red blooms. Forsythias, whether against walls or in the open, catch the eye with their stems smothered with rich yellow flowers.

Among the most magnificent of all April sights is that of the many different magnolias now coming into bloom, some with tulip-like and some with starry flowers.

There is a special charm about deciduous spring-flowering trees and shrubs, with their blossoms set off against bare branches. A selection is given opposite.

SELECTED TREES AND SHRUBS

Deciduous, in flower

Acer platanoides, Norway maple, with clustered yellow blossoms; *Amelanchier lamarckii* (*canadensis*), snowy mespilus, wreathed in starry flowers; *Chaenomeles japonica, C. speciosa* and *C.* x *superba*, flowering quinces, with many cultivars; *Cytisus purgans*, an early broom, with fragrant yellow flowers, and *C.* x *praecox*, with masses of rich cream blooms; *Corylopsis pauciflora* and *C. willmottiae*, with cowslip-scented yellow flowers; *Forsythia* x *intermedia* 'Spectabilis' (pictured on right) and many other cultivars; *Fothergilla monticola*, with scented white bottlebrush flowers; *Kerria japonica*, bearing bright yellow, buttercup-like blooms along arching stems, and its cultivars 'Pleniflora', with double flowers, and 'Variegata' ('Picta') with cream-margined leaves; *Magnolia denudata, M. kobus, M. liliiflora, M.* x *loebneri* and its cultivars, *M. salicifolia, M.* x *soulangiana* the most popular and widely grown of all the garden hybrids, with many lovely cultivars (one of which is pictured lower right), and *M. stellata*, the star magnolia, a compact shrub with fragrant white semi-double flowers; *Malus floribunda* and several other flowering crabs; ornamental *Prunus* species and varieties of many different kinds, including *P. armeniaca* (apricot), *P. avium* (gean), *P. cerasifera* (cherry plum), *P. dulcis* (*amygdalus*) (almond), *P. padus* (bird cherry), *P. persica* (peach), with many single and double flowered cultivars in a wide range of colours from white to crimson, and a large number of different flowering cherries, of which the many Japanese cultivars are perhaps the most spectacular; *Pyrus nivalis*, snow pear, and other ornamental pears; *Ribes sanguineum*, flowering currant, and cultivars; *Spiraea* x *arguta*, bridal wreath, and *S. thunbergii*, both festooned with flowers of the purest white for several weeks.

Above *Forsythia* x *intermedia* 'Spectabilis' is a very popular and reliable cultivar, awarded both a First Class Certificate and the Award of Garden Merit.

Left *Magnolia* x *soulangiana* 'Rustica Rubra' is one of the finest cultivars of the most popular magnolia hybrids, granted the Award of Garden Merit by the Royal Horticultural Society.

Left *Rhododendron fulvum* makes a large shrub or small tree, notable for its handsome, shining, dark green leaves, brown-felted beneath, and its bell-shaped pink flowers, often with a deeper blotch.

Below *Rhododendron* 'Elizabeth', among the most popular hybrids ever raised for its deep red flowers and compact growth, has received both a First Class Certificate and an Award of Garden Merit.

Among the April-flowering evergreens are many which have been brought from distant parts of the world to enrich our gardens. Perhaps the most colourful and striking now coming into bloom are *Rhododendron* species, including many azaleas, mostly from the Himalayas, China, Tibet, India and Burma, together with a large number of hybrids bred from them. Two fine examples are pictured here, and a selection is given in the list on the opposite page. All those included have been chosen for their hardiness and their suitability for gardens of modest size; all have also been granted awards for excellence from the Royal Horticultural Society.

Many other hardy evergreens which beautify our gardens with their flowers at this time of year were also brought from mountainous regions of Asia, including camellias, the Chinese *Daphne tangutica* and *Osmanthus delavayi*, and such gems from Japan as *Pieris japonica*.

Some come from the Americas, notably two brilliant orange-flowered shrubs from Chile, *Berberis darwinii* and *B. linearifolia*, and the mexican orange blossom, *Choisya ternata*, with aromatic leaves and intensely fragrant white flowers.

Evergreens, in flower

Berberis darwinii, with brilliant yellow, crimson-tinged flowers, *B. linearifolia*, with rich orange blooms, and the hybrids *B. x lologensis*, with apricot-yellow flowers, and *B. x stenophylla* and its cultivars with flowers in shades of gold; *Camellia japonica* and *C. x williamsii*, each with many cultivars in a wide range of colours; *Daphne cneorum*, garland flower, with sweetly scented rose-pink blooms, and *D. tangutica*, with fragrant flowers pink outside and white tinged with purple inside; *Erica arborea* and its cultivar 'Alpina', with scented white flowers, late-flowering cultivars of *E. carnea* (now *herbacea*), *E. x darleyensis* and *E. mediterranea* (now *erigena*), each with many cultivars; *Mahonia aquifolium*, with its long-lasting spikes of fragrant yellow flowers; *Osmanthus delavayi*, bearing an abundance of sweetly scented tubular white blossoms, and *O.* 'Burkwoodii', a hybrid from the last-named species with even more intensely fragrant flowers; *Pieris japonica* and its cultivars, with drooping sprays of waxy white flowers and striking, copper-coloured young foliage; *Skimmia japonica* and cultivars, with fragrant white flowers (followed, if plants of both sexes are present, by bright red fruits); *Viburnum x burkwoodii*, with clusters of scented white flowers opening from buds suffused with pink.

Rhododendrons in bloom include the following (with flower colours). Species: *Rhododendron augustinii* (blue), *R. campanulatum* (lavender), *R. fargesii* (warm lilac), *R. hippophaeoides* (sky blue), *R. impeditum* (blue), *R. pemakoense* (pink), *R. russatum* (purple, white throat), *R. williamsianum* (pink). Hardy hybrids: 'Bluebird', 'Blue Diamond', 'Blue Tit', 'Butterfly' (cream, crimson specks), 'Jacksonii' (rose and maroon), 'Sapphire' (lavender), 'Seta' (white and pink).

Hybrid azaleas: 'Addy Wery' (red), 'Hatsugiri' (magenta), 'Hinomayo' (clear pink), 'Kirin' (deep rose).

Climbers and Wall-plants

Clematis species now coming into bloom are among the loveliest of climbers, attaching themselves to supports by means of their twining leaf-stalks and producing masses of elegant, nodding flowers. One of the finest is *Clematis alpina*, whose violet-blue flowers bear a tuft of white in the middle; the excellent cultivar 'Frances Rivis' has larger flowers than the type, and 'Ruby' bears blooms of a glowing rose red. The evergreen *C. armandii* produces clusters of creamy white blooms in profusion. Those of its cultivar 'Apple Blossom' are, as the name suggests, attractively shaded with pink, deeper on the outside, and those of another cultivar 'Snowdrift' are pure white.

A Chinese species of outstanding beauty is *C. macropetala*, with clear blue flowers which appear almost double because of the eye-catching paler tuft of floral parts in the centre. In many places its blooms do not open until May, or even June, but in favoured localities and sheltered conditions against a wall or fence it may begin to open its flowers this month and continue to do so for several weeks. The cultivar 'Markham's Pink' has flowers the colour of strawberry ice.

Above *Rhododendron* 'Bluebird', a hybrid, raised at Bodnant, between two species from China, *R. augustinii* and *R. intricatum*, makes a highly floriferous dwarf shrub of compact habit, ideal for rock gardens and towards the front of mixed borders. It has been granted the Royal Horticultural Society's Award of Garden Merit.

Below *Bergenia* 'Morning Blush' ('Morgenrote') is one of many cultivars of these magnificent ground-covering plants, allied to the saxifrages, with large evergreen leaves. In spring stout stems arise bearing dense heads of flowers. This fine cultivar is valued not only for the size and rich colour of its flowers but for its habit of producing a second crop in early summer.

Among the most beautiful of those shrubs that are grown against a wall because they are not reliably hardy enough for the open ground are many evergreen members of the genus *Ceanothus*. Nearly all come from California and are known as californian lilacs. In mild places, with shelter from cutting winds, and given a spell of favourable weather, some of the earliest may be starting to open their first flowers towards the end of the month. In full bloom they are a magnificent sight, their stems hidden from view by massed clusters of flowers, mostly in various shades of blue. There are also some with white blossoms.

Among the earliest and most floriferous of the species popular as wall shrubs and generally available from nurseries and garden centres are *Ceanothus dentatus*, with sky-blue flowers, and *C. impressus*, with flowers of somewhat deeper blue. Of the many excellent cultivars some of the best are 'A. T. Johnson', with rich blue flowers in spring and again in autumn, 'Cascade', with bright blue flowers in long clusters, 'Delight', one of the hardiest, and 'Southmead', with dark, glossy leaves and blooms of velvety blue. All these selected cultivars make wall shrubs of great beauty and have been granted awards by the Royal Horticultural Society.

Borders and Beds

Adonis vernalis, a European native known as pheasant's eye, which may have already started to bloom in March in mild districts, will in most places now be opening its shining yellow flowers, like large buttercups, daintily displayed against bright, feathery foliage. There is also a white-flowered form.

Bergenia species and their forms and hybrids, often known as megaseas, brighten the spring garden with their dense heads of flowers carried on stout stems above the large, bold, evergreen leaves. There are many different cultivars, with flowers of pink, carmine, crimson, purple and white; a splendid example is pictured below.

Brunnera macrophylla will now be starting to open its intense blue, forget-me-not flowers borne above handsome, heart-shaped leaves. The lovely cultivar 'Variegata' has foliage splashed with pale primrose.

Species and cultivars of *Doronicum* and *Helleborus* continue to flower, as does *Primula denticulata*; details will be found in last month's notes on pages 53 and 54.

Iris unguicularis, which has flowered for some months during mild spells, is now joined by *I. innominata*, which with its hybrids has exquisitely veined flowers in shades of yellow, lilac, violet and white.

In addition to the increasing number of perennials now bringing life and colour to borders and beds, several hardy biennials sown last season will now be starting to bloom. Some may strictly speaking be more or less perennial in nature, but give the best garden value when treated as biennials. They are specially effective for bedding schemes and filling gaps before the annuals are sufficiently developed to reach the flowering stage.

Forms of *Bellis perennis*, known as double daisies, are among the earliest and most attractive. Special favourites are the selections known as 'Monstrosa', with large flowers, and the dainty 'Pomponette'.

Wallflowers (*Cheiranthus cheiri*), the most popular of spring bedding plants, come in a range both of heights, from eighteen inches (forty-five cm) to nine inches (twenty-two cm), and of colours, from blood-red to gold, with many pastel shades. The siberian wallflower (*C. × allionii*) has flowers of brilliant orange; there are golden ones too.

Another old favourite the forget-me-not (*Myosotis*) is also now opening its flowers in shades of blue, some of the best being 'Blue Ball', 'Royal Blue' and 'Ultramarine'. They are among the most popular bedding plants to associate with spring bulbs.

Above *Fritillaria imperialis*, the crown imperial, introduced from the western Himalayas several centuries ago, is among the most imposing of hardy bulbous plants. Colours range from orange-red to yellow.

Left *Narcissus* 'Red Devon', raised in Devon and registered in 1943, is a fine garden daffodil, given an Award of Merit after trials at Wisley.

SELECTED BULBS, CORMS AND TUBERS

Anemone apennina, with sky-blue flowers (also pink and white), *A. coronaria* and its many forms and hybrids, including St Brigid (mostly semi-double) and De Caen (large, single) in shades and mixtures of red, blue, mauve and white; *Bulbocodium vernum* (red-violet); *Cyclamen repandum*, last spring species to flower, in shades from palest pink to deep rose; *Erythronium dens-canis*, known as dog's-tooth violet, together with the pink-flowered *E. revolutum* and several lovely cultivars such as *E.* 'Jeanette Brickell', *E.* 'Pagoda' and *E.* 'White Beauty'; *Fritillaria imperialis*, crown imperial, (orange-red and yellow), *F. meleagris*, snake's-head, (purple chequered, also white) and many other fritillaries; *Ipheion uniflorum* (silvery white, shaded lilac) and its cultivars 'Wisley Blue', with larger and more strongly coloured blooms, and the dark-flowered 'Froyle Mill'; *Iris bucharica*, a species from central Asia with creamy yellow flowers *I. magnifica*, a large, easily grown species with flowers of pale lavender with a bright orange blotch, *I.* x *warlsind*, a splendid hybrid with blue, veined flowers with rich yellow falls, and *I. willmottiana*, a small species with pale, lavender-flecked blooms but more often grown in gardens in its white-flowered form; *Leucojum aestivum*, the summer snowflake, despite its common name, normally flowers from mid-April to early May, bearing several white, bell-like blooms with green markings at the end of a stout stem: its cultivar 'Gravetye Giant' has larger and better flowers than the type; *Muscari armeniacum*, the grape hyacinth, has clustered flowers mostly in shades of deep blue, but those of the delightful cultivar 'Cantab' are considerably paler, and there are also some white forms; some species have darker, almost black, flowers, and those of *M. macrocarpum* are a bright yellow.

Above An old chimney-pot, pictured here planted with mixed pansies, makes an attractive and unusual container for bedding plants of many kinds. Its mellow colour, warm but subdued, blends well with its surroundings and harmonizes with the brighter colours of the flowers. Its height allows the plants it contains to be enjoyed at close quarters, without stooping.

Bulbs, Corms and Tubers

A great many of the species already dealt with in the notes for March (for their descriptions see pages 54–8) may still be in bloom during April, depending on district, position and weather. To them may now be added a large number of other species which wait till the days are longer and the weather is kinder before opening their flowers. A selection of some of the more garden-worthy is given in the next column.

Many are excellent for naturalising in grass or for the front of the border, and some of the dwarf ones are invaluable in the rock garden.

Dominating April bedding schemes are the large-flowered daffodils. There are many sections, with a vast range of form and colour. They can be seen and compared in gardens and parks, at shows, and in bulb-merchants' illustrated catalogues, which contain many novelties.

The large-flowered bedding tulips are mostly at their best in late April and May, and are dealt with on page 85, but many developed from *Tulipa fosteriana* and *T. kaufmanniana* flower as early as the daffodils.

Right *Primula marginata*, native to the Maritime Alps where it grows mainly in the crevices of cliffs, is a splendid plant for sunny, rapidly draining places in rock gardens or walls.

Rock Garden and Pool

April sees the beginning of the season when the rock garden is at its most beautiful and colourful. Many of the smaller species of bulbs and corms, together with their cultivars (see previous column), will be displaying their flowers to best effect among the alpines, as will some of the low-growing shrubs, in particular many dwarf rhododendrons, including several vivid azalea hybrids (see page 67). A large number of other plants will now be coming into flower, of which the following is a selection of some garden favourites.

Alyssum (now *Aurinia*) *saxatile* makes a spectacular sight tumbling over a bank or a dry-stone wall, its blooms forming a sheet of bright yellow hiding the felted grey leaves; cultivars include the paler 'Citrinum' and the less rampant 'Compactum'.

The related *Arabis caucasica* (*albida*) makes a striking cascade with its profusion of white flowers. There are pink and red forms, also one with double flowers and another with variegated leaves.

Also related, and similar in growth, are the ever-popular aubrietas, mostly derived from *Aubrieta deltoidea*, in an array of brilliant colours, from purple to crimson, pink, lilac and violet. Some of them have white flowers.

Caltha palustris, marsh marigold, lights up the water's edge with its large golden blooms; there are single and double forms.

Corydalis lutea, yellow fumitory, normally comes into bloom next month, often taking over old walls, but *C. solida*, with purplish flowers, is earlier and less aggressive.

Draba aizoides, yellow whitlow grass, sends up stems bearing golden flowers from tufted rosettes; *D. bryoides* 'Imbricata' has denser rosettes and brighter flowers.

Right *Primula denticulata*, the drumstick primula, is a popular, reliable and easily grown species, with globose heads of mauve blooms. There are purple, pink and white forms.

Fruit

The last of the carefully wrapped and stored apples will now have been eaten, and no fresh produce can be expected from the open ground until the first soft fruits are ready for gathering, which in most gardens will not be until the latter part of May at the earliest. However, pot-grown strawberries under glass may in favourable circumstances yield some fruit by the end of this month.

Rhubarb, cooked and eaten as a dessert course though usually grown in a corner of the vegetable plot, should now be yielding a good supply of tender young stalks.

Few sights are lovelier than early fruit blossoms on leafless branches trained against walls and fences, as pictured here at Wisley on a clear April day.

Left *Lysichiton americanum*, bog arum, is a long-lived perennial for margins of pools and other wet places.

Below Plum 'Early Laxton', seen here in fan-trained form, follows its lovely blossom with yellow fruit, flushed red.

Gentians are among the rock garden's spring glories. Two of the most rewarding are the species group known as *Gentiana acaulis*, with intense blue trumpets flecked in the throat, and *G. verna*, with starry blue flowers and broader leaves.

Iberis sempervirens, perennial candytuft, produces massed white flowers from an evergreen mat; 'Little Gem' spreads less, and 'Snowflake' has the purest white blooms.

Omphalodes verna from the Alps, known as blue-eyed Mary, is usually the first of the navelworts to bloom, with sprays of sky-blue flowers and heart-shaped leaves.

Out of the many primulas suitable for rock gardens one of the most popular is *Primula auricula*, with fragrant yellow, white-centred blooms; there are many named cultivars such as 'Blue Velvet', and mixed hybrids in assorted colours.

Pulsatilla vulgaris, the pasque flower, will now be opening its enchanting silky violet blooms; there are also pink, red and white forms in cultivation.

Saxifrages, now starting their main flowering season, are dealt with on page 75.

Vegetables

In a well planned and well stocked vegetable garden there should now be plenty of fresh produce to be gathered and eaten. Asparagus will be sending up its first succulent shoots. Seakale beet (Swiss chard) and spinach beet provide leaves for gathering.

Sprouting broccoli, both purple and white, offers good pickings. Spring cabbages planted last autumn will start to form hearts towards the end of the month. Meanwhile kale, spring greens and turnip-tops provide a useful supply of leaves. Some of the hardy winter cauliflowers will now be producing heads ready for cutting.

Spring onions may now be pulled, either from cultivars such as 'White Lisbon' sown for the purpose during the previous summer or as thinnings from Japanese bulbing onions sown at the same time.

Leeks still in the ground may be dug, as may salsify, the vegetable oyster, and its black-skinned but white-fleshed relation scorzonera, which make welcome and delicious root vegetables before the first carrots come along.

Lettuces and radishes grown in a frame or greenhouse should now be providing the ingredients for early salads. Mustard and cress may be enjoyed from seed sprinkled on the surface of moist compost or peat in a small container. They can even be grown on damp flannel or blotting-paper in a shallow dish and stood first in the dark to germinate and then, when the seedlings are an inch or so (twenty-five mm) high, in a light and moderately warm place, such as the bench of a heated greenhouse or even a kitchen window-sill.

Given a good and plentiful harvest the previous year and the right conditions for storage, there may still be a supply of potatoes, onions and garlic from last season's crops.

Greenhouse and Frame

Probably the most spectacular greenhouse plants in bloom at this time of year are those of the genus *Hippeastrum*, with many magnificent cultivars. Other striking plants now in flower are the greenhouse calceolarias (pictured on page 75), with fleshy, pouched flowers in bright colours.

Above *Tulipa tarda*, a native of central Asia, where it grows on stony slopes, bears gold-centred, white-edged flowers, singly or several to a stem. It is easy to grow in well drained soil in rock gardens or at the front of the border.

Left *Agrostemma* Milas (a selection of *A. githago*) may be grown outside as a summer-flowering hardy annual from a spring sowing, or may be raised under glass to give an earlier display of its daintily marked pink blooms, which are splendid for cutting.

Above *Rehmannia angulata*, a member of the foxglove family native to China. It makes a much admired plant for the cool greenhouse, with long, fresh green, deeply lobed basal leaves, toothed at the margins, and its large, broadly two-lipped flowers of rich purplish rose, speckled and dotted in the throat. It may be grown outdoors in mild districts.

Cinerarias sown late last summer will be completing their long flowering season with a final display of massed daisy-like flowers in shades of colour from deep purple through blue, mauve, pink and red to white.

Primula × *kewensis*, with sulphur-yellow flowers, and *P. malacoides*, with lilac blooms to which breeders have added many other colours, bring the flowering season of the winter and spring greenhouse primulas to a close.

Among the showiest of plants starting into flower at the end of the month in the cool greenhouse is the butterfly flower, an annual developed from forms and hybrids of *Schizanthus pinnatus*. The intricate patterns and vivid colours of the blooms, in shades and combinations of crimson, rose, salmon-pink and old gold, have led to its popular name poor man's orchid.

True orchids, once thought to be only for the rich, are now becoming increasingly popular. Every spring more and more small greenhouses are adorned with many-flowered spikes of beautiful *Cymbidium* hybrids as gardeners discover that they thrive in cool-house conditions. Even in genera which mostly need higher temperatures there are cool-growing exceptions, such as the lovely *Vanda coerulea* and many of its hybrids.

Pleiones are gaining popularity as orchids that will grow and flower in profusion with no artificial heat. They make perfect spring subjects for the alpine house. The most commonly grown species is *Pleione formosana*, which has many cultivars in shades of lilac and mauve, with some white forms. All have beautifully fringed and marked lips. Other species and recent hybrids have extended the colour range to include reds and golds.

A great many alpine house subjects are now in flower. Several species of spring-flowering bulbs and corms are at their best under unheated glass, not because they cannot endure cold (indeed, many of them demand it before they will flower) but because they cannot stand the wet conditions that often prevail outdoors, and because inside they are safe from biting wind. Among the most valuable species coming into this category are several in the genera *Cyclamen*, *Fritillaria*, *Lachenalia*, *Muscari*, *Narcissus* and *Tulipa*.

Among the choicest plants now in bloom in the alpine house are those that form dense rosettes or cushions, from which emerge stalks bearing often small but enchanting flowers which have a special beauty all their own. The following is a list of some selected kinds to look for, chosen not only because of their appeal but because they are reliable and likely to be available from most of the alpine nurseries.

Androsace, a genus of the primrose family, has several cushion-forming species which are among the gems of the alpine house. *A. pyrenaica* makes a mound of tiny, grey-felted rosettes, each producing a white, yellow-centred flower to give a mass effect. *A. strigillosa* has larger leaves and purple flowers. *A. vandellii* (*imbricata*) forms a silvery cushion almost hidden by round, white, golden-eyed flowers.

Dionysia aretioides, of the same family, has softly hairy rosettes covered with yellow blooms; excellent cultivars include 'Grave-tye' and 'Paul Furse'.

The saxifrages make up a vast and diverse genus consisting of a many sections. The Kabschia section includes some fine alpine house plants, including the following: *Saxifraga* × *apiculata* (pale yellow) and its cultivar 'Alba'; *S. burseriana* (white); *S.* 'Jenkinsae' (pink); *S.* 'Valerie Finnis' (primrose); *S.* 'Winifred' (deep crimson).

House Plants

In addition to those mentioned on page 59, some climbers now in flower such as *Stephanotis jasminioides*, with its powerful orange-blossom scent, make neat and delightful pot plants for the home when carefully trained over a supporting framework of canes.

Above *Calceolaria* Confetti Mixed is one of the many brilliant modern selections of this popular greenhouse biennial. For a display of flowers during the spring, seed is sown the previous summer and the resulting seedlings pricked out, overwintered in a cool house, and transferred to their final pots in February or March.

What to do in April

Trees and Shrubs

Any deciduous trees and shrubs that still remain to be planted should be dealt with as soon as possible. This is particularly urgent for those lifted from the open ground, but even container-grown ones, although they suffer very much less disturbance to their roots during the process of transplanting, are best dealt with at the earliest opportunity, so that they can begin to establish themselves in their new quarters before they come into full leaf.

April is generally considered by gardeners to be the ideal month for planting evergreens of all kinds. The soil is beginning to warm up, encouraging the growth of strong new roots to draw in the amount of water needed to replace that lost by constant transpiration from the leaves. For full instructions on the correct way to plant trees and shrubs see page 199.

Because losses from transpiration are very much increased by strong winds, it is a wise precaution in exposed places to erect a temporary windbreak on the windward side of newly planted evergreens, as suggested in the notes for March on page 60.

If the weather should turn dry after planting, give the leaves a good spraying with water through a fine spray while the dry spell lasts. Mulching will also help to avoid undue loss of moisture.

If conditions were right earlier, a start may have already been made with propagating suitable shrubs by means of layering (see March notes, page 60). If not, there is still time; but the sooner it is done the better, while root formation is at its most vigorous. To the shrubs already suggested may be added rhododendrons, magnolias, hydrangeas and many others with branches flexible enough to be pegged down to the ground.

The most urgent pruning to be done at this time of year is the cutting back of shrubs which flower on the current season's growth and have not already been dealt with. See page 212 for details of what to do, together with a list of some widely-grown shrubs to which this treatment applies. It is important that the pruning of this group of shrubs should be carried out early, in order to give the new season's shoots as long a period of growth as possible so as to produce a good display of flowers and avoid straggly growths bare at the base.

A second group of shrubs that benefit from regular annual pruning consists of those which bloom on wood produced during the previous year, and therefore should be cut back as soon as flowering is over.

Forsythias are for many gardeners the first shrubs of the year to be dealt with in this way, since they usually finish flowering late this month or early next. For details of how to prune these shrubs see page 214, which also gives a list of species coming within this group.

Early-flowering heathers and rhododendrons may be tidied up by having dead heads removed as soon as flowering is over.

Hedges will be making new growth and can now be trimmed so that they start the growing season in good shape and remain dense and bushy. If necessary they should be cut hard back to remove any branches that have grown out too strongly and are spoiling the outline. Any unsightly bare patches which result will soon be hidden by new growth and further trimming later in the season can be kept to a light clipping with shears.

To retain a neat shape and avoid having to prune hard in subsequent seasons, a good plan is to trim every five or six weeks from now till the middle of September.

Climbers and Wall-plants

There is still time to plant such deciduous climbers as clematis, honeysuckle and wisteria from containers. Water them in well and apply a good mulch to the soil around the stem.

If ivy on walls is unkempt and scruffy after the winter, clip it back. Do not worry if it looks bare; it will soon cover itself with fresh growth and gain in appearance.

Roses

Complete any spring pruning that remains to be done as soon as possible. Though it is too late to plant roses from the open ground, container-grown ones may still be planted. Water them in well and give a good mulch afterwards.

Established roses may be fed with one of the specially formulated fertilizers sold for the purpose. Scatter it over the bed at the rate recommended on the packet and lightly hoe it into the surface.

Borders and Beds

Hardy annuals of all kinds may now be sown, including – if not already dealt with – the hardiest ones mentioned in the notes for March (see page 61). With the soil now warming up, conditions should be favourable for germination of all the most popular kinds.

The following is a selection of some of the most attractive and readily available of those grown in gardens as hardy annuals: sweet alyssum, clarkia, clary (*Salvia horminum*), *Dimorphotheca aurantiaca*, echium, eschscholzia (californian poppy), godetia, larkspur (annual delphinium), lavatera (mallow), *Limnanthes douglasii* (poached eggs), *Linaria maroccana* (toadflax), nasturtium (*Tropaeolum majus*), scabious, sunflower, sweet pea, sweet sultan (*Centaura imperialis*) and viscaria.

Sweet peas raised in pots or boxes from seeds sown in the autumn and overwintered in a frame may be planted out when conditions are suitable. Those sown in spring in gentle heat can also be planted after they have been thoroughly hardened off. Give them support immediately.

Any other plants that need support should also be attended to as soon as possible, while the new shoots are still small. If once allowed to flop about and become kinked they may never recover, and in any case are unlikely to give a satisfactory display. Details of various methods of support to suit different kinds of plant will be found on page 200.

Gaps among perennials caused by winter losses may be made good either with new plants or with divisions from existing ones.

Late-flowering herbaceous perennials such as Michaelmas daisies may still be bought and planted. Overgrown clumps that have been in for some years can often be restored to vigour and produce more and better flowers if they are divided and replanted; discard the worn-out centre portion and plant the strongest of the outer shoots, as shown on page 197.

Never let recently planted perennials suffer from lack of water. Not only should a good soaking be given at planting time, but if a dry spell should occur, as often happens at this time of year, water may be needed again. A good surface mulch will help to conserve moisture round the roots.

Bulbs, Corms and Tubers

Gladiolus corms may be planted in batches during the month to provide a succession of flowers both for garden display and for cutting.

Remove blooms from daffodils and tulips as soon as they fade, so as to keep the display neat and to stop the possibility of setting seed.

Rock Gardens and Pools

Hand weeding carried out now, while the weed seedlings are still small and easily removed, will save a great deal of trouble and hard work later. Dead and dying plants should be replaced and gaps filled. Garden centres and nurseries have a large selection of pot-grown plants to choose from; but hurry, or you may find the best ones gone.

Before removing plants from their pots make sure the compost is moist. If necessary give it a good watering. The soil in the planting holes should also be moist (but not sodden).

Where stone chippings on the surface have been disturbed, scatter more around the plants, particularly under the crowns.

Slugs and snails are now becoming active and hungry. A sprinkling of slug bait will help to prevent new growth from being chewed.

As the weather becomes warmer, water-lilies may be planted, together with other water and bog plants in and around the pool.

Lawns

The grass will be growing more strongly, and more frequent mowing will be needed. The blades of the mower may now be lowered, to give a closer cut, but do not overdo it. The grass should not be cut shorter than three-quarters of an inch (twenty mm).

Towards the end of the month a dressing of spring fertilizer may be given (see page 208), so long as conditions are favourable and the grass is in active growth.

If weeds are also making growth, a selective weedkiller may be applied. Many people find it easiest and most effective to give a dressing of combined fertilizer and weedkiller, as explained on page 208. Moss may be treated with lawn sand or special moss killer used strictly as instructed on the package.

Fruit

All recently planted fruit trees, particularly those against walls, where the soil tends to dry out quickly, should be given a mulch of compost, strawy manure or similar material to conserve moisture.

Continue with the spraying of fruit trees and bushes, but do *not* use pesticides when flowers are open.

Vegetables

Among the many crops that may now be sown and planted in the open are artichokes, asparagus, beetroot and leaf beet, brussels sprouts, broccoli, cabbages, calabrese, carrots, cauliflowers, kales, leeks, lettuces, onions, parsley, parsnips, peas, potatoes, radishes, salsify, summer spinach and turnips.

Sowings may be made under cover of aubergines, celery and celeriac, cucumbers, marrows, sweet corn, sweet peppers and tomatoes.

Hoe and hand-weed in good time, to give crops the best start. Remove and burn old brassica stumps.

Greenhouse and Frame

On sunny days greenhouse plants will need more air and water. Shade young plants from direct sun and start feeding established ones.

Freesias should be rested after flowering by gradually giving less water. In a cold frame dahlia tubers may be started into growth and half-hardy plants hardened off ready for planting out next month.

Plant tomatoes under glass, in the border, growing bags or large pots.

House Plants

Increased watering will now be needed. Spring-clean plants by removing dust and dead leaves.

Ferns may be divided and repotted. Many plants can now be propagated by leaf and stem cuttings and by layering, as shown on pages 192–197.

May

From these sweet-springing meads and bursting
  boughs of May,
Dream, while the innumerable choir of day
  Welcome the dawn.

Robert Bridges (1844–1930)

May is generally considered to be the month when spring has truly arrived. The often wild and uncertain weather of March and April is behind us, and a more settled period may be expected. Weather forecasts generally contain fewer references to those depressions in the west which are so often associated with mist and rain. The middle of May is on average one of the driest times of the year. In southern districts, with settled conditions, there are likely to be sunny spells, bringing a marked rise in temperature both of the ground and of the air.

All these factors, together with the increasing hours of daylight, lead to the opening of a great many flowers which have been protected in the bud during the previous less favourable weather. As a result, May is usually one of the most rewarding months of the entire year in the garden.

However, the weather can be very treacherous. A north or north-east wind may, if the sky is cloudy, lead to snow showers, particularly on high ground and in the North, or to destructive hailstorms. However, if the sky is clear there is the danger of sharp frosts, particularly destructive to open blossoms. Fruit growers dread late frosts, which can destroy the crop. Wise gardeners never trust May weather, particularly towards the end of the month, when it often turns cold and squally. Except in very mild districts it is safer to delay planting out somewhat tender plants such as outdoor tomatoes and half-hardy annuals. In cold areas, it is better to wait till the beginning of next month.

Left *Rhododendron luteum*, the popular deciduous shrub often called *Azalea pontica*, bears richly scented yellow flowers, is completely hardy and has gained an Award of Garden Merit.

What to see and enjoy in May

Trees and Shrubs

Pieris formosa forrestii, pictured on the right, with brilliant young growths and slightly scented flowers, is one of this month's most beautiful shrubs, but needs lime-free soil. In this it resembles the closely related rhododendrons, the earliest of which have now finished flowering or are past their best. There are, however, hundreds more coming into bloom in many colours, shapes and sizes, from tall, stately bushes to dwarf shrubs suitable for the rock garden.

A selection of young plants can be seen in bloom at most garden centres; to see how they will look when mature it is well worth visiting gardens which feature rhododendrons and are open to the public during the flowering season.

Though rhododendrons need lime-free soil, it is possible for gardeners with limy soil to grow the smaller ones in containers filled with lime-free compost. Among the most suitable for the purpose, as well as for planting out where the soil is suitable, are the azaleas. A small selection of early-flowering evergreen hydrids is given in the April notes (page 67), but many more are now in flower. In addition, the deciduous azaleas are coming into bloom, many of them sweetly scented and some with autumn foliage nearly as vivid as the flowers. A favourite species is pictured on the previous page. A selection of some of the best hybrids, both evergreen and deciduous, is given below.

> **AZALEA HYBRIDS**
>
> **Evergreen**
> 'Blue Danube', 'Hinocrimson' and 'Hinodegiri' (deep red), 'John Cairns' (terracotta), 'Mother's Day' (rose), 'Orange Beauty', 'Palestrina' (white, green throat), 'Rosebud' (pink, double), 'Vuyk's Rosy Red', 'Vuyk's Scarlet'.
>
> **Deciduous**
> 'Cecile' (salmon), 'Christopher Wren', 'Gibraltar' (orange), 'Homebush' (carmine), 'Klondyke' and 'Koster's Brilliant Red' (glowing orange), 'Narcissiflorum' (yellow, double), 'Norma' (rose), 'Silver Slipper' (pinkish white), 'Sunbeam' (gold).

Several trees and shrubs already dealt with in the April notes and listed on pages 65–67 will still be in flower. In cold seasons and less favoured places some may not come into bloom till this month, together with later flowering species and cultivars.

Among the most beautiful deciduous ones are still the magnolias, flowering cherries and crabs, of which *Malus* 'Aldenhamensis', with wine-red flowers, and *M. hupehensis*, with fragrant white blossoms, are two of the latest to bloom. Among the most attractive evergreens are several May-flowering cultivars of *Camellia japonica*.

Many other trees and shrubs are now starting to come into flower; a selection is given on the opposite page.

Above *Pieris formosa forrestii* is one of the most beautiful of all shrubs for lime-free soils, with slightly fragrant, glistening white, pitcher-shaped flowers and vivid young growth. Several forms have been granted awards for excellence, including the Royal Horticultural Society's Award of Garden Merit for the lovely 'Wakehurst'.

SELECTED TREES AND SHRUBS

Aesculus hippocastanum, common horse-chestnut; *Buddleja globosa*; *Ceanothus* species and cultivars; *Cercis siliquastrum*, judas tree; *Choisya ternata*, mexican orange-blossom; *Cornus nuttallii*; *Crataegus* species and cultivars, hawthorns; *Crinodendron hookerianum*, crimson-flowered lantern tree; *Daphne x burkwoodii*; *Davidia involucrata*, handkerchief tree; *Embothrium coccineum*, chilean fire bush; *Enkianthus campanulatus*; *Exochorda x macrantha*, pearl bush; *Genista hispanica*, spanish gorse, and *G. lydia*; *Halesia carolina*, snowdrop tree.

Laburnum anagyroides, *L. x watereri* and cultivars; *Paeonia* species and their varieties and hybrids, tree peonies; *Pieris formosa* and its cultivars; *Robinia pseudoacacia*, false acacia; *Sorbus aria*, whitebeam, *S. aucuparia*, mountain ash or rowan, each with several cultivars; *Syringa vulgaris*, lilac, in a large range of single- and double-flowered cultivars; *Tamarix tetrandra*, tamarisk; *Viburnum carlesii* and its cultivars and hybrids *V. x carlcephalum* and *V. x juddii*, all with sweetly scented flowers, *V. lantana*, wayfaring tree, *V. plicatum* and cultivars, japanese snowball bush.

Above *Rhododendron* 'Temple Belle', a well-established favourite dating back to 1916 and resulting from a cross between *R. orbiculare* and *R. williamsianum*, forms a neatly rounded shrub with clear rose flowers. It is hardy in the south and west, in most areas around the coast and in the more sheltered gardens inland.

The first of the large-flowered clematis hybrids, which blossom on growth made during previous years, will now be coming into bloom; many will also produce smaller flowers in the autumn on current season's growth. Among the best are the following, all of which have received awards from the Royal Horticultural Society: 'Comtesse de Bouchaud' (cyclamen pink), 'Henryi' (cream), 'Lasurstern' (deep lavender), 'Mrs. Cholmondeley' (pale blue) and 'Nelly Moser' (pale mauve pink with carmine bar).

Towards the end of the month *Lonicera periclymenum* 'Belgica', known as early dutch honeysuckle, begins to open its sweetly scented flowers, rose-purple outside and creamy yellow within. Wisterias, which may start to bloom at the same time, are dealt with in the June notes (see page 99).

Still outstanding among wall shrubs flowering now are several species of *Ceanothus* (see April notes, page 68). Another striking beauty is *Hebe hulkeana*, whose flowers of delicate lavender-blue, borne in great profusion on slender stems, are seen at their best on a sunny wall.

Roses

This month sees the flowering of some of the most charming of the shrub roses, mostly species from China and their hybrids. A selection of those which have received awards for their garden value includes the following: *Rosa hugonis*, with fern-like foliage and arching branches studded with butter-yellow flowers; *R. × cantabrigiensis*, with fragrant creamy blooms; 'Canary Bird', with deliciously scented flowers of brilliant canary yellow; *R. primula*, the incense rose, with primrose blooms; *R. willmottiae*, with flowers of lilac-pink, and its more deeply coloured cultivar 'Wisley'; *R. ecae*, with saucer-shaped bright yellow blooms which though small are borne in great abundance.

Borders and Beds

Till now most herbaceous plants to come into bloom have been low-growing ones. Now they are joined in flower by many taller plants, giving more height to the border. Listed on the next page are some of the best and most readily available.

Above *Clematis montana* 'Tetrarose' is a tetraploid form, of Dutch origin, with bronze foliage and lilac-rose blooms, considerably exceeding in size those of the normal white-flowered species, which may be seen pictured on the opposite page (top right).

Climbers and Wall-plants

This is the month when one of the most popular and delightful of all climbers, *Clematis montana*, comes into bloom, joining the earlier species dealt with in the April notes (see page 67), some of which may still be in flower. Pictured above is a tetraploid form with rose-pink blooms which are considerably larger than those typical of the species. The ordinary type is pictured on the opposite page (top right), and displays a profusion of vanilla-scented white flowers. The most widely grown form is *C. montana rubens*, with purple-tinged leaves and flowers of a soft rosy red.

Right *Clematis montana*, a vigorous climber from the Himalayan region, festooned with scented white flowers, has many cultivars which have gained the Royal Horticultural Society's Award of Garden Merit.

SELECTED HERBACEOUS PLANTS

Anchusa azurea and cultivars, with big forget-me-not flowers; *Aquilegia* species and hybrids (columbine) in many colours; *Brunnera macrophylla*; early-flowering *Centaurea hypoleuca* 'John Coutts'; *Convallaria majalis* (lily-of-the-valley); *Crambe cordifolia*; *Dicentra spectabilis* (bleeding heart); *Epimedium perralderianum* and Wisley-raised hybrid *E.* x *perralchicum*; *Euphorbia griffithii*, with its vivid cultivar 'Fireglow'. *E. myrsinites* and *E. characias wulfenii*; *Geranium macrorrhizum* cultivars, notably the rose-pink 'Ingwersen's Variety'; *Geum* 'Borisii', 'Lady Stratheden' and 'Mrs. Bradshaw'; *Incarvillea delavayi*; many intermediate and dwarf irises; *Meconopsis cambrica* (welsh poppy) with orange and yellow flowers; many species and cultivars of peony (see overleaf, page 84); *Polygonatum* x *hybridum*, garden favourite solomon's seal, with double-flowered and variegated forms; *Primula japonica*, earliest of the candelabra primulas, with many cultivars; *Nepeta mussinii* (now *N.* x *faassenii*), the popular catmint, with its first lavender blooms now starting its summer-long flowering season; *Trollius europaeus* (globe flower) and the many cultivars, with incurved flowers like large double buttercups in bright yellow or orange, of the garden hybrid *T.* x *cultorum*; *Veronica gentianoides*, with spires of palest blue flowers.

Among bedding plants brompton stocks (pictured right) join the biennials in flower (see page 69).

Right Brompton stock 'Lady' in mixed shades of red, pink and lilac, make an attractive spring bedding display with the sparkling flowers of the double daisy *Bellis perennis* 'Montana Super Giant' in the foreground.

Right *Paeonia
suffruticosa*, the
moutan peony from
China and Tibet, is a
branching shrub of
medium height, well
suited to a sunny
position in a mixed
border with enough
shelter to protect its
flowers and young
growth from late frosts.
There are many
beautiful cultivars.

Below *Paeonia broteri*,
a native of Spain and
Portugal, displaying its
cerise-pink flowers,
with golden stamens,
against bold,
handsome foliage of
cool grey-green, is one
of the earliest and
loveliest species of
herbaceous peonies to
brighten the garden
with their welcome
blooms.

Perhaps the most magnificent of all border
plants to flower during May are the early
peonies. Generally the woody kinds commonly known as tree peonies, of which an
example is pictured above, come into bloom
first. Though they are shrubs they are excellent subjects for the mixed border, where they
associate well with the herbaceous ones.

The main flowering season for most
herbaceous peonies is not until June, but in
favourable conditions several popular forms
and hybrids of *Paeonia officinalis* may be
expected to open their first flowers in the
second half of May. Perhaps the best known is
that favourite old double 'Rubra Plena', with
large, globular flowers of deepest ruby. Other
doubles include the bright pink 'Rosea
Superba Plena', the dusky maroon 'Red
Ensign' and the lovely flushed white 'Albo
Plena'. Among the most beautiful of the
single-flowered are the garnet-red 'Crimson
Globe' and the salmon-pink 'China Rose'.

Bulbs, Corms and Tubers

Daffodils, which have been such a dominant feature of the garden scene in recent months, will now be almost over, except perhaps for some of the late jonquils, with several flowers to a stem in shades from lemon-yellow to gold. Latest of the spring-flowering species is the variable *Narcissus poeticus*, bearing white, sweet-scented blooms with shallow cups coloured orange-red, or in some cases yellow with a red or green rim; the variety *recurvus*, last to flower, is the old garden favourite known as pheasant's eye.

The most popular of May-flowering bulbous plants for the garden are the large-flowered tulips, of which there is a vast range, in a dazzling array, derived from several different species and representing almost every colour except the blues.

Many of the bulbs mentioned in the April notes (see page 70) may still be in flower. Bluebells are now in full bloom, both the common species, *Hyacinthoides non-scripta*, and its Spanish counterpart *H. hispanica*, distinguished by its blue anthers. Enjoying similar open woodland conditions are the trilliums, of which the white-flowered *Trillium grandiflorum* is easiest to grow.

Some of the later-flowering fritillaries will now be in bloom. Two of the best for garden cultivation are *Fritillaria pyrenaica*, with very dark flowers, and *F. pallidiflora*, with pale yellow blooms.

Among the most striking May-flowering bulbs, attractive both in the garden and for cutting, are the alliums, or ornamental onions, bearing heads of flowers in white, yellow, rose and purple on upright stalks.

Below In the foreground of this colourful and well-planned spring bedding display at the Royal Horticultural Society's garden at Wisley is the bright orange-red tulip 'Beauty of Apeldoorn', set off to perfection by an underplanting with the wallflower 'Golden Bedder'. The blooms of an intense deep red to the left and right in the middle distance are those of the companion tulip 'Apeldoorn'.

Potentilla aurea, from the Alps, forms a spreading carpet of green with intricately divided leaves and clusters of deep yellow flowers. There is a cultivar known as 'Chrysocraspeda', with orange-tinged blooms, and a semi-double one named 'Plena'.

May is a particularly rewarding month in the rock garden. Some favourites that may have already been in bloom for several weeks will still be opening fresh flowers, such as the aubrieta pictured here, and a rich variety of new plants will all be coming into bloom at the same time. The following is a list of some of the most attractive and readily available.

SELECTED ROCK GARDEN PLANTS

Aethionema 'Warley Rose'; *Androsace primuloides* (*sarmentosa*), in many forms with blooms in shades of rose-pink and soft red; *Armeria maritima*, thrift, and several cultivars, with heads of red, pink and white flowers on short stems, and *A. juniperifolia* (*caespitosa*), of which the deep pink 'Bevan's Variety' is a fine form; *Campanula garganica*, an unusually early bell-flower, with sprays of lavender-blue flowers for many weeks, and its more deeply coloured cultivar 'W. H. Paine'; *Geranium dalmaticum*, among the first of the alpine geraniums to bloom, with shell-pink flowers, and a white-flowered form known as 'Album'; *Haberlea rhodopensis*, gracing cool north-facing positions with its lavender-lilac blooms; *Houstonia caerulea*, the charming bluetts, of which the cultivar 'Fred Millard' is outstanding with its sky-blue flowers; *Iris chamaeiris*, very dwarf and variable, and its fine cultivar 'Campbellii', with large indigo flowers; *Linum perenne* 'Alpinum', a very popular flax for rock gardens, with salver-shaped blue flowers, larger and better coloured than those of the type; *Lithospermum diffusum* (now *Lithodora diffusa*) 'Heavenly Blue' and 'Grace Ward', two favourite cultivars of this popular plant, which will produce flowers of intense blue along prostrate stems throughout the summer.

Above *Aubrieta deltoidea* 'Gurgedyke', creating a brilliant effect tumbling over a dry stone wall, is a fine example of the many splendid cultivars now available to the gardener in a wide range of colours, from palest lavender through violet and rose to purple and red, flowering with great freedom over an extended season lasting throughout the spring months.

Rock Garden and Pool

Several of the mat-forming plants, shrubby or herbaceous, which give the rock garden interest and variety will now be in bloom.

One of the most appealing is the creeping evergreen shrub *Ceanothus prostratus*, forming a dense mat almost hidden beneath masses of clear blue flowers.

Genista lydia, smothered with bright yellow blooms, can be rather too vigorous in a limited space, but *G.* (now *Chamaespartium*) *sagittalis* forms a neat mat of stems bearing close-packed clusters of golden flowers.

Helianthemum alpestre 'Serpyllifolium', with sheets of bright yellow blooms, is among the earliest cultivars of the sun roses which in the coming weeks will enliven the rock garden with their many brilliant colours.

Omphalodes cappadocica, displaying its clear blue flowers above heart-shaped leaves; *Oxalis adenophylla*, a neat, tufted plant with bright lilac-pink blooms; *Phlox douglasii* and its many cultivars, with flowers of lavender, pink, red and white, and the more vigorous *P. subulata*, also with many named forms; *Primula auricula* and its large and varied number of forms and hybrids, many grouped as *P. x pubescens* cultivars, also a wide selection of other primulas; *Ramonda myconi* (*pyrenaica*), with flowers of deep lavender; *Tiarella cordifolia*, with a dense carpet of pale green softly hairy leaves surmounted by sprays of dainty white flowers.

Of the vast number of saxifrages grown in rock gardens, those known as mossies are now at the height of their flowering season. As can be seen from the picture above, they form dense cushions made up of many green rosettes, from which arise the flowers on slender stalks. The colours range from white through pink to deep red.

From the wide range in cultivation, the following is a short selection of some tried favourites: 'Four Winds' (deep crimson), 'Gaiety' (rose pink), 'Pearly King' (white), 'Peter Pan' (crimson), 'Pixie' (rosy red), 'Sanguinea Superba' (blood-red) and 'Winston Churchill' (large-flowered, clear pink).

Many novelties appear from time to time, and a visit to a nursery to see the plants in flower would be well worth while.

Above Mossy saxifrages, at their best now, are among the easiest plants to grow and the most popular for the rock garden, where they form dense, spreading mounds made up of fresh green rosettes, crowned with starry flowers borne in clusters on stalks well above the foliage. There are many lovely cultivars available, with flowers varying from white through pink to deepest red.

Right This rock garden scene shows how an attractive and harmonious whole can be created by a balanced combination of simple materials. The stone and water provide a restful and unchanging background to the changing beauties of foliage and flowers throughout the season.

Below *Dodecatheon pauciflorum*, one of several species of shooting stars from western North America, is a member of the primrose family. It has flowers shaped like those of a cyclamen and prefers a moist spot in a position where it receives some shade from the midday sun during the summer.

Several plants for the waterside and other moist places are now beginning to flower. Among the most spectacular are the candelabra primulas, of which *Primula japonica* usually starts to bloom by the end of the month. Most, however, do not display their full splendour till June, and are dealt with on page 104.

The related and somewhat earlier shooting stars, which have been described as like cyclamen on stilts, also prefer damp places. One of the loveliest species, *Dodecatheon pauciflorum*, is pictured on the left.

In the shallows at the pool's edge the water crowfoot, *Ranunculus aquatilis*, opens its pure white buttercups, and the water hawthorn, *Aponogeton distachyus*, its heavily scented white flowers, later turning green.

Left This photograph of one of the model vegetable plots at Wisley was taken during the first week of May. The rows of young vegetables, sown as soon as the ground was in suitable condition in early spring, are now making vigorous growth and require thinning, to give those that remain room to develop. Many of those thinnings will provide some of the most welcome produce of the whole year.

Fruit

The chief appeal of the fruit garden during this month is to the sense of sight rather than that of taste. There can be few sights more breathtakingly beautiful than rows of apple trees loaded with blossom on a fine day in May. Though the particular colour mixture of pink and white known as apple-blossom is well recognized, and indeed applied to many completely different flowers, there is a wide variation from one cultivar to another. Where different ones have been planted next to each other for cross-pollination purposes the colour variations between neighbouring trees can be very attractive. Pears too provide a wonderful display with their billowing white blossoms.

Strawberries grown under glass, or in the garden with such means of protection as polythene tunnels or cloches (see page 227), should be yielding the first, and most eagerly awaited, soft fruit of the season, with a flavour incomparably more delicious than those in the shops.

In favoured districts and if the weather is kind, there may be a picking of gooseberries in the latter part of the month. They will go nicely if stewed with the rhubarb which should still be yielding plenty of tender young stalks.

Vegetables

Asparagus, esteemed by many as the most delicious of all vegetables, should now be coming into full bearing, though a few early shoots may already have appeared towards the end of last month. The great advantage of garden asparagus is not only that it can be cooked and eaten fresh but that it can be left to make a good length of succulent green stalk before being cut.

Spring cabbages will now be making solid hearts ready for use. Other brassica crops ready for cutting include sprouting broccoli and winter cauliflowers.

Lettuces of suitable kinds sown and grown on under protection should already have been providing welcome spring salads. The hardier kinds such as 'Winter Density' will now be starting to form hearts.

Other salad crops to go with the lettuces and now ready for gathering are radishes and spring onions.

Seakale beet (Swiss chard) and spinach beet continue to produce leaves, which should be picked regularly while young and tender if they are to be enjoyed at their best.

A few young carrots which were sown in a frame early in the year may well be ready for gathering towards the end of the month, while they are at their sweetest.

Above *Pelargonium*
'Albert Bainbridge' is
one of the large
number of regal
pelargoniums, in a wide
range of colours and
markings, which make
excellent and long-
flowering subjects for a
cool greenhouse or a
living-room.

Greenhouse and Frame

Although it is still only spring in the open and
there is every chance of late frosts and cold
winds, inside the greenhouse summer is already on the way. The number of different
plants that are likely to be in bloom is rapidly
increasing. The range depends on the kinds
grown, the temperatures maintained and the
time of sowing or propagating by cuttings or
other vegetative means.

While the period between starting into
growth and arriving at maturity is usually a
good deal shorter under glass than in the
open, a certain amount of time is needed
before the flowering stage can be reached.

Among the best-loved and most widely
grown plants likely to reach the flowering
stage this month from cuttings taken the
previous summer, are the regal pelargoniums,
of which a splendid example is pictured
above. These triumphs of the plant breeder's
art have been developed over the past century
or more, at first chiefly in England and France
but more recently in north America. The
fresh green softly hairy leaves form a most
attractive background to the blooms, and
there are large numbers of different cultivars,
with single or double flowers, most of them
elegantly veined or blotched, in a wide colour
range from snow white to very nearly black.

After a relative decline in the popularity of
regal pelargoniums a few years ago they are
now back in favour, and the multitude of
existing cultivars is constantly being added to
by novelties, sometimes an improvement on
previous ones and sometimes not. To give an
indication of the wide range available, the
following is a short selection of some established favourites of exceptional quality:
'Aztec' (strawberry-ice pink and white);
'Burgundy' (deep wine-red overlaid velvety
black); 'Caprice' (cherry red); 'Carisbrooke'
(extra large frilled pink flowers with maroon
blotch); 'Doris Firth' (milk-white, blotched
dark red); 'Grandma Fischer' (orange shaded
salmon-pink, with a black blotch on each
petal); 'Grand Slam' (rose-red, tinged violet);
'Lavender Grand Slam' (silvery lilac with
slight maroon marking); 'Marie Rober' (deep
purple with black flare); 'Princess of Wales'
(outstanding, with frilled flowers of glowing
pink); 'Rhodomine' (pale mauve with white
throat and maroon blotch).

Descriptions, however, convey little of the
beauty of these plants. To see the choice
available at first hand, visit a well-stocked
garden centre, or better still a nursery that
specializes in pelargoniums, where perhaps
something new and exciting may be found to
take back home.

Hydrangeas, also propagated from cuttings
last year, rested during the winter and started
into growth in February, will now be producing their handsome heads of flowers.
They are propagated in their thousands com-
mercially each year from autumn cuttings
and sold in flower at this time of year as dwarf
plants in four-inch (ten cm) pots for the
home, but they are likely to last considerably
longer in flower if placed in a cool
greenhouse.

Other plants for the house or the cool
greenhouse now beginning to flower are the
cape primroses, belonging to the genus *Streptocarpus*. They are not of the primrose family,
though their leaves are like long primrose
leaves. The beautiful trumpet-shaped flowers
of the modern hybrids range from white
through rose to blue and purple. Seed of the
hybrids will produce a mixture of colours.
Specially desirable plants may be propagated
by leaf cuttings (see page 195).

Annuals now in flower in the cool greenhouse (including some which though not truly annual are best grown as such) are mostly from later sowings of those already mentioned as coming into bloom in the previous month or two.

Cinerarias from the last sowing in August can still produce a splendid display to round off their flowering season in the greenhouse; in the cooler conditions of window boxes they may continue in flower well into June.

Another annual already mentioned as starting to flower last month, the butterfly flower or poor man's orchid, will now be in full bloom from sowings made last autumn. These striking plants, developed from *Schizanthus pinnatus*, have long been favourites for the cool greenhouse. Even the smallest and most crowded one could accommodate a few pots of the neat and compact Dwarf Bouquet mixture, only a foot (thirty cm) high and covered with flowers in tones of pink, rose, crimson, salmon and amber. The more recently introduced selection Hit Parade is little if any taller and has larger flowers with an extended range of colour, including lilac, violet, purple and white, all beautifully marked with contrasting colours. Star Parade has similar but somewhat smaller flowers.

In the alpine house several bulbous plants will be in bloom, some too tender to face late frosts, driving rain or chilly winds and some that, while hardy, grow better under glass and have flowers that can be better appreciated at eye-level on a bench. Among them are some delightful species of tulip, such as the one pictured below.

Many species of the important and increasingly popular genus *Lewisia* open their attractive flowers, mostly in shades of rose-pink, salmon and white, quite early in the month in the alpine house. Some of them bloom later in the month outside in the rock garden. In most places, however, the majority of species reach their flowering peak in June, and are dealt with on page 105.

House Plants

Many of the greenhouse plants dealt with in the last two columns may be brought indoors when in full bloom to brighten up a room while the flowers last. Too much heat, however, may cause them to drop their buds.

Among the house plants that now adorn the majority of homes, particularly of those without gardens, some now at their best include *Aphelandra squarrosa*, *Chlorophytum comosum* and *Spathiphyllum wallisii*.

Right *Tulipa maximowiczii*, a native of rocky hillsides in Central Asia, is one of several species of tulip which are well suited to cultivation in the alpine house, which offers them ideal conditions for growth and well-being, and in which their flowers are displayed to best advantage.

What to do in May

Trees and Shrubs

Evergreens may still be planted; for instructions on how to do so see page 199. Dull, showery weather is most suitable, so long as the soil is not sticky.

The availability of container-grown plants has made late planting a great deal safer than with those lifted from the open ground, since the risk of root damage is much reduced. It is, however, best to complete the planting soon, so that new roots have as much time as possible to penetrate into the surrounding soil and establish themselves before the end of the growing season.

Some shrubs, both evergreen and deciduous, become hardier as they grow older but are somewhat tender when young. These – which include several from the genera *Arbutus*, *Ceanothus*, *Choisya*, *Fuchsia* and *Hydrangea* – are safest planted out from containers in the latter half of the month when frosts are not likely to be too severe. Water the soil after planting and mulch round the plants with plenty of moisture-holding material. If there is a dry spell after planting it may be necessary to water again.

Remove faded flower heads from rhododendrons, azaleas and lilacs to prevent them wasting their energy in setting seed. Dead blooms may also be removed from heathers. To keep these plants vigorous and compact cut back the stems nearly as far as the old wood. Be careful, however, not to cut into the old wood itself.

Harder pruning is required by the group of shrubs, such as *Forsythia*, that flower in the spring on wood produced during the previous season. They should be pruned as soon as flowering is over. Full instructions are given on page 214, together with a list of shrubs in this group.

Remove damaged wood from broad-leaved evergreens (see page 214).

Climbers and Wall-plants

Because of the extra warmth and shelter that walls and fences provide, plants grown against them are likely to be making vigorous growth. New shoots should be trained into place before they become too long and while they are young and pliable.

Species of clematis that flower in spring, such as *Clematis alpina*, *C. armandii*, *C. macropetala* and *C. montana* with its several cultivars, are usually best with little or no pruning. If, however, they are becoming overcrowded or outgrowing the space available, flowering laterals may be cut back to two or three buds as soon as the blooms begin to fade.

The clematis hybrids such as 'Lasurstern', 'Nelly Moser' and the double-flowered 'Vyvyan Pennell', which produce large blooms at this time of year on the previous season's ripened wood – followed usually by smaller flowers in late summer or autumn on new wood – are generally left unpruned. Straggly and overcrowded plants may, however, be improved by a certain amount of what is known as renewal pruning.

As soon as the first lot of flowers on the previous year's growth starts to fade, cut back a third of the old shoots to about a foot (thirty cm) from the base. The result will be that vigorous new replacement shoots will grow from the cut-back wood to carry a good display of flowers next spring. Some of them may produce a few autumn blooms this year too.

Where hard pruning is practised, it is important that the plants should be well nourished if they are to produce strong new growth in place of what has been removed.

If May brings a dry spell, the soil against walls may quickly become parched, so be sure to water wall plants thoroughly before they start to flag. After watering, give a good mulch to conserve moisture.

Roses

The warmer days are likely to bring with them the first attacks by aphids, which are particularly attracted to the young growths of roses. Keep a watchful eye out for them and as soon as they are seen spray with an aphicide, as advised in the section on pests (see page 235). Watch also for signs of black spot and mildew, and if necessary spray with a suitable fungicide (see page 241). It is always best to tackle pests and diseases at the first signs of attack, not only because they are more easily dealt with in the early stages but also because the longer they are allowed to persist the more they are likely to weaken the plant's constitution.

Rolled-up leaves inhabited by caterpillars or sawfly grubs are most easily dealt with by removing and destroying them together with their contents.

Overcrowded or badly placed shoots, particularly those growing inwards towards the middle of the plant, may be removed now. This will keep the centre open and so lessen the risk of disease, besides making for plants which have a more attractive shape and display their flowers to the best effect.

If fertilizer has not yet been applied to established rose beds, do so now, hoeing it lightly into the surface of the soil.

Borders and Beds

Weeds grow rapidly at this time of year and if not tackled can soon overwhelm the less vigorous cultivated plants. It is best, therefore, to spend a little time now hoeing or hand-weeding while the weeds are still young, instead of having to spend a great deal more time on the task later on when the weeds are bigger and have a firmer hold.

Protect young shoots from slugs by sprinkling slug pellets round them.

Most border plants are now growing quite rapidly, and many of them are putting a good deal of energy into the development of flower stems. To fuel all this growth and development takes a considerable amount of food, so it is a timely help to give a top dressing with a suitable compound fertilizer (see page 183) at the recommended rate and hoe it lightly into the soil.

Many established herbaceous perennials have a tendency to produce too many shoots and as a result to become overcrowded. In such cases it is best to thin out the growths while they are still young. Simply remove the weaker shoots, especially from the centre of the plant, leaving the sturdiest ones plenty of room to develop. The appearance of the plant and the quality of the flowers should be much improved.

As shoots grow taller they become increasingly top heavy and more likely to collapse, so it is important to continue supporting them. Stake and tie them in good time, or use one of the other methods of support, as shown on page 200.

Seeds of hardy biennials, such as canterbury bells, foxgloves, sweet williams and wallflowers may now be sown in drills in a nursery bed for transplanting later. Alternatively, they may be sown in boxes. Do not give them any artificial heat if you want the plants to be hardy and sturdy.

Both hardy and half-hardy annuals may be sown outdoors in the positions where they are to flower, so as to give a colourful display in late summer and autumn. To avoid giving a spotty effect it is best to sow in groups, each of one kind.

Before sowing it is a good plan to mark out the boundary of each group with a trickle of sand. Broadcast the seed thinly and evenly over each section and rake in lightly.

Bulbs, Corms and Tubers
Remove faded flower heads from daffodils, hyacinths and tulips.

Where ground occupied by bulbs is to be used for summer bedding, lift them as soon as flowering is over. If they are to be used again they should be dug up carefully complete with their leaves. Dig a shallow trench in spare ground, lay wire-netting along this with the ends protruding, place the bulbs on this and fill in the soil to cover the base of the leaves. When these have shrivelled, lift the wire-netting with the bulbs, which can then be stored for replanting.

Dahlia tubers may now be planted; if dividing them, make sure each piece carries at least one good bud. Cover with three inches (eight cm) of soil to protect shoots from frost.

Rock Gardens and Pools
Vacant places may still be filled with pot-grown plants.

Strong growers such as aubrietas and *Alyssum* (now *Aurinia*) *saxatile* may be trimmed back to keep them tidy and compact.

With the risk of icing almost nil, now is the ideal time to put in new aquatic plants and divide old ones.

Lawns
Weather permitting, grass should now be cut at least once a week.

Give a dressing of fertilizer if this has not already been done, and apply a lawn weedkiller if needed.

Fruit
Strawberries in cloches or tunnels need ventilation whenever possible.

Remove surplus raspberry shoots, leaving only the strongest ones, and give them a good mulch.

Spray tree and soft fruits against pests and diseases, as described on page 238. Be careful, however, not to spray open blossoms or useful pollinating insects may be killed.

Vegetables
Maincrop potatoes not yet planted must be put in as soon as possible. Early ones may be earthed up.

Continue to make sowings of lettuce, radish, beet, carrots and peas to extend the cropping season. Runner and french beans may be sown, also spinach, swedes and (late in the month) sweet corn. In a nursery bed broccoli, cabbages, cauliflowers and kale may all be sown.

Plant out brussels sprouts and cabbage, also celery and celeriac, when they have been hardened off.

Greenhouse and Frame
On sunny days more ventilation will be needed. Use the top ventilators; side ones may let in cold spring draughts. An automatic opening device (see page 229) is a great help. Shading will be needed, particularly for plants in flower or with delicate foliage. More frequent watering will also be necessary.

Early in the month cucumbers, sweet corn and marrows may be sown for planting out next month.

Ensure that tomatoes making new growth are securely supported, and remove side-shoots as they appear. In unheated greenhouses tomatoes may now be planted to give a later crop.

Celery seedlings that have not yet been pricked out should be attended to; harden them off in a frame for planting out next month.

Plant tuberous begonias and gloxinias in their flowering pots. All rooted cuttings and seedlings should be potted on as necessary.

House Plants
Plants standing on sunny window-sills should be moved out of the glare or shaded by a curtain or blind during the middle of the day.

Give water as necessary, and add a liquid feed, at half the recommended strength, about every two weeks.

June

And what is so rare as a day in June?
Then, if ever, come perfect days;
Then Heaven tries earth if it be in tune,
And over it softly her warm ear lays.

James Russell Lowell (1819–1891)

The beginning of June sees the change from late spring to early summer, perhaps the most important time in the gardener's whole year. At last, except in freak seasons, the fear of frost and icy winds is past, and the half-hardy plants which will bring so much colour and life to the garden during the next two or three months can be safely planted out in the open.

A great many more of the established plants are now coming into flower, both woody and herbaceous. As yet, most of the former produce their blooms on growths made in previous seasons, but already there are some beginning to flower on this year's shoots. Chief among these are the best-loved and most widely grown of all woody flowering plants, the modern hybrid roses.

The majority of herbaceous plants are in vigorous growth, and there is a considerable increase in flowering, under the influence of the strengthening of the sun and the lengthening of the days.

With the longest day towards the end of the month, June is often the sunniest time of the year. It is also often the driest, and this, combined with the greatly increased need for water by strongly-growing plants, can lead to wilting unless a sharp watch is kept and water given if necessary, particularly to plants that have recently been put in and have not had time to establish an adequate root system.

As well as bringing out flowers, June weather brings out a host of butterflies, bees and other friendly insects on which plants depend for their pollination. Unfortunately it also brings out greenflies and other pests that need to be dealt with (see pages 231–241).

Left Pyrethrum 'Brenda' is an established favourite among the cultivars developed from *Chrysanthemum coccineum*, which give the border some of its brightest colours in early summer.

What to see and enjoy in June

Trees and Shrubs

Dates of flowering rarely fit exactly into calendar months; much depends on the nature of the season and of local conditions, as well as the length of time different species remain in flower. Many trees and shrubs mentioned in the May notes (see pages 80 and 81) will still be in bloom now; in late seasons some may not flower till this month.

Much depends on situation. The flowering period of some special favourite can be extended by planting it in different parts of the garden. Even a perfectly hardy plant may bloom weeks earlier in a warm spot against a wall than in a more exposed position. Shown here is a wisteria in the open during mid-June in full bloom, when the flowers of those on a wall are fading.

In gardens with lime-free soil the flowering season for rhododendrons still continues. Among the species now coming into bloom is the striking *Rhododendron griersonianum*, parent of many hybrids, with brilliant scarlet bell-like flowers. Another late-flowering species, which may continue to be in bloom next month, is *R. discolor*, another parent of many hybrids, with a profusion of fragrant, funnel-shaped pink flowers produced in enormous clusters, making an unforgettable sight.

More popular for small gardens than the species are the hardy hybrids, of which there are a great many in a wide range of colours. On the next page is a selection of some of the best of those which flower in June and are widely available.

Right *Wisteria floribunda* 'Macrobotrys', a particularly fine form of the japanese wisteria, bears fragrant lilac tinged purple flowers in racemes that sometimes reach more than three feet (one m) long. It is seen at its best when grown on a tall framework in the open, where the chains of blossom are able to hang free. It has received the Award of Garden Merit from the Royal Horticultural Society.

SELECTED RHODODENDRON HYBRIDS

'Alice' (rose pink, light centre), 'Bagshot Ruby', 'Blue Peter' (violet, white throat spotted maroon), 'Britannia' (glowing red), 'Cynthia' (rosy crimson, dark markings), 'Doncaster' (wine-red), 'Gomer Waterer' (white, mauve edged), 'Kluis Sensation' (scarlet, darker spots), 'Lady Clementine Mitford' (peach, pale centre), 'Mrs. A. T. de la Mare' (frilled white), 'Mrs. Charles E. Pearson' (mauve-pink), 'Mrs. G. W. Leak' (mottled rosy pink, dark splash), 'Pink Pearl' (deep lilac-pink).

Azaleas are still prominent among flowering shrubs for their brilliance. In addition to those already mentioned (see page 80) others are now coming into bloom, in particular those old favourites the late-flowering Ghent hybrids. Two of the most popular are 'Daviesii', with fragrant, pale cream blooms with a yellow flare, and 'Narcissiflorum', with double, sweetly-scented, pale yellow flowers, darker in the centre. Among the latest of all to bloom is 'Coccinea Superba', with vivid orange-red flowers.

The increasing number of trees and shrubs in bloom includes several somewhat later-flowering species of genera already included in the May notes (see page 81), such as the lovely *Buddleja alternifolia* pictured above.

Above *Buddleja alternifolia* is wreathed during June in sweet-scented lavender-blue flowers all the way along graceful stems grown during the previous season. It was introduced from China in 1915, given the Award of Garden Merit nine years later, and is now one of the best-loved and most widely planted flowering shrubs in British gardens.

Above *Solanum crispum* 'Glasnevin', a fine cultivar of the chilean potato-tree, bears clusters of flowers more freely than the type and over a longer period, starting earlier and continuing well into the autumn. Though it is also somewhat hardier, it is at its decorative best trained against a wall or fence or allowed to let its long stems scramble over a shed or other unsightly structure. It has been given the Award of Garden Merit by the Royal Horticultural Society.

There are not only several later-flowering species of genera already included in the May selection but also some cultivars that habitually bloom after others of their group. The difference may be one of weeks or only a few days, and there is usually a good deal of overlap between flowering times. It may therefore be a good plan to compare the selection which follows with that on page 81. Together they give a more complete idea of the vast range of trees and shrubs that may be seen in bloom as late spring gives way to early summer.

Several somewhat tender shrubs that may now be flowering in the open in some districts but are better with protection in less favoured places are not included in the list, but are dealt with separately under Climbers and Wall-plants opposite. Some, such as the *Solanum crispum* pictured here, are suitable not only for training against a wall but for scrambling over fences, sheds and outhouses.

Robinia hispida, pictured on the opposite page, also makes a lovely sight against a sunny wall, which offers its brittle stems protection from wind damage.

SELECTED TREES AND SHRUBS

Aesculus indica, indian horse-chestnut, pink-flushed flowers, smaller than *A. hippocastanum*; *Buddleja alternifolia*, pictured on previous page; *Cistus*, rock rose, species and hybrids; *Colutea arborescens*, bladder senna, bright yellow pea flowers; *Cornus kousa*, spangled with white-bracted flowers; *Cotoneaster lacteus*, bee-attracting milky blooms; *Cytisus scoparius*, common broom, with many cultivars and hybrids in brilliant yellows and reds; *Deutzia* species and hybrids, flowers in white and shades of pink; *Erica cinerea*, bell heather, and *E. tetralix*, cross-leaved heath, many white, pink and purple flowered cultivars; *Genista tinctoria*, golden flowered dyer's greenweed; *Kalmia latifolia*, calico bush, buds like sugar-icing stars opening out into bright pink blooms; *Kolkwitzia amabilis*, beauty bush, with the outstanding Wisley-raised cultivar 'Pink Cloud'; *Laburnum alpinum*, scotch laburnum, later to flower than the common species; *Magnolia sieboldii*, *M. tripetala* and their hybrid 'Charles Coates', creamy white fragrant blooms with crimson stamens; *Malus coronaria*, a late-flowering crab with sweetly scented shell-pink blossoms; *Neillia thibetica* (*longiracemosa*), tubular pink blooms in terminal racemes; *Olearia* x *scilloniensis*, grey leaves almost hidden by daisy-like flowers; *Philadelphus*, mock orange, many cultivars, mostly with sweet-scented white flowers, single or double; *Phlomis fruticosa*, Jerusalem sage, aromatic grey leaves and bright yellow blooms; *Potentilla arbuscula*, *P. dahurica* and *P. fruticosa*, many cultivars, flowers ranging from pale to deep yellow; *Pyracantha* species and their many cultivars, firethorns, bearing masses of white, hawthorn-like blossoms; *Rubus* x *tridel* 'Benenden', an outstanding ornamental bramble, studded along arching stems with glistening white saucer-shaped flowers containing bold central clusters composed of bright golden stamens.

Spartium junceum, spanish broom, almost leafless branches loaded with honey-scented, golden pea-flowers; *Spiraea nipponica* and *S.* x *vanhouttei*, with dense masses of pure white blooms; *Stranvaesia davidiana*, with clusters of white flowers, followed later on by bright crimson bird-proof fruits; *Syringa* x *prestoniae*, late-blooming lilac hybrids, flowers ranging from pink to purple; *Viburnum opulus* 'Roseum' ('Sterile'), the snowball tree; *Weigela florida*, with many forms and hybrids, bearing foxglove-like flowers mostly in shades from rose-pink to deep red.

Climbers and Wall-plants

Wisteria sinensis, a magnificent climber for a sunny wall, drapes itself with fragrant, mauve-lilac flowers. *W. floribunda* also now comes into bloom. Its superb cultivar 'Macrobotrys', pictured on page 96, is admirable on an open framework where its long racemes of flowers can hang free.

Clematis hybrids continue to bloom (see page 82), joined later in the month by some honeysuckles (see July notes, page 115). The self-clinging *Hydrangea petiolaris* smothers itself with flat heads of white blooms.

A non-climber now at its best against a warm wall is *Abelia floribunda*, with cherry-red tubular flowers.

Below *Robinia hispida*, the beautiful rose acacia from the south-eastern United States, has gained the Award of Merit as a shrub of distinction and charm, with its graceful, bristly stems and its large, deep pink pea-flowers. Though hardy, it is somewhat brittle and needs a sheltered position. An ideal place is against a sunny wall.

Left *Rosa* 'Nevada', a firm favourite among shrub roses, resulting from a cross between a hybrid tea and a wild species, produces its sparkling blooms in profusion during June. Later there may be intermittent bursts of flowers until the autumn.

Below Rose 'Morning Jewel', a hybrid between the popular blush white 'New Dawn' and 'Red Dandy', also produces its first flush of warm pink, semi-double blooms in June and continues to flower from time to time for several months.

Roses

June is the month when the majority of cultivated roses come into their full glory and earn their place as the best loved of all flowers in the garden.

The most popular and widely grown are those known as hybrid teas and floribundas (though many growers are now beginning to describe them by the newer terms large-flowered and cluster-flowered). These bloom on new wood made since the spring pruning and in many places normally come into flower in the latter part of the month.

Somewhat earlier to bloom are many of those known as shrub roses, which in general are pruned lightly if at all. These tend to produce their flowers on short laterals from the old wood and so do not need to make so much growth before coming into bloom. Several, such as 'Nevada', pictured above, may be grown into magnificent specimens which rival any other flowering shrub.

Many climbers, which produce their flowers in similar fashion, also come into full bloom early this month, such as the lovely 'Morning Jewel', pictured on the right.

Borders and Beds

As midsummer approaches herbaceous plants truly come into their own, providing some of the most vivid displays of colour in the gardening year. The foliage is also attractive, contributing with its varied textures and its many shades of green, from silvery and grey to emerald and bronze, just that element of coolness that is necessary to prevent the effect of all those strong flower colours together becoming garish and lacking in repose. In some cases, such as that of the pulmonarias with their silver-splashed leaves, plants which have finished flowering now earn their place for a second time by their foliage.

Other plants whose foliage continues to bring interest and variety to the border after their flowering period is over are the bergenias. Their large, round, evergreen leaves, with the texture of well cared for leather, not only make a handsome sight but form a good weed-defeating ground cover.

Among those which will have made beautiful bold foliage before producing flowers are the hostas, with leaves of various shades, from blue-grey to green and gold, some variegated and some with contrasting margins.

Many plants now in bloom combine grace of flower with elegance of foliage, such as the aquilegias, pictured here, with their fresh green, delicately divided leaves.

Below *Aquilegia* long-spurred hybrids, developed by selection and crossing of several species of columbine, provide one of the earliest decorative displays for the middle of the border. They have flowers in a wide range of colours, including white, cream, yellow, pink, red, mauve and blue, held on slender stalks above dainty foliage.

Above *Lilium* 'Pandora' is one of the many beautiful lily hybrids introduced during recent years. Derived from the species *L. tigrinum* (now *lancifolium*), it was produced at the Scottish Horticultural Research Institute, and has proved to be exceptionally early to come into bloom. It is also very floriferous, with short, sturdy stems bearing from eighteen to twenty attractive orange flowers.

In addition to the earlier peonies mentioned in the May notes (see page 84), this month sees the coming into bloom of the multitude of magnificent Chinese peonies. Mostly derived by selection and hybridization from *Paeonia lactiflora*, a native of Siberia and Mongolia, they have been developed by breeders over a very long period into probably the most sumptuous of all early summer flowering plants. Novelties appear occasionally, but the following is a selection of some of the established favourites which have stood the test of time and should not be difficult to obtain:

'Baroness Schroeder', double, very large fragrant flowers of creamy white shaded flesh pink; 'Bowl of Beauty', large single cup-shaped flowers, mallow pink with a pale yellow central cluster; 'Duchesse de Nemours', double white, rose scented; 'Karl Rosenfeld', double, rich red; 'Kelway's Supreme', double blush pink, turning white; 'Laura Dessert', double creamy white, lemon centre; 'Sarah Bernhardt', large double apple-blossom pink with paler edges; 'White Wings', single, numerous, snow-white flowers with bright yellow stamens.

The next column gives a selection of other herbaceous plants in flower. Many of those listed on page 83 may still be in bloom too.

SELECTED HERBACEOUS PLANTS

Achillea ptarmica 'The Pearl', white button flowers, *A.* 'Coronation Gold' and *A.* 'Moonshine', sulphur yellow; *Aconitum anglicum*, the early native monkshood, violet-blue flowers; *Alchemilla mollis*, lady's mantle, feathery foliage, massed starry yellow blooms; *Anthemis tinctoria*, golden marguerite, and its lemon-yellow cultivar 'E. C. Buxton'; *Anthericum liliago*, St. Bernard's lily, grassy leaves and snow white, wide lily flowers; *Aquilegia* species and hybrids (pictured on previous page); *Armeria plantaginea* 'Bees' Ruby', brilliant deep pink; *Aruncus dioicus (sylvester)*, goat's beard, plumes of creamy blossoms; *Asphodeline lutea*, king's spear, sulphur-yellow flowers in stiff spikes; *Asphodelus albus*, bold spikes of white blooms; *Astrantia maxima*, the finest masterwort, domed heads of pinkish flowers above collars of rosy bracts; *Campanula glomerata*, *C. lactiflora*, *C. latiloba* and cultivars, in several shades of blue, also pink and white; *Catananche caerulea*, lavender blue dark-eyed daisies above grassy leaves; *Chrysanthemum leucanthemum (Leucanthemum vulgare)*, ox-eye daisy; *Delphinium elatum* and the vast range of popular garden hybrids derived from it and other species; *Dianthus* cultivars of many kinds, including border carnations and pinks; *Eremurus robustus*, foxtail lily, lofty spires of scented pink flowers, and *E. stenophyllus (bungei)*, shorter and with yellow blooms; *Erigeron* cultivars, with large daisy flowers in lilac, blue, pink and magenta; *Galega officinalis* and *G.* x *hartlandii* cultivars, spires of pea flowers in white, lilac, pink and mauve; *Geranium sanguineum*, bloody cranesbill, and cultivars, with magenta, pink and white blooms; *Heuchera* species and cultivars, bells of pink, coral, scarlet and white on slender stems above rounded and often marbled leaves; bearded irises in a vast range of colour combinations.

Kniphofia, red-hot poker, early dwarf hybrids, ranging in colour from ivory through yellow to bright red; *Libertia formosa*, snow white open blooms with yellow stamens; *Linum narbonnense*, intensely blue silky flowers; lupins, derived from selections and crosses of *Lupinus polyphyllus*, in a dazzling array of self and contrasting colours; *Papaver orientale*, oriental poppy, with many cultivars in brilliant reds and pinks, also flushed white; *Penstemon barbatus*, foxglove-like flowers, scarlet and pink; *Potentilla* hybrids, single and double flowers ranging from yellow through orange to vivid scarlet.

Several more biennials are now in bloom besides those mentioned on pages 69 and 83, among them sweet williams, pictured above, Canterbury bells and foxgloves, with spikes of flowers in many shades with beautifully stippled throats, derived largely from *Digitalis purpurea* pictured on the next page.

Bulbs, Corms and Tubers

Flowering onions are opening their heads of flowers on stout stalks. Among the most popular are *Allium cernuum* (rose), *A. karataviense* (grey-pink), *A. moly* (yellow), *A. oreophilum* (*ostrowskianum*) (carmine), *A. schubertii* (deep rose). Some early lilies are in flower; one is pictured opposite. Details will be found in the July notes (page 120).

Above Sweet william Auricula-eyed, an old garden favourite developed from *Dianthus barbatus*, a short-lived perennial, is grown as a biennial to brighten up beds and borders during the early summer. It has densely packed heads of brilliantly coloured flowers marked with contrasting zones in concentric circles like small, daintily fringed auriculas.

Left *Digitalis purpurea*, the native foxglove, is a woodland plant, preferring a shady position and soil rich in organic matter. Though a perennial in suitable conditions, it is best grown as a biennial, as are the many selections derived from it, such as the tall Shirley hybrids, the less tall Excelsior mixture and the newer and shorter-spiked Foxy.

Below *Meconopsis betonicifolia*, the Himalayan blue poppy from Tibet and neighbouring lands, requires a sheltered position with some shade and rich, moist but well-drained soil.

Rock Garden and Pool

Outstanding this month among plants for the waterside or other damp spots are the candelabra primulas, with several species and many forms and hybrids, all with flowers in whorls along the stem. Among them are *Primula aurantiaca* (gold), *P. bulleyana* (orange), *P. japonica* (magenta), with cultivars such as 'Miller's Crimson' and 'Postford White', *P. pulverulenta* (deep pink, dark eye) and the lovely Bartley hybrids in pastel shades.

Another June-flowering beauty which needs moist soil and a cool spot is the blue poppy *Meconopsis betonicifolia*, pictured here.

Many rock garden plants listed on pages 86 and 87 may still be in flower. An additional selection is given on the next page.

SELECTED ROCK GARDEN PLANTS

Achillea argentea, silvery tufts, heads of white flowers, *A. aurea* and *A. tomentosa*, dense greenery with golden blooms, and *A.* 'King Edward', primrose yellow; *Ajuga reptans* cultivars, blue spikes above bronzed and coloured foliage; *Antennaria aprica*, *A. dioica* and cultivars, green carpeters with white, pink and red flowers; *Anthemis biebersteinii* (*rudolphiana*), foliage like silver lace, orange-gold blooms; *Arenaria balearica* and *A. montana*, green mats studded white flowers; *Campanula carpatica* cultivars, white, blue and purple; *Dianthus alpinus*, rose-red, also the white form 'Albus', *D. gratianopolitanus* (*caesius*), Cheddar pink, and many lovely cultivars; *Dryas octopetala*, open white blooms, and its free-flowering hybrid *D.* x *suendermannii*; *Erigeron aureus*, orange, and *E. karvinskianus* (*mucronatus*), pink and white daisies; *Erinus alpinus*, downy tufts bearing spikes of rose-pink blooms, and its white form 'Albus'; *Geranium cinereum* 'Ballerina', lilac pink flowers veined crimson against ferny foliage, *G. dalmaticum*, shell-pink or white; *Globularia cordifolia*, globe daisy, fluffy blue flower heads above dark green mats; *Gypsophila repens*, greyish trailer, sprays of pink blooms; *Helichrysum bellidioides* and *H. milfordae* (*marginatum*), mats formed of silvery rosettes with short-stalked, crisp white flowers; *Lewisia cotyledon* and its many forms and hybrids, fleshy rosettes starred with white, pink and salmon blooms; *Linum perenne* 'Alpinum', dwarf flax, with clear blue flowers; *Nierembergia repens* (*rivularis*), ground-hugging, with upturned white cup-shaped flowers; *Papaver alpinum*, alpine poppy, silky blooms of white, pink or yellow and finely divided leaves; *Potentilla aurea*, golden yellow flowers, and the hybrid 'Tonguei', apricot blotched crimson; *Thymus serpyllum*, creeping thyme, wide range of cultivars.

Some of the shrubs and sub-shrubs mentioned in May as giving variety of colour and texture to the rock garden (see page 86) flower for several weeks and may still be in bloom. One such is *Genista lydia*, pictured here, a superb shrub where there is room for it. In more restricted spaces the completely prostrate *G. pilosa* 'Procumbens', which moulds itself to any contour and flowers in a sheet of gold, is more suitable. The semi-prostrate *Cytisus* × *kewensis*, smothered in creamy blooms, is another fine shrublet.

Among the most brilliant of all shrubby plants for the rock garden now coming into flower are the rock roses, of which there is a multitude of cultivars, derived mainly from *Helianthemum nummularium*. Among the most attractive and widely available are the following: 'Ben Heckla' (coppery gold), 'Cerise Queen' (glowing red, double), 'Firedragon' (flame orange), 'Praecox' (buttercup yellow, grey foliage), 'Rose Queen' (lovely satiny rose), 'Wisley Pink' (soft pink) and 'Wisley Primrose' (extra large flowers of clear primrose yellow).

Above *Genista lydia*, a superb small shrub from the eastern Balkans, is ideally suited to the borders of rock gardens or to dry walls where there is plenty of space for its pendulous stems covered in late spring and early summer with golden flowers. It has received many awards, including the Royal Horticultural Society's First Class Certificate and Award of Garden Merit.

Right Among the chief centres of attraction in the rock garden at this time of year are the alpine bellflowers, species and cultivars of *Campanula*. Tried and trusted favourites are the many forms and hybrids grouped together under the name *C. carpatica*, now coming into flower and continuing through the summer; They make dense rounded clumps with shiny leaves, and the different forms carry upturned cup-shaped flowers in many shades of blue, from the palest lavender to the deepest azure; there are also white-flowered forms.

Even where there is not a rock garden it is possible to enjoy several of the alpines now in flower by growing them beside steps or in spaces between paving stones, where the drainage is sharp and they receive plenty of light. The following are suitable plants.

Campanula cochleariifolia, with dense mats of shining green leaves and short, erect stems bearing small bell-flowers of white, blue and lavender, and many other creeping campanulas, such as that pictured here; *Mentha requienii*, Corsican mint, with tiny peppermint-scented leaves starred with small lavender flowers; *Thymus serpyllum* in its many forms, with prostrate stems bearing small aromatic leaves and flowers of white, pink, red and purple; many forms of *Saxifraga aizoon* (now *paniculata*).

Fruit

Strawberries, the most popular and widely grown of all soft fruits, will now be in full bearing, and with favourable weather should continue to yield for several weeks.

Towards the end of the month there may be the first pickings of gooseberries, and perhaps of red and white currants. Several of the early sweet cherries will also be ripening now.

Vegetables

Asparagus may be cut until the middle of the month. Other fresh vegetables include broad and french beans, beet, cabbage, carrots, cauliflower, lettuce, onions (spring and overwintered), peas, radish, spinach, turnips and perhaps some early potatoes.

Left *Limonium suworowii*, an annual species of sea lavender from western Turkestan, makes an attractive display in a cool greenhouse, where it comes into flower in May from a sowing made in February. Further sowings made in succession till April will extend the flowering period into the autumn.

In the foreground, *Lobelia tenuior*, a trailing annual, native to western Australia and also sown in February, produces its dainty, forget-me-not blue flowers with a contrasting white eye in great abundance.

Greenhouse and Frame

Though the emphasis now that summer has begun is very much on the display outside, several greenhouse plants are now producing an abundance of bloom.

Among the most appealing are some of the annuals sown in early spring to provide flowers in the cool house by midsummer, such as *Limonium suworowii*, pictured above, with in the foreground *Lobelia tenuior*, sown at the same time.

Several favourites much used for planting out in beds and containers to make a display later in the summer are also excellent for giving a splash of colour under glass now, weeks before they begin to make a show out of doors. Among the most popular are fuchsias, begonias and pelargoniums.

In the heated greenhouse perhaps the showiest plants to come into bloom now, from tubers started into growth early in the year, are those popularly known as gloxinias, developed over many years from *Sinningia speciosa*. Their large velvety flowers range from red to pink and purple, usually with a contrasting border. *Achimenes* cultivars, of the same family and started into growth at the same time, will be opening their tubular, trumpet-mouthed flowers in red or purple.

House Plants

Many of those mentioned in the May notes (see page 91) will still be in bloom; in general, the cooler the room the longer the flowers may be expected to last. Begonias of many kinds start into bloom at this time.

What to do in June

Trees and Shrubs

Several of the shrubs that bloom on wood made during the previous year may be pruned as soon as the flowers fade, so that useless old growth is removed and new shoots to carry next season's blooms are given as long a period as possible to produce and mature their growth.

Among those that may be ready for such treatment during this month are the common broom, *Cytisus scoparius*, and the large number of cultivars derived from it. The flowered shoots can be cut back nearly to the old wood, but be careful not to cut into the old wood itself, or the stems may be killed.

Several other shrubs which flower in June, such as deutzias and weigelas, also benefit from hard pruning as soon as the flowers fade; details of how to do so, together with a list of shrubs that come within this group, will be found on page 214.

Many shrubs and sub-shrubs, such as caryopteris, lavender, rosemary, santolina and weigela, may be propagated from softwood cuttings. Take these from vigorously growing young shoots as soon as they have reached a suitable length. Prepare and insert them as explained on page 194, and place them in a closed propagating case. At this time of year rooting should be rapid, and ventilation should be given when the cuttings can be seen to be producing new growth.

As far as possible – that is to say if there is time available and the specimens are not too big to be tackled – it is still well worth while to remove faded flower heads from rhododendrons, including azaleas, and from lilacs, to stop them from wasting their energy in forming seed. Laburnums too will benefit from having their dead clusters removed. Many parents of young children also do so because the seeds are intensely poisonous.

Climbers and Wall-plants

Several half-hardy annual climbers raised under glass (including some that, while perennial by nature, are best grown as annuals) can now be planted in sheltered places against sunny walls or fences, or to scramble over pergolas or arches, where they will give a succession of flowers through the summer and autumn till the cold weather puts an end to the display.

Among those suitable for the purpose are the following: *Cobaea scandens* (cup-and-saucer plant), with purple, bell-shaped flowers set in a saucer-like calyx; *Eccremocarpus scaber* (chilean glory vine), with tubular orange-scarlet blooms; *Ipomoea* 'Heavenly Blue' (morning glory) and others with blue-and-white, pink and red flowers; *Thunbergia alata* (black-eyed susan), with orange-yellow, dark-centred flowers; *Tropaeolum peregrinum*, often called *T. canariense* (canary creeper), with fringed canary-yellow blooms borne in great profusion.

These climbers will need support right from the beginning; they grow very rapidly and their slender stems are very easily damaged. Some simple and effective methods of support are shown on page 202. The plants should be well watered in and never allowed to lack moisture at the roots, particularly when grown against walls, where the soil tends to dry out very quickly. A good mulch on the surface can be a great help in controlling this, but watering may still be needed from time to time, since as the growth of the plants increases so does the amount of moisture they extract from the soil, which may become very dry.

Established climbers and wall plants will be making rapid growth, and some of them, such as clematis and chaenomeles, may now be readily propagated by means of layering (see page 196).

Roses

The most popular garden roses, generally known as hybrid teas and floribundas, will be coming into bloom this month, and fading flowers should be regularly removed to encourage the production of new ones. Always cut back to a good strong bud or shoot.

If large, high-quality blooms are required – for exhibition purposes or for flower arranging – hybrid tea roses may be disbudded by taking off all side-buds from the flower stem, leaving just the terminal one.

Watch out for suckers growing from the rootstock, and as soon as any make their appearance remove them. If left they may take over and replace the named cultivar. Never take the easy way of cutting them off at ground level; that will only cause even more to spring up. Scoop away enough soil to find where the sucker joins the root and pull it right off at that point.

Continue to keep an eye open for signs of attack by aphids and other pests or by disease, and spray as soon as an attack is noticed, before the trouble has time to spread.

Borders and Beds

As soon as the blooms fade on early-flowering herbaceous perennials it is best to cut off the spent flower-stems. Some may produce a further crop of flowers later on; also both the plants and their neighbours will benefit from more light and air.

Plant out half-hardy annuals raised under glass as soon as possible. For those without facilities for raising them, a wide range can be bought at nurseries and garden centres. Some of the most popular are from the following genera: *Ageratum, Antirrhinum, Arctotis, Aster, Cosmos, Dianthus, Heliotropium, Lobelia, Nemesia, Nicotiana, Petunia, Phlox, Salpiglossis, Salvia, Tagetes, Verbena* and *Zinnia*.

It should now be safe to plant out pelargoniums for a summer display, either in beds or in decorative containers (see pages 218–19).

Biennials and perennials sown in the open during the past month or so may now need thinning to give them room to develop. The thinnings need not be wasted; they may be planted in a nursery bed, six inches (fifteen cm) apart, to grow on till they can be put into their flowering quarters.

Bulbs, Corms and Tubers
Remaining bulbs from spring-bedding schemes should be lifted.

Dahlia tubers not yet planted out should be put in as soon as possible. All those which need support should be staked at the time of planting.

Rock Gardens and Pools
Cut back old flowered stems of alpine phlox, aubrietas and other trailing plants to keep them trim and avoid seeding.

Continue with weeding, and remove algae from pools before they grow into large unmanageable masses.

Complete the planting of aquatics and alpines as soon as possible, to give them a good season of growth.

Lawns
With the grass growing rapidly, increase the frequency of mowing if possible to twice a week. If there should be a long dry spell raise the mower blades to make the cut less close, and remove the grass-box for the time being.

Any isolated weeds still left after spring treatment with weedkiller may be dealt with by spot treatment. If the grass was not fed in the spring a lawn fertilizer may now be applied at the recommended rate. Should it be necessary to water the lawn, and there are no restrictions on doing so, give a good soaking, preferably with a sprinkler (see page 204).

Fruit
Inspect apple and pear trees and remove any misshapen, undersized or damaged fruits. If further thinning is needed, leave it till next month, since many fruits usually fall off naturally during the June drop.

Strawberries will be in full production this month and straw, or special mats (see page 224), should be placed under the plants to prevent the fruit from being soiled.

Fruits trained against walls should be watered if necessary; light rain may not be enough in such positions. Mulching helps to conserve moisture.

Vegetables
Several of the less hardy plants raised under glass may be planted out in the open early in the month, so long as they have been properly hardened off. Among them are aubergines, cucumbers, marrows, peppers, sweet corn and tomatoes. Of these it is still possible to sow marrows and sweet corn direct into the ground with a reasonable chance of a useful late crop.

If celery and celeriac have not already been planted out, do so as soon as possible. Being plants with high moisture requirements, they should be watered in extra well if the weather is dry.

Crops which are generally sown in a nursery bed in the open ground and later planted out in their final positions include brussels sprouts, sprouting broccoli, summer and winter cabbages, cauliflowers, kales and leeks.

Continue to make regular sowings of lettuces and radishes to keep up the supply of salads. Other crops of which further sowings may be made include runner and french beans, beetroot, leaf beets, carrots, chicory (sugar-loaf and witloof), Chinese cabbage, endive, peas, spinach (summer and New Zealand), swedes and turnips.

Keep on with weeding, by hoeing and by hand, and do any necessary thinning. Earth-up maincrop potatoes when the plants reach a height of about nine inches (twenty-two cm), drawing soil up around the stems to prevent tubers from being exposed to light.

Greenhouse and Frame
On summer days, when temperatures under glass can rise very rapidly, as much ventilation as possible should be given. To help keep things cool and to prevent the air from becoming unduly dry, greenhouse floors and benches should be damped down twice daily on hot days.

A great many cool greenhouse plants will benefit from a spell out of doors during the summer, in a spot with some shade from the midday sun. Plunge them, up to the rims of their pots, in shingle, ashes, peat or failing these well-drained soil. Do not neglect to water the plants as often as necessary.

Cinerarias and *Primula malacoides* may be sown to produce plants for flowering in the cool greenhouse in the early months of next year.

Continue to pot on seedlings and rooted cuttings as required.

Secure stems of tomatoes to their supports as they grow, and remove side shoots as soon as they appear.

House Plants
Leaves of foliage plants will greatly appreciate a light spraying or gentle sponging with clean tepid water to freshen them up and remove dust. On warm days when there is fine rain (but *not* a heavy downpour), many plants may be stood outside for an hour of two, where they will benefit from fresh rainwater and fresh air.

Continue to remove old leaves and to feed and water as necessary.

Watch out for aphids and other pests and deal with them without delay, before they can multiply.

July

Hot July brings thunder showers,
Apricots and gillyflowers.

Sara Coleridge (1802–1852)

July is often the hottest month of the year. Though the longest day was last month and the hours of daylight are already beginning to decrease, there is always a time-lag before the soil can warm up to reach its maximum temperature, which usually occurs in the latter half of this month. The highest temperatures are normally recorded in the south, and some distance inland. Places near the sea tend to escape the extremes of heat in the summer, just as they escape the extremes of cold in the winter.

July can also be a month of higher than average rainfall, especially when the wind is from the west. A wet St Swithin's day on the fifteenth of the month is said, according to folklore, to be followed by forty days of rain. Though there may be little scientific evidence for the belief, it is true that there is a strong tendency for weather conditions, whether wet or dry, to remain the same for weeks on end.

While plants under glass probably need more frequent watering in July than at any other time, those in the open generally need less than they did during the past month or more, both because of the increased rainfall and because those most at risk from drought – the annuals and bedding plants – should by now have developed a rooting system which enables them to draw water from the deeper layers of soil.

Heavy, and very often sudden, thunderstorms may be expected at this time of year. They can cause havoc, especially to the herbaceous plants which are such an important feature of the garden in July. That is why the successful gardener will have made sure that everything that needs support has been attended to, and so avoided smashed down plants and flowers splashed with mud.

Left *Mesembryanthemum criniflorum* (now *Dorotheanthus bellidiformis*) Yellow Ice is a selection of the livingstone daisy, usually grown as a half-hardy annual.

What to see and enjoy in July

Trees and Shrubs

Though the main focus in many gardens is on herbaceous plants and roses, plenty of trees and shrubs are also now coming into flower.

The large and handsome *Rhododendron auriculatum* produces its scented white blooms, and from *R. kaempferi* come such July-flowering cultivars as 'Daimio' and 'Mikado', in shades of salmon-pink.

Hydrangea × *macrophylla*, a large group of garden favourites, is in two sections. Hortensias, otherwise known as mop-headed hydrangeas, produce large round heads of sterile florets. Lacecaps produce flat heads of small fertile flowers surrounded by larger florets. There are many cultivars of each kind, from white and pink to blue (only made possible in alkaline soils by the use of a blueing agent).

SELECTED TREES AND SHRUBS

Aesculus parviflora, the shrubby horse-chestnut, whose spreading, slender stems bear white blossoms with red anthers; *Buddleja davidii*, butterfly bush, in many cultivars with tassels of flowers from white through red to purple; *Calluna vulgaris*, scottish heather or ling, single and double-flowered cultivars in white, pink and mauve; *Castanea sativa*, sweet chestnut, pale yellow cord-like catkins and sharply toothed, shining leaves; *Catalpa bignonioides*, indian bean tree, wide spreading, with white, foxglove-like flowers flecked yellow and purple, and its outstanding cultivar 'Aurea' with large, gleaming yellow leaves.

Right *Iberis umbellata* Dwarf Fairy Mixed, a distinctive selection of the popular hardy annual candytuft, is miniature and compact, with rounded clusters of brightly coloured flowers in many shades of pink, carmine, lavender and white. It comes into bloom very rapidly from seed and makes an attractive display if grown in bold patches as an edging to borders and beds. Successive sowings from early to late spring will produce flowers throughout the summer and early autumn.

Daboecia cantabrica, irish heath, several cultivars with very showy white, pink and rose-purple, pitcher-shaped blooms; *Desfontainea spinosa*, scarlet-yellow trumpet-shaped flowers against holly-like leaves; *Deutzia monbeigii*, dense grey foliage and glistening, starry white blooms; *Erica ciliaris*, Dorset heath, several cultivars with white, pink and rosy red flowers, and *E. vagans*, cornish heath, with a large number of cultivars bearing long sprays of cerise, red, rose and lilac flowers; *Escallonia* cultivars in a wide range with small polished leaves and tubular blooms mostly in varied pink, rose-red and crimson, also white; *Eucryphia glutinosa*, with erect branches carrying a profusion of white flowers; *Hebe* species and cultivars, evergreens surviving most winters except in the coldest parts, with flowers in many shades of white, pink, violet and blue, displayed against handsome foliage.

Above Rose 'Dorothy Perkins', among the best known and most widely grown of all ramblers, was raised in the United States and introduced in 1901. Its parents were *Rosa wichuraiana* and 'Madame Gabriel Luizet', a hybrid perpetual.

Left Rose 'Dutch Gold', one of the newer hybrid tea roses, notable for its large, fragrant blooms of rich golden yellow, which gained it a Gold Medal in trials in Holland.

Above *Hydrangea* x *macrophylla* 'Madame A. Riverain' is one of the large number of cultivars belonging to the group known as mop-headed hydrangeas, or hortensias. The large globular heads are composed of sterile florets, which are mostly in shades of pink, red or blue, according to the cultivar and to the nature of the soil in which it is grown.

Hedysarum multijugum, with sea-green, feathery foliage and rosy magenta pea-flowers in long racemes; *Hoheria lyallii*, with large silvery-grey leaves and fragrant, translucent white blooms; *Hypericum androsaemum, H. forrestii, H.* x *inodorum* 'Elstead', the superb large-flowered *H.* 'Hidcote' and the ground-covering *H. calycinum*, rose of Sharon, all with brilliant yellow petals and conspicuous stamens forming a central brush; *Indigofera gerardiana (heterantha)*, with elegant compound foliage and a display all through the summer of rosy purple pea flowers; *Koelreuteria paniculata*, golden-rain tree, wide-spreading with divided, willow-pattern leaves and yellow flowers, to be followed later by bronze, bladder-like fruits.

Lavandula angustifolia (spica), old english lavender, many cultivars, dwarf and tall, with flowers from pale greyish blue to the deepest purple, also some with white and pale pink blooms, and *L. stoechas*, the intensely aromatic french lavender with crowded flower-heads of dark purple; *Leycesteria formosa*, flowering nutmeg, with cascades of small white flowers nearly hidden by showy wine-red bracts; *Liriodendron tulipifera*, tulip tree, greenish yellow tulip-like blooms with orange centres; *Nandina domestica*, chinese sacred bamboo, erect stems, large pinnate leaves and long terminal heads of white flowers followed in autumn by scarlet berries; *Olearia* x *haastii*, the favourite daisy bush, rounded in shape, with oval leaves green above and grey beneath, smothered in fragrant white flowers; *Phygelius capensis*, cape figwort, tiers of dangling tubular scarlet blooms with yellow throats; *Romneya coulteri*, californian tree poppy, sub-shrub bearing deeply cut bluish green leaves and large, silky white poppy flowers with a central boss of golden stamens, and its hybrid, the more robust *R.* x *hybrida*; *Santolina chamaecyparissus*, cotton lavender, dense mound of small, finely dissected, silver-grey leaves surmounted this month by yellow button flowers, and the somewhat larger *S. neapolitana* with more feathery foliage; *Sorbaria (Spiraea) aitchisonii*, elegant red-tinted stems bearing long ash-like leaves and creamy white plumes of tiny flowers; *Spiraea* x *billiardii, S.* x *bumalda, S. japonica* and cultivars, sharply toothed leaves and flattened heads of pink, ruby and crimson blooms; *Styrax japonica*, large shrub or small tree with pendulous, bell-like white flowers along the spreading branches; *Yucca filamentosa* and its yellow-striped cultivar 'Variegata', *Y. flaccida* and *Y. gloriosa*, Adam's needle; all with large clumps of narrow, pointed, sword-like leaves from which arise tall, densely packed spires of ivory white, drooping flowers resembling lilies.

Left *Lilium regale*, among the most popular and easily grown of all lily species, bears large, fragrant, funnel-shaped flowers in loose clusters, pure white inside with sulphur-yellow centres. It thrives in full sun, grows well in most garden soils, and increases rapidly.

Below One of a selection of promising new lily seedlings grown at Wisley in order to assess and compare their qualities as garden plants.

Climbers and Wall-plants

Several subjects mentioned in the June notes (page 99) will still be producing flowers, some of the showiest being the *Clematis* hybrids, which now begin to include those such as 'Jackmanii' and 'Ville de Lyon' that bloom on the current season's wood.

Many honeysuckles are now coming into bloom, scenting the air with their powerful yet delicate fragrance. Among the most popular are *Lonicera periclymenum* 'Serotina', producing flowers from now until the autumn, *L.* × *americana*, with white flowers turning to yellow flushed deep rose, 'Dropmore Scarlet', with large leaves setting off bright red tubular blooms, *L. japonica* cultivars, evergreen and with particularly sweet-smelling flowers, and *L.* × *tellmanniana*, an outstanding hybrid with oval leaves and clusters of eight to twelve rich golden flowers opening from rose-pink buds.

Another favourite sweet-smelling twiner or scrambler is *Jasminum officinale*, the common white jasmine, with feathery leaves composed of from five to nine leaflets and terminal clusters of white, scented flowers.

Roses

The most popular garden roses – generally known as hybrid teas and floribundas, and also called large-flowered and cluster-flowered – are still in full bloom. Many later cultivars are now opening their first flowers, joined by several climbers; some attractive examples are pictured on page 113. Careful and prompt attention to the removal of fading blooms will ensure as long a flowering season as possible.

Borders and Beds

There is an enormous range of herbaceous plants now in flower. Many of those already mentioned in pages 102–3 will still be in bloom, especially if dead-heading is regularly carried out. In addition, many are now coming into flower for the first time, including several of the taller ones at the back of the border, which have by now reached their full flowering height. A selected list of some of the most popular perennials is given below and in the columns which follow.

> ### SELECTED HERBACEOUS PLANTS
>
> *Aconitum* x *bicolor* cultivars, flowers from ivory to violet and navy blue, many of them two-toned; *Alstroemeria aurantiaca*, peruvian lily, rich orange, beautifully marked lily flowers, and *A. ligtu*, pink, with many hybrids in varied shades including salmon and copper; *Campanula persicifolia*, with lilac bellflowers, and cultivars from white to sky-blue; *Centranthus ruber*, red valerian, fleshy leaves and crowded heads of small rose-pink blooms, also forms with white and deep red flowers; *Chrysanthemum maximum*, shasta daisy, many cultivars, such as the anemone-centred 'Wirral Supreme', splendid for garden display and for cutting; *Coreopsis grandiflora* 'Mayfield Giant', large golden daisies set against dense, finely cut foliage; *Dictamnus albus*, burning bush, stiffly upright stems with aromatic leaves and white flowers with long stamens, also mauve-flowered forms; *Echinacea purpurea*, deep mauve daisies.

Above This ornamental terracotta pot provides an appropriate container for an attractive summer display of half-hardy annuals, made up of royal purple petunias and trailing lobelias in a matching colour, set off by the slender, cascading stems of a decorative ivy with variegated leaves.

Eccremocarpus scaber is a rapidly growing climber clinging by leaf tendrils and now opening its orange or scarlet tubular flowers. An extremely vigorous twiner is that generally known as *Polygonum baldschuanicum*, though very often in fact *P. (Bilderdykia) aubertii*, the russian vine, foaming with masses of tiny creamy blossoms, and ideal for covering unsightly sheds or tree-stumps.

Trachelospermum jasminoides, an attractive twining plant for south or west aspects, produces clusters of intensely fragrant, white jasmine-like flowers set against the dark green, narrow oval, shining foliage.

A magnificent evergreen summer-flowering shrub for a sunny wall with plenty of space is *Magnolia grandiflora*, with large leaves like polished leather and huge, creamy white, deliciously fragrant flowers.

Echinops ritro, globe thistle, handsome prickly leaves and spherical steel-blue flower heads on stout stems; *Eryngium* x *oliverianum*, a sea holly hybrid with deeply cut leaves and branched stems carrying deep blue flower-heads like large thimbles; *Gaillardia* x *grandiflora*, garden hybrids with large, flamboyant daisy flowers in yellows and reds with dark centres; *Galega* x *hartlandii*, goat's rue hybrids with feathery leaves and pea-flowers on shades of mauve., pink, violet and lilac; *Geranium endressii* 'Wargrave Pink', fine cultivar of this popular Pyrenean species, with bright salmon-pink flowers, and the hybrid *G*. 'Russell Prichard', with pastel pink flowers, produced in succession until the autumn; *Gypsophila paniculata* 'Bristol Fairy', with double white blooms, and the double pink 'Rosy Veil'; *Helenium bigelovii* 'Aurantiacum', rich yellow, and other cultivars in mahogany, red and gold; *Hemerocallis* hybrids, day lilies, with trumpet flowers in yellow, orange, terracotta, maroon and pink; *Hosta fortunei* and *H. sieboldiana*, early among the plantain lilies to open their pale lilac flowers on stems above the broad, ribbed leaves; *Lavatera olbia* 'Rosea', the most popular tree mallow, sub-shrubby and with clear rose-pink flowers; *Liatris spicata* 'Kobold', vivid mauve blooms in dense spires; *Linaria purpurea*, a toadflax with spikes of small, snapdragon-like lilac blooms, and its pink-flowered cultivar 'Canon Went'; *Linum narbonnense*, the most popular perennial flax, deep blue flowers; *Lychnis chalcedonica*, maltese cross, bright scarlet blooms in flat heads; *Lysimachia punctata*, yellow loosestrife, spires of shining yellow stars; *Macleaya microcarpa (cordata)*, plume poppy, grey-green lobed foliage and plumes of many small buff or pink flushed blooms; *Monarda didyma*, bergamot, otherwise known as bee balm, with pointed, aromatic, mint-like leaves and heads of rich red, hooded flowers with deep crimson calyces; there are also several lovely forms with flowers of various shades of pink, from rose to salmon.

Oenothera cultivars, including 'Fireworks', with brilliant yellow, red-stemmed flowers; *Polygonum bistorta* 'Superbum', blooms forming light pink pokers above broad foliage; *Rheum palmatum*, fluffy spires of rosy red blooms and large rhubarb leaves; *Salvia nemorosa* forms and hybrids, with dense erect spikes of violet-blue flowers; *Scabiosa caucasica*, lavender blue and perfect for cutting, with cultivars from dark blue to white; *Sidalcea malviflora* and its many cultivars, with small, hollyhock-like flowers, from pink to red, in elegant spikes; *Solidago* 'Goldenmosa', a fine dwarf golden rod, and 'Lemore', with primrose-yellow blooms thriving in sun or in part shade.

Above *Penstemon* Scarlet and White is one of many selections of attractive border plants, related to the foxgloves and with somewhat similar flowers. Though perennial and sometimes surviving the winter, border penstemons are usually grown as annuals, readily propagated from seed or cuttings.

Above Two favourite half-hardy annuals make a colourful summer display.

Salpiglossis Friendship, in the background, is a popular selection, with upward facing flowers in shades of blue, red, rose and gold, mostly veined in contrasting colours.

The tawny orange blooms in the foreground are of a free-flowering selection of french marigolds, derived from *Tagetes patula*.

Stachys olympica (*lanata*), lamb's ears, woolly grey with magenta flowers; *Stokesia laevis* 'Blue Star', clusters of sky-blue flowers *Thalictrum aquilegiifolium*, meadow rue, graceful foliage and heads of fluffy purplish flowers, also paler and white forms; *Tradescantia*, spiderwort, forms with flowers from deep purple through pale blue to white with blue centre; *Veratrum nigrum*, large, ribbed leaves and maroon, star-like flowers; *Verbascum phoeniceum*, purple mullein, and its many hybrids, with flowers from purple and pink to amber, yellow and white; *Veronica incana*, *V. spicata* and their forms and hybrids, compact plants with dense spikes of violet-blue, pink and white flowers, and *V. teucrium* cultivars such as the well named 'Royal Blue'.

A very large number of hardy annuals will now be in flower. The following are some of the most popular, both for beds and the mixed border: *Alyssum maritimum*, *Calendula officinalis* (pot marigold), *Centaurea cyanus* (cornflower), *Chrysanthemum carinatum*, *Clarkia elegans*, *Convolvulus minor*, *Delphinium*, (annual larkspur), *Dimorphotheca aurantiaca*, *Echium plantaginum*, *Eschscholzia* (californian poppy), *Godetia*, *Helichrysum bracteatum* (straw flower), *Lavatera* (mallow), *Limnanthes douglasii*, *Linaria* (toadflax), *Linum grandiflorum* (flax), *Matthiola bicornis* (night-scented stock), mignonette (*Reseda odorata*), nasturtium (*Tropaeolum majus*), *Nigella damascena* (love-in-a-mist), poppy (*Papaver rhoeas*), scabious (*Scabiosa atropurpurea*), sweet pea (*Lathyrus odoratus*), sweet sultan (*Centaurea imperialis*), *Viscaria oculata* (*Silene coeli-rosa*).

To extend their flowering season, remove fading blooms regularly.

Above The white flowers are those of *Lavatera trimestris* 'Mont Blanc', a lovely hardy annual mallow. In the foreground are brilliant modern F₁ hybrid zonal pelargoniums.

There are also many half-hardy annuals, raised under glass and planted out in beds or containers, which should now be in bloom. They provide some of the most colourful and attractive flowers in the garden during the summer, as can be seen from the pictures on this and the three previous pages. A selection from the wide range of garden favourites would include many from the following genera: *Ageratum, Begonia, Cosmos* (Cosmea), *Gazania, Impatiens, Lobelia, Mesembryanthemum* (livingstone daisy), *Nemesia, Nicotiana, Petunia, Phlox, Portulaca, Salvia, Tagetes* (french and african marigolds), *Verbena* and *Zinnia*.

Right *Dianthus* Queens Court, an outstanding F₁ hybrid selection of the annual pink, produces a lavish display of elegantly fringed flowers in an exceptionally wide range of rich and glowing colours.

Above *Hemerocallis* 'Jane Russell' is an established favourite among the large number of hybrid day lilies produced by breeders over many years from combinations of several parent species. With their long, arching leaves, day lilies are among the stateliest of border plants, and the many cultivars bear flowers ranging from yellow and gold to orange, pink and red. Some are scented, particularly among the yellows.

Bulbs, Corms and Tubers

Lilies are among the most beautiful bulbous plants now in flower. One of the earliest species is that old cottage garden favourite *Lilium candidum*, the madonna lily, with white, bowl-shaped flowers. Other popular species flowering now include *L. martagon*, turk's head, *L. pardalinum* and *L. regale*.

More usual nowadays, however, are the hybrids, of which there are large numbers to choose from, with flowers of many different shapes and colours, from white through palest yellow to deepest red.

Others now in bloom include *Galtonia candicans* and *Iris xiphioides* (now *latifolia*). Some gladioli may also start to flower by the latter half of the month.

Rock Garden and Pool

Valuable for their fern-like leaves and graceful plumes of tiny blossoms are many garden forms of *Astilbe*; an example is pictured opposite. Tall ones are suited to the border, but dwarf species such as *A. chinensis* and *A. glaberrima* are excellent for moist places in the rock garden.

SELECTED ROCK GARDEN PLANTS

Acantholimon glumaceum, sprays of pink blooms above deep green cushions; *Achillea umbellata*, heads of white flowers held well clear of tufted silvery foliage; *Asperula nitida* and *A. gussonii*, forming dense mats with flesh-pink flowers; *Campanula cochlearifolia* (*pusilla*), creeping stems and violet-blue bellflowers, and *C. portenschlagiana* (*muralis*), amethyst; *Convolvulus mauritanicus*, for warm, protected places, bearing wide blue flowers with white throats; *Cyananthus lobatus*, radiating stems ending in single large, deep blue flowers, also a white-flowered form; *Dianthus arvernensis*, dense grey foliage studded with bright pink blooms on short stems, also a lovely form with pure white flowers; *Diascia cordata*, deep pink blooms on stalks above prostrate leafy stems, and the hybrid 'Ruby Field', with salmon-pink flowers; *Gentiana asclepiadea*, willow gentian, arched leafy stems bearing clusters of blue flowers, stippled inside, and *G. septemfida*, with large bell-shaped blooms in shades of blue and purple, according to cultivar; *Geranium renardii*, velvety leaves and pale lilac flowers with darker lines, and *G. sessiliflorum* 'Nigricans' with small white flowers and chocolate-brown leaves; *Geum montanum*, large golden blooms held on stems above softly hairy tufts; *Globularia repens* (*nana*), dense mat with tiny leaves and short-stalked round heads of fluffy blue flowers; *Horminum pyrenaicum*, forming a rosette of evergreen, toothed leaves and arching stems bearing deep mauve blooms, also pink and albino forms; *Hypericum olympicum* (*polyphyllum*), low dome of fresh green foliage and large, shining, golden flowers, and *H. coris*, dwarf shrublet with smaller flowers and tiny leaves; *Leontopodium alpinum*, the well-known edelweiss, with narrow, downy foliage and densely clustered flower-heads with an appearance like that of creamy grey flannel.

Left *Astilbe* 'Federsee' is one of the group of garden hybrids known collectively as *A.* x *arendsii* and excellent for the waterside and other damp places. There are many cultivars, with attractive ferny foliage and plumes of flowers ranging in colour from deep red through many shades of pink to white.

Below *Santolina chamaecyparissus*, cotton lavender, is a dwarf sub-shrub with finely divided, silvery foliage and button-like yellow flower heads.

Micromeria corsica, silvery cushions decked with tiny coral-pink flowers; *Oenothera missouriensis*, prostrate, with reddish buds opening into large, lemon-yellow blooms; *Penstemon pinifolius*, narrow leaves and sprays of scarlet flowers, and *P. scouleri*, leathery leaves and lavender blooms; *Sedum spathulifolium*, with fleshy, purplish leaves covered in fine white powder and carrying clear yellow flowers in branched heads; *Sempervivum arachnoideum*, the popular cobweb houseleek with many forms, making neat rosettes of green and pinkish leaves webbed in silvery threads and bearing pink flowers on reddish stems.

There are many other species, forms and hybrids now in bloom, including many garden favourites; several species have now been transferred by the botanists to the genus *Jovibarba*.

The garden pool and its surroundings are now at their best. In the pool itself probably the loveliest of all plants are the water-lilies, with their handsome round floating leaves and their cupped, many-petalled flowers in various colours. Among the species one of the most attractive is *Nymphaea alba*, the common white water-lily, native to lakes and ponds throughout much of Europe, including the British Isles. It is a variable species, with considerable differences in the size of leaves and flowers. Some selected garden forms are of outstanding beauty.

Most cultivated water-lilies are not true species but hybrids, of mixed and often uncertain parentage. To see what is available from the very wide range it is best to visit a specialist nursery where the plants are in flower and where advice may be sought on the best ones for different depths of water.

Among the most popular cultivars are the following: 'Aurora', buff yellow, changing to copper, 'Charles de Meurville', deep pink, darkening, 'Conqueror', rosy crimson, 'Escarboucle', brilliant red, 'Firecrest', scented, pink, red stamens, 'Sunrise', primrose yellow.

In the soil around the edges of pools, and in other damp places, the most striking and colourful plants to come into flower are the bog irises. The far eastern species *Iris laevigata*, which will grow in shallow water, reaches a height of eighteen inches (forty-five cm) and carries many broad flowers of a clear, soft shade of lavender. It looks specially appealing when interplanted with its white form 'Alba'. There is a beautiful cultivar named 'Variegata', whose smooth green leaves are striped with cream.

The taller species *I. kaempferi* (*ensata*), has given rise, through centuries of selection and breeding in Japan, and more recently in the United States, to a multitude of different flower sizes, shapes and colours, from silvery white through lilacs and pinks to deep purples, often with contrasting bands and sometimes delicately veined. They are available in mixed lots, or a choice can be made by visiting a nursery this month while they are in flower.

Other waterside plants now in bloom include monkey musks, derived largely from *Mimulus guttatus*, in dappled yellows and reds.

Right Globe artichokes, grown mainly as vegetables, are decorative enough to be grown also as border plants. Their long, arching, much divided leaves, like those of a giant thistle and with a silvery sheen when young, make an impressive feature. If some of the swelling buds are allowed to develop beyond the edible stage, they open into handsome purple flower heads which, cut with long stems, are excellent for home decoration.

Fruit

Most soft fruits are now in full bearing. Strawberries should continue to give a good crop till at least the middle of the month, and raspberries are now ripening. All the currants – red, white and black – are ready for picking, and gooseberries too. It is rather early for most blackberries, but tayberries, boysenberries and loganberries may have some ripe fruit before the end of the month.

Of the stone fruit, several cherries will be ready to pick, as will early cultivars of apricots, peaches and nectarines, especially against a sunny wall, together with the first plums.

By the end of the month the earliest cultivars of apples and pears may have some ripe fruit ready for picking in favourable seasons and locations. Lift the fruit and give a slight twist; only if it parts easily from the spur is it ready to be picked. Unlike late kinds, which improve with storage, early kinds are best eaten straight away.

Vegetables

The vegetable garden is now at its most productive. Globe artichokes should be cut while the tops are still tender, before the flowers develop too far. Other crops ready to be gathered include the following: beans (broad, french and runner), beetroot and leaf beets, cabbages, carrots, self-blanching celery, courgettes, cucumbers, kohl rabi, lettuces, marrows, salad and bulb onions, peas, radishes, spinach, sweet corn and turnips. First early potatoes may be dug as required, one or two plants at a time, leaving the remainder to continue growing.

Greenhouse

Among the showiest annuals now in flower from early spring sowing are the plumed celosias (pictured above right), of which seedsmen offer several selections.

Joining the african violets and gloxinias in flower in the warm house are cultivars of two other popular gesneriads: *Achimenes*, hot water plant, with tubular to trumpet-shaped flowers ranging from rosy pink through lavender to purplish blue, and *Rechsteineria cardinalis* (*Gesneria macrantha*), with handsome leaves and bright scarlet flowers.

House Plants

A large number of plants now in bloom can be used to brighten up the home, either produced specially for the purpose or brought in from the greenhouse while their flowering period lasts.

Among the more spectacular of these plants is *Anthurium scherzerianum*, often sold as the flamingo flower. It has long, handsome leaves, but the most striking feature is the shining, waxy spathe shaped like a painter's palette and brilliant scarlet in colour. Protruding above it is a fleshy, orange-red spike bearing the tiny flowers, called the spadix, which is curled round rather like a pig's tail and persists for a long time.

An attractive plant at home in a cool room is *Cuphea ignea*, known as the mexican cigar plant. It produces a succession of tubular, bright scarlet flowers, the mouth of the tube purplish black edged with white. Another popular plant for a continuous display is *Beloperone guttata*, the shrimp plant, with brownish pink overlapping bracts almost hiding small white flowers.

Above *Celosia* Fairy Fountains, a popular selection of one of the showiest greenhouse annuals, produces bushy, compact plants of uniform height bearing several feathery plumes of vivid colours, including shades of yellow, gold, orange, salmon, pink, scarlet, ruby and bronze. Sown in heat in early spring, it will come into flower in the greenhouse by midsummer. In mild and sheltered places plants may be bedded outside for the summer.

What to do in July

Trees and Shrubs

Some shrubs which flower mainly from one-year-old wood, such as species of *Deutzia* and *Philadelphus*, may continue to bloom into July. They should be pruned as soon as the flowers fade, together with others in the same group not yet attended to; for details see page 214.

Many shrubs and sub-shrubs may still be propagated from softwood cuttings, such as those mentioned in the June notes (see page 108). In the second half of this month it will be possible to propagate several shrubs from cuttings of semi-ripe wood (see page 193).

Many garden hedges such as beech, holly, hornbeam and yew will, if cut back towards the end of July, soon produce enough new growth to cover up the cuts and will stay neat and attractive for the rest of the season, or at least need no further trimming till well into the autumn.

Climbers and Wall-plants

Clematis shoots are now in vigorous growth and should be regularly secured to their supports to prevent them from flopping and being damaged. Hybrids that bloom in spring and early summer on side-shoots from old wood, such as popular 'Nelly Moser' and 'William Kennett', may be kept well furnished by some renewal pruning. Immediately after the first flush of flowers cut back between a quarter and a third of the old stems to about a foot (thirty cm) from the base. Given a good supply of food and moisture, the pruned stems will produce strong new replacement growths.

Shrubs trained against walls, such as evergreen *Ceanothus* species, should have the main shoots tied in as they develop to prevent them from coming away from the wall. Shoots growing forward from the main framework should be cut to four or five inches (ten – thirteen cm).

Roses

The chief task at present continues to be the removal of faded blooms. Cut back to a good strong bud or new shoot (see page 216). Remove all suckers from the rootstock, right back to their point of origin, as explained on page 108.

To keep up the production of strong flowering growth, give a dressing of rose fertilizer at the rate recommended in the instructions.

Continue to watch for signs of attack by pests and diseases, and spray as necessary.

Borders and Beds

Make a regular practice of removing flowers to prevent the formation of seed and to channel energy into the production of more blooms. If seed is required for sowing, it is best to leave a special plant for the purpose and remove flowers from the rest. In some cases, such as sweet peas, freshly opened blooms may be cut for home decoration. With the rest, remove the flowers as soon as they fade.

If lavender flowers are required for drying it is best to gather them before they are fully expanded; otherwise they may fall.

If spring-sown biennials and perennials have not been thinned or transferred to a nursery bed (see page 109) they should be attended to now. This will produce strong plants for setting out in the autumn in their flowering positions.

Bearded irises that have been in the same position for more than three or four years will benefit from being divided. Cut out and discard the bare middle portions of rhizome and replant healthy outer pieces, four or five inches (ten–thirteen cm) long, with a good fan of new leaves. Cut off the top half of the foliage, to lessen water loss and prevent rocking by wind. Leave the top of the rhizomes exposed and make the soil firm round the roots.

Border carnations may be propagated by layering (see page 196) as soon as their shoots have reached a suitable length. Water them well and see that they do not lack moisture if the weather should turn dry. They should be well rooted and ready to be severed and transplanted early in the autumn.

Outdoor chrysanthemums often make an excessive number of growths. For blooms of good size and quality it is advisable to do some thinning, started by removing weak and crowded shoots. Make sure that those which remain are given any necessary support in good time, as shown on page 200.

Bulbs, Corms and Tubers

Any remaining tulips and hyacinths used for bedding should be lifted for storing and replanting in the autumn.

Daffodils and bulbous irises may also be lifted if the ground is required for other purposes or if they are overcrowded; otherwise they can be left where they are to flower again next year.

Tall gladioli should be staked in good time, both to keep their stems straight and to prevent them from being toppled by strong winds.

Autumn crocuses, such as *Crocus sativus* and *C. speciosus*, may now be planted, as may colchicums and sternbergias. All of these will make a welcome show of colourful, sparkling blooms when the main summer display is over and the days are getting shorter.

Rock Garden and Pool

Trailers that are growing with too much vigour should be trimmed back after flowering, not only to keep them tidy but to prevent them from overwhelming less aggressive plants.

If the weather turns hot and dry it may be necessary to water plants growing in exposed positions to prevent them from flagging.

Many favourite alpines that tend to be short-lived, such as aquilegias and primulas, may be increased by seed sown in pots or pans as soon as it is ripe. It should germinate well in a cold frame or a suitable place in the open, shaded from the direct rays of the sun.

Keep pools filled by replacing water lost by evaporation. It is very important that the soil in which moisture-loving pool-side plants are growing should be kept damp. The easiest way is to fill the pool through a hose till it overflows. This has the added advantage that it enables debris to be floated from the surface.

Lawns

Continue with regular mowing. Water if necessary (and if there are no restrictions) and treat any remaining weeds with a suitable weedkiller. Give a dressing of lawn fertilizer, if this has not already been done, to boost growth.

Though fungal diseases are more likely to attack grass in the autumn, fusarium may appear now if the weather turns humid. At the first sign of white mould on the surface treat affected patches with an appropriate fungicide.

Fruit

Apples and pears in restricted forms such as cordons and espaliers need summer pruning. The date will depend on the season and local conditions, but usually pears are ready by the middle of the month and apples a week or two later.

Shorten laterals back to about five fully developed leaves, but leave leaders unpruned. Deal with the most developed laterals first and leave the less developed ones till later. The whole operation will take two or three weeks.

It is best to prune black currants as soon as possible after the last fruits

have been picked.

Since next year's crop will be borne on the new shoots produced during the course of the current season, the aim is to remove up to a third of the old wood each year and so produce a regular supply of young wood. The method of pruning is shown on page 217.

Strawberry plants which have finished fruiting should be cleaned and tidied. Remove the straw and any weeds, together with all dead leaves and runners not needed for producing new plants. Layered runners (see page 197) may be transplanted as soon as they are well rooted.

Continue to tie in new shoots of wall-trained peaches and nectarines and give a fine spraying with water on dry days. Early kinds of these and other stone fruits should be netted in good time against birds, which start pecking fruit some time before it is ripe enough to eat.

Vegetables

Among the spring-sown vegetables that should be transplanted into their final quarters as soon as possible – if this has not already been done – are sprouting broccoli and calabrese, brussels sprouts, cabbages (autumn and winter), cauliflowers, kale and leeks.

Further sowings may be made in the open ground of french beans, beetroot and leaf beets, carrots, chicory (sugar loaf), chinese cabbage, endive, autumn lettuces, salad onions, parsley, peas (early dwarf kinds), radishes (summer and winter kinds), winter spinach and turnips (intended for storage).

In northern districts spring cabbages are best sown towards the end of this month. In the south they may be sown in August.

Outdoor tomatoes grown on a single stem must be tied to the stake as growth progresses. Remove all

side-shoots as soon as they appear at the junction of leaf-stalks and stem.

In warm, humid weather potatoes are in danger of being attacked by blight, so it is a wise precaution to spray the plants against the disease in good time. The same spray may be used on outdoor tomatoes, which are also subject to attack.

Celery and celeriac have high moisture requirements and should never be allowed to suffer from lack of water during dry spells.

Greenhouse and Frame

During hot weather it is important to ventilate freely and shade if necessary to prevent overheating. Damp down regularly to keep the air moist. Dryness is not only bad for growth but encourages such pests as red spider mite.

Pelargoniums, fuchsias and other plants raised from spring cuttings should be potted on as necessary. Cinerarias and primulas sown last month must be pricked off (see page 198) before they become overcrowded.

Secure tomatoes to their supports and remove side-shoots.

Brompton stocks may be sown in a cold frame to provide plants which will flower next year.

House Plants

Continue to water and feed plants as necessary. To counteract the dry atmosphere of most rooms it is helpful to place bowls or pans of water near the plants. With those which are best when surrounded with humid air, such as african violets, it is a good plan to stand them in pans or deep saucers filled with pebbles or coarse gravel kept wet.

On warm days many house plants will benefit from being stood outside. Hardier ones may be put out for several weeks, shaded from the hot sun and plunged to the rim of the pot in moist peat, shingle or soil.

August

And August came the fainting year to mend
With fruit and grain.

William Morris (1834–1896)

For many people August is the holiday month, when for a week or two they can get away from the usual routine and the familiar surroundings. It is also a splendid opportunity to gather plenty of new ideas for garden improvement by visiting some of the large number of gardens open to the public at this time of year in and near most holiday resorts, at home or abroad.

Many of the plants which have become important features of our gardens through late summer and into the autumn, extending the range of colour and the flowering season, have been developed from discoveries made by observant gardeners during their travels. Several of these valuable late-flowering plants, such as that pictured here, originated from species native to warmer parts of the world. Some are short-lived and doubtfully hardy in all but the most favoured localities, but many of them are easily propagated from cuttings taken now (see pages 192–5) and planted out next year to fill gaps left by the casualties of winter.

Though the weather experienced during July – whether wet or dry, thundery or calm – often persists into August, the hours of daylight are becoming noticeably shorter. As a result there tends to be a considerable drop in temperature during the longer nights as the month advances. Heavy dews can occur, followed in the mornings by misty, damp conditions, which unfortunately for gardeners may encourage plant diseases.

Winds may turn changeable later in the month. At times when they blow from the north or north-east they are likely to bring clear skies, leading to heat loss, so that temperatures – particularly in low-lying places in the north – drop during the night to near freezing point. There is then a distinct feeling of autumn in the air.

Left Penstemons are among the most attractive plants commonly grown as half-hardy subjects for borders and beds. In favoured conditions they may survive quite severe winters.

What to see and enjoy in August

Left *Cotinus coggygria*, a native of central and southern Europe to the Caucasus, is known as the smoke tree from the appearance of its loose, much branched plumes, covered in silky hairs, on which the tiny flowers are borne. At first pink or brownish, these turn hazy grey, resembling clouds of smoke. There are many forms, with smooth, rounded leaves which vary from green to deep purplish bronze; in the autumn the foliage turns brilliant shades of red and orange. Two forms have been given an Award of Garden Merit by the Royal Horticultural Society.

Right *Hibiscus syriacus* 'Hamabo' is one of the most beautiful cultivars of this hardy member of the mallow family, introduced long ago from eastern Asia and still among the most valuable late flowering garden shrubs, opening its large trumpet-shaped blooms in succession over several weeks, till well into the autumn. This outstanding cultivar has received the Award of Garden Merit from the Royal Horticultural Society.

Trees and Shrubs

Though herbaceous plants are still predominant in a great number of gardens this month, flowering shrubs have an important part to play in giving balance to the picture. Some of the most valuable are those which produce clouds of blooms, small individually and quiet in colour, which form a restful contrast to the vivid flowers of most of the bedding and border plants.

One of the loveliest is *Cotinus coggygria*, pictured above, known as the smoke tree from the appearance of its haze of tiny flowers suffused with pink. Of the named cultivars, 'Atropurpureus' has darker flowers, 'Royal Purple' has deep wine-red foliage, and 'Flame' is notable for its autumn leaves, which turn brilliant orange before falling.

Among other species with pleasing foliage setting off attractive masses of small, quiet-toned flowers is *Aralia elata* (japanese angelica tree), a large, suckering shrub with bold, divided leaves and billowing white blossoms. Another is *Clethra alnifolia* (sweet pepper bush), of which the cultivar 'Paniculata' is a favourite form, bearing upright plumes of creamy white, sweetly scented bell-shaped blooms above fresh green saw-toothed foliage. Yet another is *Itea ilicifolia*, a bushy evergreen for a sheltered site, with large, holly-like leaves and greenish white fragrant flowers in long, pendulous catkin-like racemes.

A selection of other shrubs in bloom, in addition to many of those listed in July (pages 112–4), is given on the next page.

Left *Fuchsia* 'Corallina', a hardy and vigorous cultivar, highly commended in trials at Wisley, blooms profusely over a long period. Though its top growth, like that of many other hardy fuchsias, may be killed during severe winters, strong new stems will usually shoot up from the base in spring, to form a robust and attractive shrub by flowering time.

SELECTED TREES AND SHRUBS

Caryopteris x *clandonensis*, greyish aromatic leaves and violet-blue flowers; *Ceanothus* 'Gloire de Versailles', masses of powder-blue flowers, and other deciduous cultivars such as the darker 'Topaz'; *Ceratostigma willmottianum*, rich blue flowers till autumn; *Clerodendrum trichotomum*, fragrant white starry flowers, to be followed later by china-blue berries, in deep crimson calyces; *Dorycnium hirsutum*, silvery hairy, low-growing sub-shrub bearing terminal heads of white pea-flowers flushed pink; *Fuchsia magellanica* and the many hardy cultivars derived from it and other species in a great variety of colour combinations; *Hebe* 'Autumn Glory', intense violet-blue flowers borne continuously till October; *Hibiscus syriacus* cultivars, blue, purple, red, pink and white blooms with dark central markings (pictured on left); *Perovskia atriplicifolia*, spires of lavender-blue flowers; *Tamarix gallica* and *T. pentandra*, feathery foliage and pink flowers.

Roses

A vast array of the popular hybrid tea (or large-flowered) and floribunda (or cluster-flowered) roses will still be in bloom, particularly if regular dead-heading has been carried out. A fine example of the latter is pictured on the left.

Many climbers and ramblers are now at their best. Among the loveliest of all is the old garden favourite 'Mermaid', bearing large, single, primrose-yellow blooms, with a central boss of amber stamens, in succession until late autumn.

Left Rose 'City of Leeds', one of the finest salmon-pink floribunda roses ever introduced, was awarded a Gold Medal by the Royal National Rose Society in 1965.

Below *Portulaca* Double Daydream Mixture is a brilliantly coloured modern selection of one of the favourite half-hardy annuals, popular for a bedding display throughout the summer.

Climbers and Wall-plants

Among the most magnificent woody climbers to flower during August and September is the trumpet vine, *Campsis radicans*, which has clinging aerial roots and needs a sunny position, against a wall or scrambling over sheds or old tree-trunks. Its handsome leaves are divided into many sharply-toothed leaflets and its bright orange and scarlet trumpet-shaped blooms are borne in terminal clusters. *C. grandiflora* (*chinensis*) carries larger flowers somewhat deeper in colour. The cultivar 'Madame Galen', resulting from a cross between the two species, has blooms of a rich salmon-red.

A brilliant evergreen suitable for a shaded wall in favoured places is *Berberidopsis corallina*, with leathery, spine-toothed leaves and hanging clusters of ruby flowers.

Herbaceous climbers which flower now on new growth sent up from the base during the current season include *Tropaeolum speciosum*, specially good in cool northern districts, with bright scarlet long-stalked blooms, and *Lathyrus latifolius* (everlasting pea), an old cottage-garden favourite with winged stems bearing leaves made up of elliptic leaflets and rosy purple pea-flowers. There are also red, violet and white forms.

Borders and Beds

Some of the brightest colours in the garden during August are provided by the half-hardy annuals, planted out in May or early June and now at the height of their flowering season. A list of some of the most popular is given on page 119. Among the most eye-catching are *Portulaca*, pictured on the left, and *Zinnia* and *Celosia*, pictured overleaf on page 132.

Most of the annuals to flower so far have been of moderate size, suitable for bedding or for the front of the border, but now those two giants among cottage-garden favourites, hollyhocks and sunflowers, will be coming into bloom.

Prominent among perennials are the earliest outdoor chrysanthemums; a fine example is pictured overleaf. A selection of the many other perennials now in flower is given in the following columns.

SELECTED HERBACEOUS PLANTS

Acanthus spinosus, stately arching leaves, deeply divided and spiny, with long spikes of soft mauve hooded flowers; *Agapanthus campanulatus* forms and hybrids, flowers in many shades of blue (see picture), also white; *Anaphalis triplinervis* (pearl everlasting), tufted grey foliage and wide heads of crisp white blooms with yellow centres; *Asclepias speciosa*, clusters of starry flowers of a soft lilac-pink; *Aster* x *frikartii* 'Wonder of Stafa', large single flowers of lavender blue with golden stamens, and the dwarfer and somewhat paler *A. thomsonii* 'Nanus'; *Cimicifuga cordifolia* (*americana*), tall stems with plumes of creamy white flowers.

Above *Agapanthus* 'Dorothy Palmer' is one of many fine cultivars, derived largely from selected forms of *A. campanulatus*, known collectively as Headbourne Hybrids. These are now more widely grown than the species, being generally hardier and bearing flowers of excellent form in many shades of blue; there are also some whites.

The orange flowers at the back are of *Curtonus paniculatus*.

Left *Zinnia* Yoga Mixed is one of the many attractive modern selections of the popular dahlia-flowered zinnias, grown extensively as half-hardy annuals for bedding purposes, giving a succession of colourful blooms through the summer.

Celosia Pampus Plume Mixed, on the left, is a brilliant selection of another popular half-hardy annual for summer bedding, with feathery heads of bright flowers.

Below 'Yvonne Arnaud' is a chrysanthemum popular for outdoor cultivation, valued for the earliness of its richly coloured flowers.

Clematis heracleifolia, non-climbing species, sweetly scented blue, hyacinth-like blooms, and the taller hybrid *C.* x *durandii*, with larger and more intensely coloured flowers; *Coreopsis verticillata*, bushy growth with fresh green finely cut foliage, covered with a succession of bright yellow daisies; *Gentiana asclepiadea* (willow gentian), pictured opposite, with graceful, slender stems, willow-like foliage and numerous rich blue flowers in the axils of the upper leaves; *Helenium autumnale* cultivars, branching stems bearing knob-centred flower-heads ranging from bright yellow to deep reddish brown; *Helianthus decapetalus* and *H.* x *multiflorus*, perennial sunflowers with many fine cultivars.

Heliopsis scabra 'Golden Plume', fully double, perfectly formed flowers of rich golden yellow, excellent for cutting; *Hosta* 'Royal Standard', late-flowering hybrid with ivory, sweetly scented blooms; *Ligularia dentata* (*L.* or *Senecio clivorum*), branched heads of bright orange daisies, its cultivar 'Desdemona' with brownish leaves, purple-red beneath, the superb hybrid 'Gregynog Gold', with great conical spikes of vivid orange-yellow flowers, and *L. przewalskii*, with dark, deeply lobed leaves and slender spires of clear, brilliant yellow blooms; *Liriope muscari* (*platyphylla*), tufted grassy foliage and wiry stems bearing dense columns of small bright lilac-blue bells resembling grape hyacinth blooms and forming columns of colour.

Platycodon grandiflorus (balloon flower), blue-green leaves on stems carrying large round buds which open into wide bell-flowers of blue, white or soft pink; *Polygonum amplexicaule*, long upright spikes of numerous small ruby-red blooms rising from a large leafy clump; *Rudbeckia fulgida* (coneflower) cultivars 'Goldsturm', orange blooms with dark centres, and 'Autumn Sun', clear lemon yellow; *Sedum maximum* 'Atropurpureum', succulent deep maroon leaves and flat flower-heads of small red stars, and *S.* 'Vera Jameson', purplish leaves and pinkish heads; *Zauschneria californica*, for warm places, a blaze of trumpet-shaped scarlet flowers in slender sprays held well above the greyish foliage.

Above *Gentiana asclepiadea*, the willow gentian, is a magnificent border plant, thriving in shade and in cool, moist soil. It is vigorous in growth and in flowering, with long, arching stems bearing many pairs of clear blue flowers in the axils of the upper, willow-like leaves.

Above Apple 'St Edmund's Pippin', shown here grown in the form of an espalier, is highly decorative in flower and fruit; it is also one of the finest flavoured dessert apples, with juicy, pale yellow flesh. This fine old garden cultivar was awarded a First Class Certificate by the Royal Horticultural Society in 1875 and is still considered by many to be the best early russet apple.

Bulbs, Corms and Tubers

Gladioli are now at the height of their flowering season. Most commonly grown are the large-flowered hybrids, with tall spikes of flamboyant blooms in a vast range of colours, to which new introductions are constantly being added. Equally free-flowering but more restrained in growth are the dainty primulinus and butterfly hybrids.

Many subjects dealt with last month (page 120) will still be producing blooms, including several more lilies. Others now coming into flower include *Crocosmia* × *crocosmiiflora*, the garden montbretias, in various tawny and red shades, *C. masonorum*, with brilliant vermilion flowers, and the similar but taller *Curtonus paniculatus*, pictured in the background on page 131.

Crinum × *powellii*, a variable hybrid with deliciously scented trumpet flowers of pink or white, is in its best forms among the loveliest of all bulbous plants to bloom in August, particularly suitable and free-flowering against a warm wall.

Dahlias, in a vast range of sizes, shapes and colours, are now in full bloom.

Rock Garden and Pool

Though the main display may now be over, a well-planned rock garden, with plants carefully chosen to provide a succession of flower, will still have much to offer in interest and pleasure. According to season, district and aspect, many of the subjects mentioned in the notes for July (see pages 120–1) may still be in bloom.

To continue the display, a selection of later flowering subjects is given below. Since many of them are variable, it is best to visit a specialist nursery or two where they can be seen in flower. Most are obtainable as container-grown plants, so that they can be taken home and transplanted with little or no root disturbance to fill gaps in the display that are now apparent.

SELECTED ROCK GARDEN PLANTS

Aster alpinus, dwarf species with greyish leaves and purple-blue, golden centred flowers, also mauve, pink and white forms; *Crepis aurea*, coppery orange dandelion-like blooms, and *C. incana*, similar flowers of pale pink; *Dianthus knappii*, clusters of glowing yellow blooms, short lived but easy from seed; *Gentiana septemfida*, clustered trumpet-shaped flowers, deep blue in the best forms, with paler spots inside, and *G. farreri* hybrids, variable but in good forms producing trumpets of intense azure, spotted greenish blue and shading to white in the throat; *Polygonum affine*, forming mats from which rise stems bearing dense spikes of rosy flowers, two good cultivars being 'Donald Lowndes' and 'Darjeeling Red', with more deeply coloured blooms; *Sedum cauticolum*, large heads of crimson-cerise flowers above bluish grey leaves on drooping stems, *S. kamtschaticum*, mat-forming with bright yellow flowers, and its more commonly grown cultivar 'Variegatum' with white-margined leaves; *Silene schafta*, a most useful and attractive late-flowering catchfly, making neat tufts of pointed oval foliage from which appear sprays of rosy magenta flowers in succession until well into the autumn.

In the pool many water-lilies will still be opening their beautiful blooms of many different colours (see page 122). In moist soil around the pool bog irises will have come to the end of their flowering season, while the monkey musks continue to open new flowers for a few more weeks.

In shallow water at the pool's edge an attractive plant now coming into bloom is the vigorous but compact *Pontederia cordata* (pickerel weed), with heart-shaped glossy leaves, often marked with maroon, and dense spikes of striking purplish blue flowers, each with a yellow eye on the upper petal, set off by a surrounding of silky white hairs. Another handsome marginal plant is *Cyperus longus* (sweet galingale), with dark, ribbed leaves and reddish brown plumes; *C. vegetus* is more compact and less invasive.

Fruit

Maincrop strawberries will have yielded their final pickings by the latter part of last month, but the so-called perpetual-fruiting, or re-montant, kinds are now coming into full bearing and with good cultivation and favourable weather should continue to crop till late autumn. There may be a last picking of summer-fruiting raspberries and some late currants and gooseberries, and blackberries, loganberries and boysenberries should be at their most fruitful.

Other fruits now ready for picking include early cultivars of apples and pears, the last sweet cherries, followed by the acid kinds, mid-season peaches and nectarines, the first outdoor figs, many plums, dessert and culinary, gages and perhaps a few early damsons, in favourable seasons and sunny places.

Below This circular herb garden is both decorative and practical. Set in paving and with a brick surround, it is easy to reach for gathering in any weather without getting muddy feet.

Among the herbs used in this bed are chives, curry plant (*Helichrysum angustifolium*), parsley, spearmint, sage and thyme.

Above *Coleus* Hercules is a selection of one of the most popular greenhouse plants, grown for the brilliance of the multi-coloured leaves. Though perennial, it is mainly grown as an annual, easily raised from seed; a small packet yields a wide range of different colours and patterns. Specially attractive forms may be propagated by cuttings.

Vegetables

Freshly picked herbs, with their aroma developed through the warm days of summer, add that little extra flavour to food that dried ones never quite seem to match. Garden – and kitchen – favourites among perennial kinds include bergamot, chives, fennel, pot marjoram, mint, rosemary, sage, winter savory and thyme. Those grown as annuals include basil, chervil, sweet or knotted marjoram and summer savory.

Culinary herbs are often grown in odd corners of the vegetable garden, or in the case of some low-growing kinds in the front of the border. Some, however, are apt to become invasive. An attractive and at the same time practical way to grow them is in a bed of their own in a paved area, where they are easily gathered and where they make a decorative feature, as in the example pictured on the previous page.

The vegetable garden should still be in full production. With good planning and successional sowings, all the crops listed in the notes for July (see page 123) will continue to yield fresh produce. Summer cauliflowers sown in the spring will be ready for cutting, as will calabrese.

Onions, both large-bulbed and pickling, will be ready for harvesting when the leaves start to turn colour and bend over. Their relatives shallots and garlic should also be ready for gathering. Before storing any of them make sure they are thoroughly dried.

Outdoor tomatoes, sweet peppers and aubergines should have fruit ready to pick during this month.

Greenhouse

Many plants grown for their coloured leaves, such as that pictured on the left, are at their most vivid now. Of those grown for their flowers, one of the loveliest for the cool greenhouse during the late summer and early autumn is *Campanula isophylla*. A native of Italy, it is hardy outdoors only in the most favoured places. Its fresh green, heart-shaped leaves, borne on slender, semi-prostrate stems, are almost hidden for several weeks by a profusion of wide open, broadly star-shaped flowers of an attractive lilac-blue, greyish in the centre. People without a greenhouse, or even a garden, can still enjoy this delightful plant in the home, for which purpose it is produced and sold in large quantities every summer. There are forms with white flowers and with variegated leaves.

For warmer conditions, either in the greenhouse or in the home, some of the most handsome plants coming into flower this month are several members of the pineapple family, known as bromeliads. Among the easiest and most attractive is *Aechmea fasciata*, with bold, grey-green leaves forming a vase, from the centre of which appears a conical head of blue flowers, turning rose, between showy shell-pink bracts. Others now in flower include *Vriesia splendens*, from the centre of whose dark green leaves, boldly marked with deep purple cross-bands, rises a sword-like flowering stem carrying a spike of flaming red bracts enclosing small yellow flowers.

Below *Begonia semperflorens* 'Frilly Red', commended after trials at Wisley, is a splendid addition to the many forms of this extremely attractive plant, grown not only for its value in the greenhouse and the home but for bedding out to provide a continuous display throughout the summer.

House Plants

Though there are plenty of suitable house plants that bloom now, many people make more use of cut flowers for home decoration at this time of year, preferring pot plants that produce their blooms when there are few outside and those available from florists are at their most expensive.

For people with gardens a very large number of the summer-flowering border plants included in the selections given on pages 116–18 and 131–3 will provide blooms that last well in water if cut when they are just opening. For those who buy them from shops or market stalls some of the best now available are asters, carnations, chrysanthemums, dahlias, gladioli, lilies and roses.

Many plants now in flower in the greenhouse, or as part of the summer-bedding display, are also suitable for rooms, balconies, window-boxes, urns and other containers. Among the favourites for these purposes are the many forms and hybrids of *Begonia semperflorens*, of which an attractive example is pictured below. The glossy leaves range in colour from bright green and reddish brown to deep purple. The flowers, which are produced freely over a long period, range from pure white through cream, with or without a cerise border, to rose pink, blood red and deep scarlet.

A compact, bushy pot plant in bloom from now to the autumn is *Exacum affine*, covered in fragrant blue flowers with gold stamens.

What to do in August

Trees and Shrubs

Several shrubs which have now finished flowering may benefit from pruning. As always, start by removing overcrowded, damaged, weak and unproductive old wood. After that the remaining shoots may be shortened. The process is pictured and explained on page 214, where there is also a list of shrubs included in this pruning group.

Most evergreen flowering shrubs need no regular pruning except perhaps for the removal of spent blooms from those not intended to produce fruits, but some which are becoming untidy or outgrowing their available space may require harder pruning, particularly those such as escallonias grown as informal hedges. Do not, however, cut more than necessary; the lighter the trimming, the more flowers there will be next season.

With formal hedges the slower growing evergreens such as yew and holly may require no further trimming if they have already been attended to (see page 124). Faster growing subjects such as privet and Lonicera nitida will still need clipping to keep them dense and tidy. It is best to complete the season's trimming by the end of this month, particularly in cold districts. Hedges trimmed too late may produce soft new growth which is liable to be damaged by the first severe autumn frosts.

A very large number of shrubs may be propagated by means of cuttings taken now from semi-ripe wood. The method of carrying out this operation is explained and pictured on page 192, together with a list of some of the more popular shrubs that may be propagated in this way.

Heathers of all kinds may be propagated from the short side shoots now available in abundance, which can easily be rooted in two parts of sand and one part of peat.

Many successful gardeners like to start the process of propagating shrubs such as rhododendrons and azaleas by means of layering as soon as the right material is available, while the soil is full of summer warmth and the pliable young shoots are in an ideal state to start the initiation of roots. Hydrangeas may also be propagated in this way, as may many other shrubs which have produced flexible young shoots that can be readily bent down to soil level.

The technique of layering, which is demonstrated in detail on page 196, has the advantage for many amateurs that it does not require the use of a propagating case, which is needed for the striking of leafy cuttings. The layered shoots should be left to grow till the end of next season, by which time they should have produced a good root system and be ready for severing from the parent plant and transferring to a new site. If by then they are not sufficiently well rooted, they may be left for another year before being severed and transplanted.

Climbers and Wall-plants

Continue to tie in new growths, particularly the slender stems of rapidly growing climbers such as clematis, which can easily snap off if not given support in good time.

Wall shrubs such as Ceanothus should continue to be trained in as necessary to prevent them from coming away from the wall, and shoots growing forward should be trimmed back (see page 124).

An important operation to be carried out early in the month is the pruning of Wisteria, which if not attended to can become an untidy mass of tangled growth. Shorten side shoots to four or five leaves, as shown on page 215. Plants that have filled the available space should have extension growths cut back too.

Roses

An important operation to be undertaken at this time of year is the pruning of rambler roses, including such old garden favourites as 'Dorothy Perkins', derived from Rosa wichuraiana, which flower in the summer on side-shoots of long canes produced from the base during the previous growing season. As soon as possible after flowering is over, cut the shoots that have bloomed down to the base. Train in new basal growths to replace them, as near the horizontal as possible, as shown on page 216. If there are two few new canes, one or two of the strongest old ones may be kept; cut back their side shoots to between four and six inches (ten–fifteen cm).

Some others, such as 'Albertine', produce few if any new shoots from the base; most of them arise from the old wood. In their case, cut out completely one or two old stems and train in any new basal shoots to replace them. The other old stems should be cut back to a point where a strong new shoot originates. Train the new shoots as near to the horizontal as possible.

Short laterals which have flowered make useful material for cuttings. They may be inserted in the open ground. Sharp sand will assist rooting, particularly if the soil is inclined to be heavy.

Continue to remove spent blooms of bush and standard roses as before to encourage the production of more flowers. Continue also to watch for signs of pests and diseases, and take action against them at once.

In dry weather give water as necessary, and if possible apply a good mulch to assist the retention of moisture in the soil. Not only is this necessary to the strength and vigour of the plants but it assists in keeping them healthy. Dryness at the roots is a factor in disorders and diseases such as mildew.

Borders and Beds

To keep up the vigour of sweet peas they should be watered as necessary during dry weather. Give a good mulch afterwards. Pick the flowers regularly to maintain the production of new ones. If the plants are grown as cordons they may be carefully released when they have reached the top of their supports, taken along horizontally, close to the ground, to another support a short distance away and trained up that instead.

Continue with the removal of faded flower heads from plants both in borders and beds and in containers. Some plants will now be finishing their flowering season; cut back the old, unsightly flowering stems and remove the unnecessary supports.

Outdoor chrysanthemums will now be forming their flower buds. To produce large, well-shaped blooms of good quality, it is necessary to restrict them to one to each stem. The process consists of removing all secondary buds and side-shoots, leaving only the central bud to flower. In order to avoid damaging the stem it is best to wait till the side-shoots are about three quarters of an inch (two cm) long before removing them. Do this by giving them a sharp pull sideways.

The disbudding of outdoor chrysanthemums should be completed by the end of the third week to make sure of flowering before it is too late in the autumn. Earwigs, which can do considerable damage, may be trapped in inverted flower-pots filled with hay and placed on canes. The pests crawl into them during the day and can be removed and destroyed.

In favourable soil conditions many hardy annuals may now be sown, to bloom earlier than spring-sown ones, including *Calendula*, candytuft, cornflower, *Echium*, *Eschscholtzia*, larkspur, *Lavatera*, *Nigella*, poppy and scabious.

Pelargoniums grown as bedding or container plants will root readily from cuttings taken this month. Choose plump, sturdy shoots about four inches (ten cm) long, trim them with a sharp blade just below a joint, insert them in a pot of sandy compost and place them in a cold frame, greenhouse or other sheltered spot, shaded from direct sun.

Bulbs, Corms and Tubers

This month is a good time to plant bulbs of that lovely old cottage-garden favourite *Lilium candidum*, known as the madonna lily. Choose a well drained site which gets a fair amount of sunshine, and plant so that the tops of the bulbs come just below the surface of the soil. *Lilium tigrinum* (now *lancifolium*) and its hybrids produce small bulbils in the axils of the leaves; these may be grown on by planting them, barely covered, in trays of sandy compost.

Daffodil bulbs that were lifted after flowering and placed in store may be replanted towards the end of the month. New bulbs of these and other spring-flowering subjects, for bedding or forcing in containers, should be ordered now for planting in the autumn.

Rock Garden and Pool

Many plants in the rock garden will be producing new shoots after earlier trimming, and these will provide excellent cuttings for propagation, as shown on pages 192–4.

Old flowering stems of rushes and other waterside plants should be cut down to prevent them from seeding.

Be sure to keep the pool filled, to make up for loss by evaporation.

Lawns

In cold northern districts grass seed should be sown by the end of the month, to make new lawns or to fill in bare patches in existing ones. For details see page 207.

Fruit

As soon as the last fruit has been picked, summer-fruiting raspberries and black currants should be pruned, as shown on page 217. Support autumn-fruiting raspberries as necessary and remove surplus canes.

Strawberry runners may be planted out when they are rooted.

Vegetables

Spring cabbages should be sown in the south during the first two weeks. Other crops that can now be sown in the open include chinese cabbages, endive, winter lettuces, japanese and salad onions, parsley, radishes (summer and winter), winter spinach and turnips.

A last sowing may be made in the open of beetroots and carrots, to be covered later with cloches.

Brussels sprouts and other tall brassica crops may need staking.

Single stemmed tomatoes are best stopped when four or five flower trusses have been formed.

Greenhouse and Frame

Cyclamen tubers rested during the summer may be started into growth again. Knock them from their pots, remove old soil and replant them in fresh potting compost. Water them well and place them on the bench or staging. New plants may be raised from seed sown now in pots or pans placed in a shaded cold frame or outside against a north wall and brought in later in the autumn.

Other coolhouse subjects that can be sown now include cinerarias, schizanthus and stocks.

House plants

While away on holiday, if there is nobody to attend to watering it is possible to tide pot plants over by standing them in large plastic bags with a little water in the bottom. Blow into the bags to inflate them and seal tightly with rubber bands.

September

Up from the meadows rich with corn,
Clear in the cool September morn.

John Greenleaf Whittier (1807–1892)

September is a month which gardeners regard with mixed feelings. In some ways it is the most rewarding month of the year, a time of harvest, with plenty of vegetables still to be gathered fresh and others safely in store, and with ripening fruit to be picked. On the other hand the summer display is coming to an end and the days are noticeably shorter; by the end of the month the hours of darkness will exceed those of daylight.

A well-planned garden will include those plants that extend the flowering season by coming into flower as the days grow shorter, such as chrysanthemums and Michaelmas daisies, available nowadays in a wide range of forms and colours. To add variety and interest ornamental berries are now making their appearance, many rivalling the flowers in their brilliance.

There is often a tendency for the weather of last month to persist into this. If August was dull and wet, the likelihood is that September will remain the same. However, with the reduction in both the duration and the intensity of light, daytime temperatures will drop considerably lower and conditions are likely to become clammy, with an increased risk of fungal disease. If on the other hand August ended with a dry and sunny spell, September will probably begin in the same way, and daytime temperatures may be high. With clear skies, however, there will be no clouds to act as a blanket and as a result temperatures may plunge during the night, bringing dew and morning mist, with perhaps a touch of frost, particularly in low-lying places.

The last part of the month often brings strong winds, giving a foretaste of autumn gales. It is wise not to wait for the winds to start but to go round in advance and make sure that all ties and stakes are secure.

Left *Polygonum vaccinifolium,* a mat-forming species from the Himalayas, is a favourite among alpines for its dense spikes of rose-pink flowers from late summer throughout the autumn.

What to see and enjoy in September

Trees and Shrubs

As summer turns to autumn, several trees and shrubs that gave pleasure earlier in the year with a display of flowers make a second contribution to the garden scene with a striking display of foliage or fruit. The most vivid autumnal tints among the leaves do not usually appear until the end of the month and continue through October, but quite early in the month the fruits of some species, such as the rowan tree pictured on the right, are at their brightest and best, before any of them start to fall or birds begin to take them. There may still be plenty of other food for the birds to eat this month.

Though much depends on season and location, many flowering trees and shrubs already mentioned (see pages 112–14 and 128–9) may still be in bloom. The popular garden hydrangeas belonging to the hortensia and lacecap groups (see page 112) will most likely have been giving an attractive display for many weeks already and may continue to do so right through to late autumn, when the heads become papery in texture. Many people then cut them, allow them to dry and make use of them for decoration in the home during the winter.

Other hydrangeas now come into bloom, joining the hortensias and lacecaps. These late-flowering hydrangeas include *Hydrangea involucrata*, a dwarf species with small fertile flowers of blue or rosy lilac surrounded by larger white or tinted ray florets, and *H. paniculata*, stronger growing, with large leaves and flowering shoots ending in broad, tapering panicles of creamy white blooms. *H. villosa*, one of the finest of all late-flowering shrubs, forms a medium tall, rounded bush with densely hairy stems, long pointed leaves – green on top and with greyish bristles below – and large, flattened heads of pale purple or lilac-blue flowers spangled with larger and paler florets. These are borne both terminally and in the angles of leaves and stems, so that the whole shrub is a mass of bloom, making one of the truly memorable sights of late summer and autumn.

Several other shrubs may be expected to come into flower as the month progresses. A selection of popular and readily available ones is given in the next column.

SELECTED TREES AND SHRUBS

Abelia x *grandiflora*, semi-evergreen and hardy, slightly fragrant pink and white flowers in abundance till late autumn; *Elsholtzia stauntonii*, mint-scented leaves and lilac-purple blooms in profusion; *Erica terminalis*, rose-pink flowers, turning russet, in terminal heads; *Eucryphia* x *nymansensis*, shiny evergreen leaves and white blooms with prominent yellow stamens; *Lespedeza thunbergii*, arching wand-like stems, weighed down by a profusion of purple pea-flowers; *Osmanthus heterophyllus*, dense, rounded bush with glossy green, holly-like leaves and clusters of small, sweetly scented white blooms; *Sophora japonica* (japanese pagoda tree), medium to tall, with elegant ash-like leaves and large terminal clusters of white, wisteria-like flowers on mature trees.

Above *Sorbus pohuashanensis*, perhaps the finest of all rowans from China, makes a splendid tree, laden in the autumn with conspicuous bunches of bright fruits, displayed against the imposing leaves made up of many sharply toothed leaflets. It is very hardy and easily grown, and an Award of Merit has been granted by the Royal Horticultural Society.

Left *Ceratostigma plumbaginoides*, a sub-shrubby perennial, is valuable for its continuous production of deep blue flowers in terminal clusters until very late in the season, when the foliage takes on reddish tints. It is excellent for the rock garden or dry wall; it also makes a useful ground-cover plant.

Climbers and Wall-plants

Many clematis hybrids of the groups which produce their blooms on the current season's growth(see page 115) continue to flower well into the autumn. They may now be joined by some of the hybrids belonging to groups that produce their main display of bloom in early summer on short growths from the old wood (see the selection on page 82). Several of these give a second crop of smaller flowers on new growth in the autumn. A species now in bloom is *Clematis flammula*, with sweetly scented white flowers.

The passion flower, *Passiflora caerulea*, displays its intricately constructed flowers on a warm wall; though not reliably hardy it is easily raised from cuttings or seed.

One of the loveliest climbers, commonly grown from seed as an annual, is the morning glory, *Ipomoea tricolor* (*rubro-caerulea*), with sky-blue flowers. There are reddish purple forms, and 'Flying Saucers', pictured here, has striped blooms.

Left *Ipomoea* Flying Saucers is a popular selection of the morning glory, a favourite half-hardy twining plant with wide trumpet-shaped flowers. It is ideal for growing up strings or wires fixed to a sunny wall, and is easily raised from seed sown under glass in spring and planted out when the danger of frost is past.

Above *Sedum spectabile*, a hardy perennial native to China, is invaluable for its late flowering. It makes a splendid plant for the front of a border with its compact growth and smooth, fleshy, greyish leaves. These are surmounted in early autumn by flat heads of small flowers of an unusual dusty pink. There are several forms, some of which have received an Award of Merit from the Royal Horticultural Society.

Roses

Most of the ramblers and climbers that have one flush of bloom during the season will now have finished flowering. The climbing sports of the popular repeat-flowering hybrid tea and floribunda roses should, however, still be producing blooms. The non-climbing originals from which they arose will also still be in flower. This successional flowering is most likely to have been achieved if care has been taken throughout the summer to remove blooms as soon as they begin to fade, before energy is diverted into forming seed instead of producing new flowers.

Borders and Beds

A large proportion of the herbaceous plants that started into bloom earlier in the summer should also be continuing to produce flowers if dead-heading has been regularly carried out. Many of them will be found in the selections on pages 116–18 and 131–3.

Many others will, however, now have finished flowering for the season. At the same time there are some species that do not start flowering till September. One is *Sedum spectabile*, pictured above, with fleshy leaves and heads of mauve-pink flowers. There are choice forms with more vivid colouring.

Michaelmas daisies come into their own this month, bringing brightness and colour to the autumn border, particularly to those places towards the back which might otherwise have little to attract the eye after many of the earlier plants have finished flowering. In addition to their value in the garden, Michaelmas daisies are also of the greatest value as cut flowers, either as part of a mixed arrangement or, as many flower arrangers prefer, in a vase by themselves.

The term Michaelmas daisy is strictly applied to the species *Aster novi-belgii* from the eastern United States, but it is also used more generally by nurserymen for several other species and in particular for the vast number of garden forms developed by selection and hybridization over a long period and by now of first importance to the border during the autumn.

The flowers range in colour from white and pale pink through rose and crimson to purple, violet and lavender. Established favourites include the following cultivars: 'Ada Ballard' (lavender-blue, double), 'Crimson Brocade' (intense ruby, double), 'Eventide' (deep blue, semi-double), 'Lady Frances' (deep pink), 'Marie Ballard' (powder blue), 'Royal Velvet' (deep violet) and 'Winston Churchill' (beetroot red). Dwarf cultivars, suitable for the front of the border, include 'Jenny' (violet, double), 'Rose Bonnet' (pink, double) and 'Starlight' (clear cyclamen red). Novelties are constantly being added. The best way to make a choice is to see them in bloom.

Another welcome source of bright colour is the selections and hybrids derived from *Phlox paniculata*, also from the eastern United States. Favourite cultivars include 'Border Gem' (rich violet-blue), 'Brigadier' (brilliant orange-red), 'Eventide' (mauve-blue, shaded lilac), 'Firefly' (peach pink, crimson eye) and the lovely 'Graf Zeppelin' (white, carmine eye).

Another invaluable late-flowering border plant is *Anemone* × *hybrida*, known as the japanese anemone, with saucer-shaped blooms held on branched stems above dark green, lobed leaves. There are several cultivars, with flowers ranging in colour from white through pale pink to deep rose.

A favourite perennial for a late display is *Limonium latifolium* (*Statice latifolia*), with a rosette of dark, leathery leaves and branching stems bearing clouds of small lavender-blue flowers of a papery texture, remaining decorative when dried.

Lythrum salicaria, purple loosestrife, gives a long display of purplish pink flowers in tall spires; those of the cultivar 'Firecandle' are bright rosy red.

Other perennials valuable for late flowering include *Physostegia* 'Vivid', with brilliant lilac-pink blooms, and *Veronica virginica*, with erect stems bearing spikes of pink, pale blue or white flowers.

Many bedding plants continue to contribute their bright splashes of colour throughout the month till the frosts. A pleasing example is pictured on the left.

Above Among the most brilliantly coloured bedding plants still in bloom are those known as busy lizzie, derived from *Impatiens walleriana*, of which seedsmen and nurserymen offer many selections, developed for their compact growth and freedom of flowering. Seen also are some white and red flowers of petunias.

Right *Aster* 'Professor A. Kippenberg' is one of the finest dwarf michaelmas daisies, with semi-double mauve-blue flowers, particularly suitable for the front of the border and small gardens.

Of the smaller species suitable for naturalising, for the front of the border or for suitable places in the rock garden, *Colchicum autumnale*, known as naked ladies or incorrectly as the autumn crocus, is usually first of its genus to flower. Others follow, including the splendid *C. speciosum*, with large goblet-shaped flowers. Several lovely forms and hybrids exist, some with pure white blooms and others, such as that pictured on the left, of brighter colour.

Among true autumn crocuses now coming into bloom is the popular and easily grown *Crocus speciosus*, with large globose flowers of purple, lavender and white, with orange stigmas. There are several named cultivars.

Left *Colchicum* 'Princess Astrid' is one of the earliest of many large-flowered hybrids and garden forms.

Below *Amaryllis belladonna*, native to southern Africa, is one of the most beautiful of autumn flowering bulbous plants, requiring a sheltered position.

Bulbs, Corms and Tubers

Some of the most rewarding of all the taller species in this category come into flower during the late summer and early autumn. Among the most beautiful is the old favourite long known to gardeners as *Acidanthera bicolor* but now classified as *Gladiolus callianthus*. Its large white blooms, blotched deep maroon in the centre and borne in graceful spikes above sword-like leaves, are intensely fragrant. As cut flowers they will fill a room with their sweet perfume.

A magnificent sight, particularly suited to a south-facing wall, is *Amaryllis belladonna*, with scented trumpet flowers of mauve-pink turning deeper after opening. There are several fine cultivars, one of which is pictured on the right.

The closely related *Nerine bowdenii*, also from South Africa and needing a sunny wall in all but the mildest places, carries elegant flowers with narrow, curving petals on a stout stem. Their colour varies from pink to white; the form known as 'Fenwick's Variety' has larger flowers of a deeper rose-pink, and there are several other selected forms.

Rock Garden and Pool

Though the flowering season has now come to an end for a large number of alpine and water plants, several of those mentioned on pages 105, 120–1 and 134 with a long period of bloom may still be continuing to produce flowers this month.

In addition there are some plants that wait until late in the season before they come into flower. One of these welcome species is the mat-forming *Polygonum vaccinifolium* (pictured at the beginning of this chapter on pages 140–1), with numerous spikes of small, bright red flowers. Another plant invaluable for its late flowering is the sub-shrubby *Ceratostigma plumbaginoides*, pictured on page 143, whose deep blue flowers continue to appear right through to November, set off against the attractive leaves, which take on reddish tints as the season advances.

Autumn-flowering bulbs (see opposite page) are now starting to make their contribution to the interest and appeal of rock gardens and grassy slopes and banks.

Fruit

By now the early soft fruits will have been gathered, but blackberries should be giving good pickings and repeat-fruiting strawberries will be in full bearing, together with autumn raspberries.

Late nectarines and peaches will be ripe for picking, also apricots, figs and grapes. Many plums and damsons will be ready, as will several of the mid-season apples and pears, both dessert and culinary.

Vegetables

With successional sowings and regular gathering, most of the crops listed on page 123 should still be yielding fresh produce. Early and second-early potatoes will all have been harvested, and the maincrop ones should be lifted, allowed to dry thoroughly and stored in a dark and frostproof place.

The first of the chinese cabbages sown during the summer will be ready for cutting. Their densely packed, juicy leaves with wide white midribs and prominent veins make them a most useful dual-purpose vegetable, both for autumn salads and for cooking like ordinary cabbages.

Greenhouse

Many of the summer-flowering greenhouse plants already dealt with on pages 107, 123 and 136 will still be giving a display. Fuchsias are among the most popular; both established favourites and novelties in a wide range of colour combinations may be seen at the many flower shows which feature them at this time of the year.

House Plants

Many begonias will be providing a succession of bloom, together with several of the other subjects mentioned on page 137. Late-blooming border plants such as Michaelmas daisies and chrysanthemums provide ideal cut flowers for the home.

Flower arrangers can create striking effects by using the coloured leaves of ornamental kale, either by themselves or mixed with flowers. Plants from a spring sowing are now at their most brilliant, as can be seen in the picture above.

Above Ornamental kale, raised from a spring sowing in the open ground, makes a colourful display in the autumn garden. The frilled leaves, in many different shades and combinations of colour, may be used in floral arrangements in the home to create unusual and striking effects.

What to do in September

Trees and Shrubs

A large number of evergreen shrubs may be propagated this month from stem cuttings taken from growth made during the current season. These may be either cut just below a joint or taken with a heel of older wood, as shown on page 193. Although at this time of year there is unlikely to be much, if any, new growth above ground, below the surface roots should soon start to form. By next spring, when new shoot growth begins, there should be a well enough developed root system to ensure that the new plant is given a good start to its first full season of growth.

It is generally agreed that the latter part of this month, or the early part of next, is the best time to transplant evergreens. The reason is that there is still enough warmth in the soil to encourage root action but at the same time the shorter daylight hours and cooler weather limit the amount of transpiration and so reduce the danger of excessive loss of water through the leaves. After planting, and staking if necessary (see pages 199–200), give a thorough watering and spread a thick mulch of organic material over the surface of the ground round the plant to conserve moisture. In exposed places it is wise to erect a wind-break in order to cut down the force of drying winds, and so limit water loss, which can lead to severe leaf-scorch and defoliation.

There are anti-desiccant sprays which may be applied to the foliage of evergreens before transplanting them so as to reduce transpiration. It is also a good idea to spray the foliage with water during spells of dry weather.

If ordering trees and shrubs to be planted during late autumn or winter do so in good time. The rule is first come first served, and those whose orders are received late are likely to be disappointed.

Climbers and Wall-plants

Many container-grown plants are obtainable from nurseries and garden centres for planting out this month, while there is still some summer warmth in the ground to encourage new roots to penetrate the surrounding soil.

It is particularly important that plants grown against walls should not be allowed to become dry at the roots after planting. The same wall which provides shelter for plants that would be too tender for the open ground may also prevent rain from reaching the soil beside it. It is also capable during dry weather of drawing large quantities of moisture from the ground and evaporating it into the air.

Secure the plants to suitable supports without delay. On page 202 will be found examples of some of the methods of support that may be used for the purpose.

Roses

The pruning of ramblers and climbers which have passed out of flower should be completed early in the month, so that the new growths made during this season may be tied in to replace as much of the old wood as possible.

The increased light and air help to ripen the new growth and ensure a good display of flowers next year. For pruning details refer to the August notes (page 138) and to the practical section on page 216.

Cuttings of side shoots taken from the wood that has been pruned from ramblers and climbers may be used for propagating new plants, as explained on page 138.

Continue to remove faded blooms from bush and standard roses. When cutting flowers for home decoration, do so just as they start to open.

Spray against mildew if necessary, and against aphids if they are troublesome.

Borders and Beds

If a new border is to be made, the ground should be dug as soon as possible, to allow time for the soil to settle before planting time later in the autumn.

Perennials and biennials raised earlier in the season may now be planted out into their flowering positions, preferably during dull weather. Do not let them suffer from dryness if there is no rain.

On well-drained soil in favoured localities there is still time to sow several of the hardiest annuals (see list on page 139) to flower early next season.

Bulbs, Corms and Tubers

Among the large number of spring-flowering bulbs and corms that may be planted now are many species and hybrids of *Narcissus* (including the daffodils), *Crocus*, *Chionodoxa* (glory of the snow), *Eranthis* (winter aconite), *Erythronium* (dog's-tooth violet), *Muscari* (grape hyacinth) and *Scilla*. Details of how to plant are given on pages 198–9. The smaller kinds are excellent for naturalizing in grass, for the rock garden and for the front of the border. Large ones, including tulips and hyacinths, are much used for spring bedding and are usually planted later, when the summer bedding has been cleared away completely.

If you wish to transplant lilies (except *Lilium candidum*, see page 139) delay till the very end of the month, or if possible well into October, otherwise the bulbs are liable to die from desiccation.

Rock Garden and Pool

This month is an excellent time to construct rock gardens and pools (see pages 188–9) before severe weather sets in. Plants may be put in from pots with little disturbance to the roots and should soon become established in their new quarters.

Lawns

As growth slows down, mowing will not be needed as frequently as it was during the summer. Also the height of the cut should be increased by raising the blades of the mower to a quarter of an inch (six mm) above the summer level.

Towards the end of this month or early next month is the ideal time for spiking the lawn, after first giving it a thorough raking to remove the matted growth which tends to build up over the surface during the growing season. A top dressing may then be applied. For details of autumn lawn treatment see page 208.

September is also the ideal month to sow grass seeds to form a new lawn or renovate bare patches in an existing one. Autumn sowing usually results in sturdier young plants, with a well established root system which enables them to withstand summer drought better than those sown in the spring. Full instructions for raising lawns from seed will be found on page 207.

Fruit

The planting of strawberries should be completed as soon as possible, while there is still warmth in the soil to assist rooting. Those planted early this month may be allowed to bear fruit next year, but those planted after the middle of the month should have their blossoms removed when they appear in the spring so that they can concentrate on forming strong plants to fruit the following year.

Complete the pruning of currants and summer-fruiting raspberries, and make sure that autumn-fruiting raspberries are securely tied to their supports. As soon as the last blackberries and loganberries have been picked the old canes which have borne the fruit should be cut off at ground level and the new canes which have grown this season trained in to take their place.

Vegetables

Sowings of lettuces may still be made in the open to overwinter as seedlings, for use next spring. Winter radish and turnips to provide green tops can also be sown.

Cover late-sown carrots, endive, lettuce and radish with cloches in the latter half of the month.

Gather all remaining outdoor tomatoes and finish ripening them indoors. If the plants are healthy put them on the compost heap; if not, burn them. The same applies to potato plants after the crop has been lifted.

Continue to earth-up trench celery. Also earth-up winter brassicas to give them support.

Spring cabbages may be planted out from the middle of the month.

Greenhouse and Frame

By the middle of the month tender flowering plants such as pelargoniums and heliotropes which have been grown outside for summer display should be brought under glass. Those in containers may be moved intact, those bedded out may be carefully lifted and planted in pots of good soil or compost.

Violets may be transferred to frames to produce a welcome succession of flowers during the winter, protected from beating rain and splashes of mud which often disfigure those outside.

Antirrhinums may be sown about the middle of the month and overwintered under unheated glass for planting out in the spring. Sweet peas too may be sown in pots or boxes in a cold frame to be planted out for an early display.

Towards the end of the month pot-grown chrysanthemums with their flower-buds well advanced should be placed in a cool, well ventilated house. Those growing in the open ground may be lifted, potted up and treated similarly.

House plants

Any repotting that needs to be done should be attended to during the first half of the month, before growth slows down as the autumn progresses. If the repotting cannot be done at this time it is best to wait till the spring, when vigorous growth starts again.

As the days become shorter and the sun sinks lower in the sky, the amount of light coming through the windows is considerably reduced. Plants that require plenty of light should benefit from being moved if necessary to a south-facing window.

Be careful, however, not to place tender plants too close to the glass, especially during chilly nights. Also avoid standing them in places where there is a likelihood of cold draughts.

Most house plants will now need less frequent watering and feeding than they did during the height of the summer. This particularly applies to cacti and succulents, which are liable to develop rot if their conditions are too wet.

On the other hand, if room heating has to be increased as the weather turns colder there is the danger that the air may become very dry, with the result that some plants may suffer. Arid conditions also encourage attacks by red spider mites, which infest the undersides of the leaves and suck sap from them, causing them to turn yellow and wither.

There are various methods of restoring moisture to the air in heated rooms. Humidifiers can be bought, either free-standing or to hang on radiators. A simple and cheap method is to fill bowls or pans with water and place them around the house. An excellent way of providing plants with a humid micro-climate round their leaves is to stand the pots on a layer of gravel in a tray filled with water to just below the surface of the gravel.

October

Bright October was come,
  The misty-bright October.

Arthur Hugh Clough (1819–1861)

Although there is often a spell of warm weather, known as St Luke's summer, in mid-October, there can be no escaping the fact that autumn has arrived. The days are already shorter than the nights and becoming shorter still, the sun is lower in the sky and declining in strength, and the main floral display is over.

For a short time, however, gardens containing well-chosen trees and shrubs provide perhaps the most spectacular display of the year as the foliage develops its vivid autumn colours in a wide range and combination of reds, yellows and golds.

The spectacle, however brilliant, does not usually last very long. Before the month is over there are likely to be gale-force winds which whip off the leaves and scatter them about the garden. One of the most important October tasks is to gather them up and put them to use by stacking them or adding them to the compost heap.

If left ungathered, they may clog drains, smother small plants – especially choice alpines – and cause them to rot, encourage worms on lawns and become a real danger on paths and steps when autumn rains turn them wet and slippery.

The latter part of October often brings dense cloud and long periods of heavy rain, which may saturate the ground and lead to flooding. If the sky clears there is the likelihood of a sharp frost, making the soil hard with ice. It is therefore best to seize every chance of digging vacant ground as early as possible when the weather is fine and the soil is in a favourable condition, neither sticky nor hard. The reason is not only that the task will be easier and more agreeable but that soil dug early in the autumn receives the benefit of maximum exposure to wintry conditions.

Left *Nyssa sylvatica*, a North American tree needing lime-free soil and noted for its brilliant autumn colour, has gained the Royal Horticultural Society's Award of Garden Merit.

What to see and enjoy in October

Trees and Shrubs

There is a vast range of trees and shrubs which round off the growing season with a dazzling display of autumn foliage. The following are some of the most attractive and popular. To make sure of choosing the best coloured forms, see what is available while still in leaf before buying.

SELECTED TREES AND SHRUBS

For autumn foliage

Acer palmatum cultivars (see pictures opposite), shades of yellow, orange and red, *A. platanoides*, rich gold, *A. rubrum* 'Schlesingeri', orange yellow and scarlet, and several other maples; *Aesculus flava*, horse-chestnut leaves turning bright orange; *Amelanchier lamarckii*, glowing orange-red; *Berberis thunbergii*, *B. wilsoniae* and cultivars, deciduous barberries of exceptional brilliance; *Betula pendula* and other birches, leaves turning clear yellow; *Carpinus betulus*, hornbeam, old gold; *Callicarpa bodinieri*, rose-purple foliage and violet coloured berries; *Ceratostigma willmottianum*, leaves becoming purplish red while still in flower; *Cercidiphyllum japonicum*, heart-shaped leaves turn smoky pink or creamy yellow, dependent on soil and season; *Cornus florida*, large leaves colouring brilliant scarlet; *Cotinus coggygria* 'Flame', turning bright orange-pink, and several deeper red cultivars; *Cotoneaster bullatus*, *C. divaricatus*, *C. horizontalis* and others, with dark leaves turning shades of bright red and orange and with prolific vivid red berries; *Crataegus pedicellata*, scarlet hawthorn, with saw-toothed heart shaped leaves changing through bright yellow to vermilion, and *C. prunifolia*, with dark, shiny foliage turning orange and scarlet before the fruits develop their rich crimson colouring; *Enkianthus campanulatus*, with small to medium elliptical leaves in fiery reds and golds; *Euonymus alatus* and *E. europaeus*, two spindleberries with foliage changing to an eye-catching rosy pink shading to scarlet.

Fothergilla monticola, large hazel-like leaves giving vivid sunset tints; *Fraxinus excelsior* 'Jaspidea' ('Aurea'), golden ash, leaves paling to clear yellow, and *F. oxycarpa* 'Raywood', foliage turning plum purple; *Hamamelis mollis*, chinese witch hazel, and cultivars, all with soft, hairy leaves assuming shades of yellow; *Koelreuteria paniculata*, golden-rain tree, with feathery leaves turning bright yellow and bronzy bladder-like fruits; *Liquidambar styraciflua*, sweet gum, brilliant maple-like leaves (pictured above); *Liriodendron tulipifera*, tulip tree, unusually shaped leaves turning butter yellow; *Malus coronaria* 'Charlottae', *M. tschonoskii* and many other ornamental crabs, with leaves of yellow, orange, scarlet and purple; *Nyssa sylvatica*, handsome foliage turning rich orange, scarlet and gold (pictured on previous page); *Parrotia persica*, deep green leaves colouring to brilliant red and gold.

Above *Liquidambar styraciflua*, the sweet gum from the eastern United States, is a handsome large tree for lime-free soil, noted for the brilliant autumn colouring of its maple-like foliage. Its outstanding qualities have gained it the Award of Garden Merit from the Royal Horticultural Society.

Populus alba, white poplar, *P.* 'Serotina Aurea', golden poplar, *P. tremula*, aspen, and other poplars, splendid trees where there is space, noted for the bright yellows and golds of their autumn foliage; *Prunus avium, P.* x *hillieri* 'Spire', *P. incisa, P. sargentii* and several other ornamental cherries, with leaves turning rich shades of crimson; *Quercus rubra* (*borealis maxima*), the red oak, with sharply pointed and lobed foliage which on lime-free soils turns scarlet and then russet brown before falling; *Rhamnus frangula*, alder buckthorn, a large shrub or small tree with small ovate leaves becoming clear yellow.

Below *Acer palmatum* 'Dissectum Atropurpureum', with finely cut, richly coloured leaves, has received the Royal Horticultural Society's Award of Garden Merit.

Right *Acer palmatum* 'Senkaki', with coral-red young shoots and autumn foliage turning canary yellow, has also been granted the Royal Horticultural Society's Award of Garden Merit.

Rhododendron luteum (*Azalea pontica*), the common yellow-flowered azalea, and other species, together with the vast number of deciduous azalea hybrids, many with brilliant leaf colours rivalling those of their flowers; *Rhus typhina*, stag's-horn sumach, brown felted stems and pinnate leaves turning yellow, orange and scarlet; *Ribes odoratum* (*aureum*), buffalo currant, coarsely toothed foliage turning gold; *Sorbus aucuparia, S. commixta, S.* 'Embley', *S.* 'Joseph Rock' and many other mountain ashes, with fern-like leaves, developing orange, copper, crimson and purple tones, and bunches of red, orange or yellow berries; *Spiraea prunifolia*, finely toothed, shiny oval leaves turning orange or red; *Stephanandra incisa*, deeply lobed foliage changing to golden yellow; *Viburnum lantana*, wayfaring tree, leaves often colouring rich crimson, and *V. opulus*, guelder rose, maple-like foliage in shades of red and orange.

Above *Schizostylis coccinea* 'Major', a fine form of the kaffir lily, has gained the Royal Horticultural Society's Award of Merit. It thrives in moist, fertile soil, forming clumps of narrow, sword-like leaves and producing spikes of starry red flowers till the frosts.

Though most conifers and related plants are evergreen a few are deciduous, and these now add their distinctive colours and textures to the autumn scene. The fan-shaped leaves of *Ginkgo biloba*, the maidenhair tree, change to gold before falling, and the clustered needles of the larches turn the colour of old parchment. The feathery foliage of *Metasequoia glyptostroboides*, the dawn redwood, changes from grass-green to coppery pink and old gold, and the frond-like foliage of its family relation *Taxodium distichum*, the swamp cypress, turns bronze.

The leaves of some evergreen conifers also start to take on winter hues, such as *Cryptomeria japonica* 'Elegans', whose tawny green foliage becomes coppery bronze.

Depending on site and season, several of the trees and shrubs mentioned as flowering during the past month or more (see pages 128–9 and 142) may still be in bloom. To them may now be added *Arbutus unedo*, the strawberry tree, an evergreen with dark shiny leaves and pendent ivory-coloured flowers appearing at the same time as the ripening orange-red, strawberry-like fruit. Other evergreens now coming into bloom may include *Elaeagnus* × *ebbingei* and *E. pungens*, with fragrant silvery flowers followed in favourable conditions by egg-shaped red or orange fruits, and *Fatsia japonica*, with globular heads of creamy white flowers held above the large, handsome, glossy leaves with seven or nine deeply palmate lobes.

Climbers and Wall-plants

Among climbers there is little or nothing to rival the blazing autumn foliage of *Parthenocissus quinquefolia*, the true virginia creeper, and such other species as *P. henryana* and *P. tricuspidata*, with sharply lobed and divided leaves which turn brilliant shades of orange, scarlet and ruby. Of the closely related ornamental vines, perhaps the most breath-taking is *Vitis coignetiae*, whose huge leaves, with rust-coloured down on the underside, become intense crimson before finally falling.

Celastrus orbiculatus, a vigorous twiner with spiny shoots, suitable for growing over walls, hedges and tall shrubs or trees, gives a two-fold display: the rounded leaves turn a clear yellow and the brownish seed-capsules split open to show glistening scarlet fruits against a golden lining. To produce fruits, male and female plants are needed, or there are highly desirable hermaphrodite forms in cultivation.

Many clematis hybrids which bloom on the current season's growth, such as the popular 'Jackmanii', may still be in flower, and several that bloomed in early summer on short growths from the old wood produce an autumn crop of smaller flowers. Two late-flowering species are *Clematis tangutica*, with yellow lantern-shaped blooms, and its near relative *C. orientalis*, bearing flowers with four waxy sepals like orange peel; both species have ferny foliage and follow their flowers with attractive seed-heads that end in softly silky plumes.

Roses

Many of the popular hybrid garden roses may still be producing blooms, especially if regular dead-heading has been carried out. Of the many shrub roses bearing attractive fruits, one of the most brilliant is *Rosa moyesii*, with large, flagon-shaped hips (heps) of bright crimson. Others include *R. rubiginosa* with oval fruits, *R. glauca* (*rubrifolia*), with mahogany-red fruits, *R. rugosa*, with large, shining, tomato-shaped fruits against the clear yellow of its autumn foliage, and hybrid musk roses such as 'Wilhelm', with bright orange-red fruits.

Borders and Beds

The summer bedding is now over, and although several herbaceous perennials such as the Michaelmas daisies continue to produce flowers till the hard frosts, only a few more now join them, such as the very late *Kniphofia rooperi* (pictured right). This is when suitable bulbs such as that pictured opposite can bring new life to the border; a selection is given on the next page.

Above *Kniphofia rooperi*, the last red hot poker to bloom, brightens the autumn border with its rounded heads of flowers, pinkish red opening to sulphur yellow. It has gained an Award of Merit from the Royal Horticultural Society.

Left *Cyclamen hederifolium* (*neapolitanum*), autumn flowering and with marbled leaves, has gained several awards, including a First Class Certificate and an Award of Garden Merit.

Above *Gentiana sino-ornata*, a favourite autumn-flowering rock garden plant, is native to China and demands lime-free soil. When established it produces its azure blue trumpets in such profusion as to hide the foliage. This delightful species, with several variants, has gained several awards, including a First Class Certificate and an Award of Garden Merit.

Bulbs, Corms and Tubers

Several more autumn-flowering species now join those included in the notes for September (see page 146). Among the most striking is *Schizostylis coccinea*, pictured on page 154, hardy in favoured situations and needing full sun and plenty of moisture.

Other species coming into bloom include *Cyclamen hederifolium* (usually sold as *C. neapolitanum*), pictured on the previous page. Several more autumn crocuses will be flowering, among them *Crocus sativus*, a fine form of which is pictured opposite, and *C. kotschyanus*, often listed as *C. zonatus*, with large rosy lilac flowers marked with orange spots at the base of the petals.

Colchicum byzantinum, mauve-flowered with crimson-tipped stigmas, and *C. cilicicum*, with darker petals and purple-tipped stigmas, join the earlier species in bloom.

Others now in flower include *Leucojum autumnale*, autumn snowflake, with pinkish white bells borne on slender stems.

Scilla autumnalis, a late-flowering bulbous plant found growing wild in short grass over much of western Europe, is not a spectacular garden plant, but its numerous small, starry flowers, somewhat variable in colour from pale blue through mauve to pinkish lilac, and borne on short stems usually before the leaves appear, have a quiet charm.

Another pleasing bulbous plant valuable for its late blooms is *Zephyranthes candida*, admirable for a warm sheltered spot, with pure white flowers and rush-like leaves.

Rock Garden

Gentiana sino-ornata, pictured on the left, is generally agreed to be the finest of all autumn-flowering gentians, with brilliant blue trumpets perfectly displayed against mid-green leaves. Given lime-free soil, it is also one of the easiest to grow.

Many of the smaller autumn-flowering bulbs (see previous column) are among the most valuable and attractive occupants of the rock garden at this time of year.

Fruit

Among fresh fruits that can be gathered this month are still the repeat-fruiting (otherwise known as perpetual or remontant) strawberries, which should continue to yield until the frosts. If bad weather threatens, the season can be extended by covering the plants with cloches. Other fruits to be picked include autumn-fruiting raspberries, blackberries and their hybrids, apples, pears, plums and damsons, melons, grapes, nuts and perhaps some late figs.

Vegetables

If sowings have been made in succession to keep up the supply, most of the crops listed on pages 123 and 147 may still be gathered. To them may be added the first brussels sprouts, trench celery and celeriac, parsnips and winter spinach.

Though tomatoes are tastiest when picked ripe from the growing plant, before the onset of frosts cut the plants down and put them under cover to ripen as much remaining fruit as possible. If that cannot be done, pick off the fruits, wrap them in paper and put them in a drawer or cupboard to ripen.

Greenhouse and Frame

In the alpine house or frame many bulbous and cormous plants are now in flower, some a little too tender to stand outdoors during the lengthening and increasingly chilly nights and others fully hardy but apt to suffer in the heavy rains which often occur at this time of year. These include several of the autumn-flowering crocuses already mentioned, such as that shown on the left.

Among favourite greenhouse plants now in bloom are the chrysanthemums, both the large flowered kinds in which the number of blooms is restricted by disbudding and the increasingly popular ones, such as that shown below, which are not disbudded and produce a massed display of flowers.

House Plants

In addition to the many flowering and foliage plants already mentioned in the previous month's notes (see page 147), several others should now be available from florists and an increasing number of other shops. Among them are the brilliant florists' azaleas and Cape heaths, also *Solanum capsicastrum*, popularly known as the winter cherry, with its cheerful red fruits.

Above *Crocus sativus*, the saffron crocus, produces handsome flowers with very large orange stigmas, from which saffron is obtained. Though it can be grown in a warm spot outdoors, it does well in the alpine house.

Right Charm chrysanthemum 'Yellowhammer' is one of the colourful range of these popular pot plants for the greenhouse or home, with masses of long-lasting flowers.

What to do in October

Trees and Shrubs

The planting of evergreens, including conifers, should be completed as early as possible in the month. At the same time sites should be prepared for deciduous trees and shrubs, so that the soil will have a few weeks to settle before the time comes for planting them late this month or during November. Dig the ground at least two spits deep and in all but the richest soils incorporate plenty of well-rotted manure or garden compost into the lower spit.

It is wise to examine all stakes and ties giving support to tall subjects and renew them if they show signs of being loose or defective. At this time of year the weather can be very uncertain, periods of calm suddenly giving way to violent storms which can do great damage if anything has been left insecure. It is better to spend some time now making things safe before the storm rather than being sorry afterwards.

This is the ideal time of year to propagate a large number of shrubs from hardwood cuttings. Details, including the best type of wood to choose for the purpose, are given on page 192, together with a selection of some of the garden favourites that may be increased in this way. In the majority of cases the new plants propagated by this means should be suitable for transferring to their permanent positions by the end of next year's growing season.

Fallen leaves should never be wasted; they represent a valuable source of organic material both to incorporate in the soil to improve its texture and water-holding capacity and to use as a surface mulch. They may be made into a stack to form leaf-mould, but in a small garden it is usually neater, quicker and less space-demanding to put them on the compost heap (see page 183), mixed with other waste vegetable matter from garden and kitchen.

Climbers and Wall-plants

Though plants grown against walls and fences are not usually as liable to damage by autumn gales as those in the open, it is just as important that they should be made as secure as possible. Their sheltered position encourages tall, rapid growth and they tend to grow outwards from the wall, so that they are easily beaten down by the heavy rains common at this time of year. Later they may be made top-heavy by ice or snow and torn from the wall. To prevent this a few minutes devoted to examining supports and ties and renewing them if necessary will be time well spent. Some examples of suitable methods of support are given on page 202.

If new climbers and wall shrubs are to be put in, prepare the ground well in advance so that it will have settled down when the time comes to plant them. If they are to be grown against the house, be sure when digging the ground that soil is not allowed to block air-bricks or ventilation grilles. Be careful also not to leave earth resting against the wall above the damp-proof course or it may be the means of conducting moisture up from the ground, penetrating the wall and leading to rising damp which can cause serious damage to the structure.

Roses

It is important to make sure that all ramblers and climbers are firmly secured to prevent them from whipping about in the autumn winds and becoming damaged. Make sure also that all stakes and ties supporting standard roses are intact and strong enough to withstand high winds.

Though most bush roses grown in gardens are given their main pruning in the spring, it is a wise precaution to shorten tall shoots now, so as to lessen the risk of harm caused by wind rocking the plant and loosening the roots.

Borders and Beds

The last of the summer-bedding plants will need to be cleared away during this month. Put all suitable remains on the compost heap, as shown on page 183.

The space vacated by the summer bedding plants may be used for a cheerful display next spring by replanting with wallflowers, polyanthus and garden primroses, which are available in a wide range of bright colours.

Among other bedding plants which may now be transferred to their flowering positions from a nursery bed, or be bought ready for planting out from a nursery or garden centre, are several garden favourites grown as hardy biennials, such as Canterbury bells, forget-me-nots and sweet williams.

October is also a good month to plant most herbaceous perennials, provided that the soil is light and well drained. If, however, the soil is heavy and inclined to remain wet, it is much safer to delay planting till the spring, when the ground is becoming warmer and drier. This is particularly so where plants are divided and replanted (see page 197), since cold, wet soil is more conducive to rotting than to healing and re-establishment.

Annuals sown during last month or late August should be thinned to about two or three inches (five–seven cm) apart to keep them sturdy and prevent them from becoming overcrowded and spindly.

Pelargoniums (commonly known as geraniums) in pots or other containers which have been giving a summer display outdoors should be brought in when hard weather threatens and placed in a frost-free room or greenhouse. It is time also to lift stock plants of early-flowering chrysanthemums from the ground and place them in a cool greenhouse or frame to remain there during the winter.

Bulbs, Corms and Tubers

If the ground is in a workable condition, take the opportunity to complete the planting of most kinds of lilies in the early part of the month. For details of how to plant them see page 198. In heavy soils, particularly where drainage is inclined to be sluggish, it is a wise precaution to stand the bulbs on a layer of sharp sand. It is also possible to propagate lilies now by means of bulb scales (see page 197).

Most hardy spring-flowering bulbs may be planted now, in the fronts of the borders, in rock gardens, in grass for naturalising or in display beds (see page 198). Planting of bedding tulips is usually delayed until next month.

Hyacinths and daffodils intended to flower early in the new year for room decoration may be planted in bowls of fibre or pots of compost and stood in a cool, dark place such as a cupboard till the shoots are about an inch (two and a half cm) long, and then brought into the light.

As soon as frost blackens the foliage of dahlias, cut off the stems to within an inch or two (three–five cm) above the tubers. Dig up the tubers, allow them to dry off thoroughly and store them for the winter in trays or boxes in a dry, cool, frost-proof place such as an outhouse or shed. Packing peat round the tubers gives them protection and prevents them from drying out too much. Tuberous begonias, gladioli and the less hardy montbretias may be lifted and stored in similar conditions.

Rock Garden and Pool

The chief task in the rock garden this month is to gather up fallen leaves, so that they do not smother small plants and encourage decay. In the pool too, leaves and other debris should be removed before they decay and foul the water, making it harmful to plant life and to fish.

Lawns

If the lawn has not yet been raked and spiked, as recommended in the notes for September (see page 149), it should be attended to before the ground becomes wet from autumn rains or hardened by frost. The job may be somewhat tedious, but the benefits make it well worth while, particularly where the soil is heavy or the lawn has been used for games throughout the summer. A compacted surface puts the finer grasses at a disadvantage against the coarser ones, and also favours disease.

This is the ideal month for laying turf, either to make a new lawn or to repair worn and damaged patches in an existing one. Details will be found on pages 206–8.

Fruit

If strawberries were not planted earlier there is still time, but do so as soon as possible. With such late planting, it will be best to remove blossoms next spring so as to build up strong plants for fruiting the following year.

Complete the pruning of currants and gooseberries if this has not already been done. New plants can be propagated from hardwood cuttings (see page 192 for details).

Prepare the ground in good time for fruit trees that are to be planted next month.

Vegetables

Asparagus foliage will now be turning yellow. Cut the plants down to ground level and remove them before any berries start to drop.

Finish earthing-up trench celery before severe frosts begin.

Lift and store beetroot, carrots and any remaining potatoes.

A start may be made with digging vacant ground (see pages 184–5) so that it has as long as possible to weather during the winter, ready for raking down next spring.

Greenhouse and Frame

An important task this month is the removal of dirt from the glass, together with any shading that was painted or sprayed over it in the spring to prevent overheating of the greenhouse or scorching of leaves. What is needed now and through the winter is as much light as possible.

Less watering and damping down will be needed. To avoid cold draughts admit air through top ventilators rather than side ones. Nights, particularly when the sky is clear, are likely to become cold enough to call for some artificial heat, even in cool houses, where the temperature is not usually allowed to drop below forty-five °F (seven °C). To conserve heat and keep fuel bills down, insulation may be increased by lining the greenhouse with plastic sheeting, as explained on page 229.

Sweet peas may be sown in pots or boxes in a cold frame to give early plants for setting out next spring.

House Plants

As the length and intensity of daylight decrease still further, the amount of illumination admitted into the home through the windows is considerably reduced. Though many of the foliage plants which have become so popular for home decoration are tolerant of – and even prefer – some degree of shade, few will thrive unless they receive a fair amount of light, without which they tend to become pallid and spindly. It may therefore be necessary to bring them closer to the window during the autumn and winter months. Be careful, however, not to place them too near the glass on chilly nights, and avoid exposing them to cold draughts. Though in general less water is needed than during the growing season, do not let plants suffer from the drying effects of increased room heating; for ways to overcome the problem see page 149.

November

No warmth, no cheerfulness, no healthful ease,
No comfortable feel in any member –
No shade, no shine, no butterflies, no bees,
No fruits, no flowers, no leaves, no birds, –
  November

Thomas Hood (1799–1845)

The old idea that there is little or nothing worth looking at among hardy garden plants in November may once have had some truth, but nowadays it is hopelessly out of date. During the century and a half since the lines above were written, the scene in November has been transformed by the wealth of beautiful new plants brought to us by explorers from remote places to brighten our gardens as the days become shorter. A superb example is *Pyracantha rogersiana*, pictured here, which was introduced to western gardens from China in 1911, and which can now be bought at any nursery or garden centre (where you should also find a wide choice of other seasonally attractive plants).

As daylight hours decrease and the sun sinks lower, chillier weather can be expected, with spells of heavy rain, mist and fog, interspersed with clear periods, bringing night frosts. Strong winds are frequent, taking the last leaves from the deciduous trees and shrubs and, often combined with squally rain, driving gardeners indoors. Here time can be usefully spent noting down the past season's successes and failures, while they are still fresh in the memory, and starting to plan how things can be improved next year.

A fine day in early November, lit by a last burst of autumn sunshine, creates garden pictures all its own. It also gives the opportunity for digging the ground in comfort, leaving the whole winter for the weather to break down the soil and get it into good condition in time for sowing next spring. Digging completed this month produces better results and saves effort later.

Left *Pyracantha rogersiana flava*, a fine firethorn from China, has gained both a First Class Certificate and the Award of Garden Merit from the Royal Horticultural Society.

What to see and enjoy in November

Trees and Shrubs

Most of the autumn foliage will by now have fallen from deciduous trees and shrubs, though a few leaves may show last splashes of red or gold before the wind carries them away.

In many cases, the loss of foliage reveals the beauty of the bark, either by its pattern or by its colouring, or by a mixture of both. Among the cool shades are the pale grey of the beech and the silver of the birch; among the warmer colours are the reddish brown of the common cherry and the polished metallic copper-red of the related *Prunus serrula* from China.

The outer bark of some species, both deciduous and evergreen, peels off in patches, to display a warm cinnamon-red surface beneath. Among the most striking of these species are the paperbark maple, *Acer griseum*, and in favourable districts *Arbutus andrachne*. The hybrid between this and the strawberry tree, known as *Arbutus × andrachnoides*, which is more intense in colour and hardier, flowers in late autumn and winter, its ivory white, pitcher-shaped blooms carried in nodding terminal panicles.

In mild localities few species can rival the chilean myrtle, *Myrtus luma (apiculata)*, a small tree whose cinnamon-coloured outer bark peels to expose an inner surface resembling thick cream. Snakebark maples are a striking blue-green, streaked with white, pink and pale jade. Most brilliant of all are the young stems of the dogwoods *Cornus alba* (bright ruby red) and *C. stolonifera* 'Flaviramea' (clear greenish yellow), together with those of the ornamental brambles, such as *Rubus cockburnianus*, coated with shining white, and many willows, including the golden willow, *Salix alba* 'Vitellina', and the violet willow, *S. daphnoides*. A selection is given in the next column, together with some that flower this month and several whose berries and other fruits make a cheerful November display, examples of which are pictured here.

As the light weakens, variegated leaves show their value in brightening even the dullest day. A selection of these and other evergreens appears in the notes for December (see page 170).

SELECTED TREES AND SHRUBS

In flower
Autumn cherry *Prunus subhirtella* 'Autumnalis'; late-flowering heather *Calluna vulgaris* 'Durfordii'; *Erica carnea* (now *herbacea*) and *E. mediterranea* (now *erigena*); *Mahonia × media* cultivars; *Elaeagnus macrophylla, E. pungens* and cultivars; sweet-scented shrubby honeysuckle *Lonicera standishii*; *Viburnum farreri* and *V. × bodnantense*.

Beautiful bark
Many maples, including *Acer davidii, A. griseum* and *A. grosseri*; *Arbutus × andrachnoides*; most species of *Betula*; dogwoods *Cornus alba* and *C. stolonifera*; *Prunus serrula*; *Salix alba* and *S. daphnoides*.

Decorative fruits
A wide variety from many genera, including *Aucuba*; *Berberis*; *Callicarpa*; *Cotoneaster*; *Crataegus* (hawthorn); *Euonymus*; *Malus*; *Pernettya*; *Pyracantha*; *Sorbus*; *Symphoricarpos* (snowberry).

Above *Erica mediterranea* (now *erigena*) has many fine cultivars, a choice of which will give flowers at intervals from now till spring. The background foliage is of *Mahonia napaulensis*, carrying flower buds which will begin to open early next year.

Right *Mahonia* 'Charity's Sister' is one of several magnificent hybrids, belonging to the *M. × media* group, which brighten the garden during late autumn and early winter with their sprays of fragrant yellow flowers in terminal clusters above the bold and handsome foliage.

Climbers and Wall-plants

Very few of these plants produce flowers in November, except winter jasmine, *Jasminum nudiflorum*, which, though perfectly hardy, is perhaps seen at its best against a wall. Here it will display to perfection a succession of bright yellow flowers along its arching green stems from now right through the winter.

The ivy's greenish flowers, appearing now, attract little notice, but several cultivars of *Hedera helix*, *H. canariensis* and *H. colchica*, particularly variegated ones splashed with cream, silvery grey and gold, make a welcome sight on dull walls.

Many shrubs with colourful fruits (see the list opposite) are ideal against walls.

Roses

A late bud or two may appear which will flower in a vase of water indoors. Many shrub roses still carry beautiful fuits. A selection of decorative hips is given in the October notes on page 155.

Above *Ilex aquifolium* 'Ferox Argentea' (variegated hedgehog holly) being male has no berries. *Pyracantha* 'Mohave' in the background is a firethorn with an abundance of berries of an intense red.

Borders and Beds

In the traditional herbaceous border – confined strictly to perennials which die right down in the autumn and spend the winter as roots and other underground storage organs protected by their covering of soil – there was little to look at in November. That was why in the grand gardens of the past such borders were placed at a distance from the house, so that nobody need see such a depressing sight in the winter.

In the modern small garden, where everything is in sight of the house the whole year round, the mixed border, containing plants of all kinds, is much to be preferred. Planned with care and imagination, as can be seen from these pictures of Wisley in November, mixed borders provide interest and beauty at all times. Even during what is often thought of as one of the deadest border months of the year there can be a great deal that is attractive to the eye.

Among the few border plants that may be found flowering in November is the latest of the Michaelmas daisies to bloom, *Aster grandiflorus*, sometimes called the Christmas daisy, from the eastern United States. In sheltered spots its deep violet flowers may even persist into December. In mild places the late sunflowers, *Helianthus atrorubens*, also from the eastern United States, may produce some last blooms now. The fine cultivar 'Monarch' has large, semi-double flowers of rich golden yellow.

Hosta tardiflora, a dwarf plantain lily from Japan, may continue to open its large, deep mauve, bell-like flowers. However, even when flowering is finished the thick glossy, dark-green leaves make a striking border feature, and form the perfect background to some of the autumn flowering bulbs, notably colchicums and crocuses.

During mild spells *Iris unguicularis* (still sometimes known as *Iris stylosa*), produces from among its dense, grassy tuft of leaves – attractive in themselves – a succession of lavender-coloured flowers, beautifully veined and deliciously scented. Should the weather become threatening, the flowers are excellent for cutting as home decoration; they last well in a vase of water.

Below *Cortaderia selloana* (pampas grass) with its silvery plumes, gives height to this mixture of grasses, sedges and other stately plants.

Bulbs and Corms

November is a month when a great many bulbs and corms are in bloom. These are ideal subjects for many different parts of the garden, such as the front of the mixed border, the rock garden, in the light shade of trees and shrubs, or naturalized in grass.

Among the most attractive and rewarding are many species and cultivars both of the true crocus and of what is commonly called the autumn crocus but is botanically known as *Colchicum*. Others include many delightful cyclamen, the completely hardy autumn snowdrop, and some that are best against a sunny wall, such as the South African *Nerine* and *Schizostylis*. Some of the choicest are listed below.

SELECTED BULBS AND CORMS
In flower
Cyclamen cilicium (fragrant), *C. coum*, *C. hederifolium* (often called *neapolitanum*); *Colchicum* species and cultivars; *Crocus speciosus* and cultivars, *C. cancellatus*, *C. medius*, *C. nudiflorus*; *Galanthus reginae-olgae* (autumn snowdrop); *Nerine bowdenii*; *Schizostylis coccinea* and cultivars; *Sternbergia clusiana* and *S. lutea*.

Left *Euonymus europaeus*, the spindle-tree, is native to country hedgerows, and has many splendid cultivars, of which 'Red Cascade', given the Award of Garden Merit by the Royal Horticultural Society, is one of the finest. Its profusion of rosy-red fruits will later split, exposing a bright orange covering to the seed inside.

Rock Gardens and Pools

Two glories of the rock garden at this time of year, with no competition from other blue flowers, are the late-flowering *Gentiana sino-ornata*, with intense azure trumpets, and hybrids of *G. farreri*, with luminous Cambridge-blue flowers. Many bulbs and corms also provide late flowers; a selection will be found on the facing page.

In the water garden, little is to be seen in flower, but some of the plants around the margin with bold, sword-like foliage make a handsome sight in the autumn sun.

Lawns

A last stroll may be enjoyed, and perhaps a last game or two played, before winter weather makes it wisest to keep off the grass. Springy turf, repaying good treatment by absence of bare patches and moss, is better looked at than trodden on when bad weather sets in.

Fruit

Though there is no fruit to be enjoyed fresh from the garden, some of the finest apple and pear cultivars are now starting to develop peak eating quality in store. Inspect all stored fruits once a week to ensure they have not been attacked by storage rots.

Vegetables

Among the many kinds which can be enjoyed fresh from a well-stocked vegetable garden (and some of which are said to be sweeter for a touch of frost) are the following: brussels sprouts, cabbage, carrots, celery, leeks, parsnips, radishes, spinach beet and swedes. Many others are available from stores that are vermin proof and waterproof.

Greenhouse

Whatever the weather outside, there are plenty of excellent plants to make a pleasing display under glass. From a large selection of suitable kinds, some of the most popular are the magnificent cyclamen developed from *C. persicum* (pictured below); begonias of many types; colourful cultivars of *Primula obconica* and *P. sinensis*; the bright red massed flowers of *Kalanchoe blossfeldiana*; and capsicums, otherwise known as winter cherries, with shining scarlet berries.

House Plants

Of the many flowering kinds some of the most attractive are cultivars of *Aphelandra*, *Begonia*, *Cyclamen*, *Euphorbia pulcherrima* (poinsettia), *Impatiens* (busy lizzie) and *Saintpaulia* (african violet).

Right The large-flowered florist's cyclamen, developed by breeders over many years from its parent *Cyclamen persicum*, an Eastern Mediterranean species, is a firm favourite among pot-plants both for the greenhouse and for the home. Here it is represented by two outstanding cultivars. The paler one is called 'Pastourelle' and the deeper pink one 'Orion'. In front is the spider plant, *Chlorophytum capense* 'Variegatum'.

What to do in November

Trees and Shrubs

November is normally one of the best times of the year for planting deciduous trees and shrubs, in particular those dug up from the open ground. (With container-grown plants the timing is not so important, since they do not suffer the same root damage.) However carefully the roots have been lifted from the ground, they are bound to have been torn in the process, so it is important that they should be replanted without delay in comfortable conditions where healing can take place and new roots be encouraged to grow.

In November (and as early in the month as possible) the soil is usually in just the right condition for planting: it has not become either wet or frozen hard. Staking is necessary at the time of planting to guard against coming winter gales, which can cause havoc to newly-transplanted trees – particularly standards and other tall specimens – before they have had time to produce anchoring roots. Full instructions on correct planting and staking, including preparation of the site, are given on pages 199–200.

If your order should arrive during a spell when conditions are unfavourable for planting, the package may be temporarily placed, intact, in a cool but frostproof place such as a shed or garage, or the plants may be 'heeled in' (see page 199) till conditions are right.

If planting cannot be completed by the end of the month, it is best to put it off till a fine spell, when the soil is not frozen or sticky.

Recently planted subjects, in particular those with shallow roots such as young heathers, are likely to be lifted if the ground freezes, leaving the roots liable to be damaged or even killed. So after a sharp frost it is wise to inspect them and if necessary firm the soil round them again.

November is an ideal time to prune deciduous hedges, such as beech, hawthorn and blackthorn. All – or nearly all – the foliage has fallen, so unsightly slicing of leaves is avoided and it is possible to see clearly which stems to cut back. The operation is necessary since, if they are not checked, these hedging plants will try to grow into trees and become bare and leggy at the base. Do not be afraid to prune hard; the wounds will be hidden by new growth next season. Details of how to prune such hedges are given on page 215.

Climbers and Wall-plants

All the reliably hardy ones, such as most species and cultivars of clematis, jasmine (summer and winter), honeysuckle, Virginia creeper and the many other decorative vines, may also be planted in November. Methods of planting, support and after-care are given on pages 198–9.

On a house wall, be careful not to place such plants where they might obscure air-bricks and so impede ventilation. Do not plant wall-shrubs with the base of the stem right up against the wall, but some distance from it. Then if snow falls before the plant is well established, the weight will tend to incline the shrub towards the wall instead of tearing it away; besides, the nearer to the wall the drier the soil becomes.

Plants that are situated close to a wall can only too easily suffer from lack of water, especially in their early stages, before they have had time to send out strong new roots into the surrounding soil; and this can happen even when there is ample moisture in the rest of the garden. The main reason is that the shelter of a wall may effectively prevent rain from reaching quite a wide strip beside it. It is therefore very important that the soil in which wall plants are to be grown should have plenty of moisture-holding material incorporated into it, such as peat or garden compost (see page 83). Water the soil thoroughly after planting has been completed. Should further watering be needed, give a good soaking, so that the water gets well down into the ground. Watering the surface only encourages shallow rooting, which makes the plants more vulnerable to drought than ever. A good thick mulch with organic matter will help greatly to keep the soil moist. Many climbers such as clematis, prefer to have their roots in cool, moist soil, and a mulch of large stones round the base can create these conditions.

Roses

A start may now be made with the pruning of most garden roses in the usual bush and standard forms. The majority of gardeners in the British Isles prefer to do the final pruning in spring – traditionally March – when the likelihood of really severe frost is past. There is then little danger that freezing through the cuts will seriously damage the tissues, leading to die-back and even perhaps killing the plant.

It is, however, an excellent idea to shorten the longest of the current season's shoots now, before winter winds, tugging at the top-growth, rock the plant in the ground, not only loosening it but allowing the roots to be flooded and frozen. A full, step-by-step explanation of how to prune roses is given on page 216.

Rose planting may also be carried out now. An illustrated guide to how to do so will be found on page 199.

Borders and Beds

The end of the flowering season for herbaceous perennials signals that the time has come for the annual autumn clean-up – as important for the garden border as the annual spring cleaning is for the home.

The first thing to do is to cut off

the dead tops of the plants – old flower-heads, withered leaves and stems – particularly any that show signs of decay. Unless they are obviously diseased (in which case they are safest burnt), they should be removed to the compost heap (see page 183 for details of how to build one), where they will be transformed into a useful, soil-enriching substance. If left where they are, they will only provide perfect winter quarters and breeding grounds for pests and diseases.

Do not overdo things, though: leaves that remain green should be left alone; they still have a function to perform in nourishing the underground parts of the plant, where reserves of food are stored on which the plant relies in order to start the next year's growth.

If you are intending to make new beds and borders, or to remake old ones, digging should be done as soon as possible, so that the soil will be able to benefit from exposure to winter weather and so be in the right condition to receive the plants when the time comes to put them into the ground next spring. Details of different types of soil and their correct treatment will be found on page 182, and a step-by-step illustrated guide to the easiest and best way to dig is given on pages 184–5.

The best time for planting is generally thought to be the spring, when the soil is beginning to warm up and so encourage quick rooting. However, there is still time to do some planting earlier in the autumn, while there is warmth left in the ground from the summer, but the earlier the better. If you need to clear some ground for digging but it contains a cherished plant, move this without delay into new quarters – even if these are only temporary – until a more suitable place can be made ready. Overgrown clumps

may be split up before being replanted, as shown on page 197.

Bulbs and Corms
If tulips and hyacinths were not planted out last month, there is still time to do so, but try to get it done as soon as possible, while the ground is still easy and pleasant to work. How to plant is shown on page 198.

Rock Gardens and Pools
Fallen leaves and debris should be removed from the rock garden before they can decay and cause damage. Pricking over the soil with a hand fork and sprinkling small chippings or sharp shingle over the surface will help to combat fungal attack through damp at soil level.

Some alpine plants, particularly those with woolly leaves, are vulnerable to winter rain, which causes rot. A pane of glass, supported above such plants by sticks or wire, will provide protection. Leave the sides completely open; plenty of fresh air is essential.

Remove dead and decaying leaves from the pool before they foul the water. As winter approaches, fruit-cage netting has its uses to cover the pool and prevent leaves from falling in – and to stop fish from being carried off by hungry birds. Even cats can be a nuisance around garden ponds; their instinct is to hook out fish.

Lawns
If you are planning to produce a new lawn from seed, digging should be completed as soon as possible, in order to allow winter frosts to produce the best soil conditions by sowing time next spring.

Established lawns may be given a last mowing early in the month, before the mower is serviced and put away for the winter. Spiking the surface (see page 208), if not already finished, should be completed soon,

before trampling on the ground does more harm than good.

Fruit
In favourable conditions, fruit-trees and bushes may be planted (see page 199 for details).

Pruning may be started on apples and pears (as shown on page 217), but is best left to the spring, if done at all, with cherries, plums and peaches.

Grape vines, both inside and out, should be pruned as soon as possible after leaf-fall, to avoid bleeding when the sap rises next spring.

Vegetables
The main operations this month are those concerned with getting the soil into condition for next year's crops: improving, digging and enriching (pages 182–5).

Order your seeds and plan next season's rotation (page 220).

Hardy peas and broad beans may be sown in the south.

Greenhouse and Frame
Glass needs a thorough washing to increase light. Open the ventilators on clear, mild days, but shut them during cold or foggy spells.

Early bulbs may be brought in from the plunge bed when their containers are well filled with roots, but keep them rather cool. Chrysanthemums should be cut hard back after flowering, to produce suckers for use as cuttings.

Chicory and rhubarb may be forced in darkness under the staging. Mustard and cress may be sown in trays of moist peat.

House Plants
To avoid drawn and spindly growth, give plants plenty of light, but move them away from the window on cold nights. Keep foliage plants fairly dry, but those in flower, such as cyclamen and bulbs, should not lack water, or blossom buds may wither and drop.

December

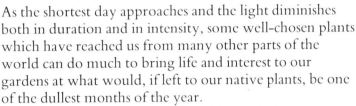

What freezings have I felt, what dark days seen.
What old December's bareness every where.

William Shakespeare (1564–1616)

As the shortest day approaches and the light diminishes both in duration and in intensity, some well-chosen plants which have reached us from many other parts of the world can do much to bring life and interest to our gardens at what would, if left to our native plants, be one of the dullest months of the year.

Some of the most effective of these plants come from the southern hemisphere, where the seasons are reversed, their summer being our winter. Many have striking foliage which continues to give pleasure long after the flowers have faded, such as the New Zealand flax, *Phormium tenax*, pictured here at the end of the season in the trial grounds at Wisley, where several different cultivars have been grown so that quality and performance may be compared. The contrasts between them become more marked as the effects of winter appear in the changing colours of the tall, sword-like leaves.

Against the bare branches of deciduous trees, a rich variety of colour is provided by the foliage of the many different conifers available to gardeners nowadays: a vast range of shades of green, together with golds, blue-greys and silvery tints. There is also a wide variety of form and colour in the cones many of them bear, both to be admired on the trees and to bring inside for home decoration.

As the weather becomes chillier, many happy and profitable hours can be spent indoors studying the catalogues provided by seedsmen and nurserymen. On fine days a visit to a local garden centre, where you can see the actual plants and make your individual choice, will prove pleasurable and worthwhile. Visits to botanical gardens will also suggest ideas for using plants; do not forget to take a notebook with you.

Left *Phormium tenax*, known as New Zealand flax, has many fine cultivars, of which some are pictured on trial at Wisley, with foliage of green, yellow, bronze, purple and wine-red.

What to see and enjoy in December

Trees and Shrubs

Those kinds that can be expected to bloom during December are few in number, but perhaps their flowers are all the more valued in our gardens for that very reason. The autumn cherry continues to produce its white, semi-double blossoms, which not only brighten the winter scene outdoors but are useful as cut sprays for indoor decoration.

In favourable conditions the wintersweet will be opening the first of its waxy, straw-coloured, deliciously scented flowers. These will perfume a room if a shoot carrying blossom buds is cut off and brought inside just as the buds are beginning to open.

Several varieties of the winter-flowering heaths are in bloom, as are some witch hazels, shrubby honeysuckles, viburnums and mahonias, in particular *Mahonia × media* cultivars. *Garrya elliptica* the tassel tree, pictured here, displays an abundance of grey-green catkins, which lengthen throughout the winter and early spring.

The colourful and patterned bark and the attractive fruits of many species and varieties (see page 162) continue to brighten the December picture. It is noticeable that as the month advances and food becomes scarcer, hungry birds devour the red berries first. Consequently, those kinds with yellow and orange coloured fruits give a longer-lasting display.

Fortunately, there are varieties with such fruits in most of the popular species, including several yellow-fruited hollies, which make excellent Christmas decorations for the house when all the red-berried ones have been completely stripped.

Among the many kinds of mountain ash and whitebeam are *Sorbus aucuparia* 'Fructu luteo', with amber berries, *S. cashmiriana*, with fruits like white marbles, *S. discolor*, with creamy yellow fruits, and *S. hupehensis*, with bunches of white berries, tinged pink.

A rich variety of leaf texture and hue is displayed by the many garden conifers, from tall, fast-growing trees to dense, dwarf shrubs which increase hardly at all.

Beauty of leaf is also displayed by a large number of variegated evergreens. A selection of the genera in which they may be found is given in the next column.

SELECTED TREES AND SHRUBS

In flower

Prunus subhirtella 'Autumnalis'; *Chimonanthus praecox*; *Erica carnea* (now *herbacea*) and *E. × darleyensis*; *Crataegus monogyna* 'Biflora'; *Hamamelis mollis*; *Mahonia × media*; *Lonicera fragrantissima* and *L. standishii*; *Viburnum × bodnantense*, *V. farreri* and *V. tinus*.

Beautiful Bark
(See the list on page 162.)

Decorative Fruits
(For genera see the table on page 162.)

Variegated Evergreens
A large selection of attractive varieties, some of the finest being in the following genera: *Aucuba*; *Daphne*; *Elaeagnus*; *Euonymus*; *Ilex*; *Ligustrum*; *Osmanthus*; *Pachysandra*; *Rhamnus*; *Vaccinium*; *Vinca*; and several variegated conifers.

Above *Garrya elliptica*, known popularly as the tassel tree, has perhaps the showiest of all catkins, which appear during the autumn and lengthen through the winter. The male form, given the Award of Garden Merit, has longer catkins than the female and in early spring they produce abundant yellow pollen, set off against the grey-green of the delicately fringed tassels and the dark, oval, leathery leaves.

Right *Berberis* 'Bunch o' Grapes' is a striking example of the many magnificent named varieties belonging to this large and important genus of garden shrubs including several that combine both abundance and brilliance of berries with great richness of leaf colouring towards the end of the year.

Below *Elaeagnus pungens*, introduced into our gardens from its native Japan, has several cultivars with variegated foliage, of which 'Maculata', with gold-splashed leaves, has gained a First Class Certificate and the Award of Garden Merit of the Royal Horticultural Society.

Climbers and Wall-plants

The winter jasmine, *Jasminum nudiflorum*, is among our most widely grown wall-plants since its introduction from China last century. It continues to produce its bright yellow flowers. Though hard frost may spoil some, others will take their place.

Of the few climbers that bloom during winter, the evergreen fern-leaved clematis (full name *Clematis cirrhosa* var. *balearica*) is particularly appealing, with its dainty, cream coloured flowers spotted purplish red.

Variegated cultivars of ivy (*Hedera*), and of many other evergreens listed in the table opposite, continue to mask dull walls and fences in an attractive way.

Roses

Several shrub roses still display their colourful fruits (see the list on page 155), both to brighten the garden and to bring indoors for winter decoration.

Borders and Beds

Coming as they do when there are fewer border plants in flower than at any other time of the year, the Christmas roses and their close relatives belonging to the genus *Helleborus* are particularly welcome. They are not strictly herbaceous plants, because they do not die down during the winter; their dark, handsome, evergreen leaves survive the harshest weather unharmed, making the perfect setting for what are undoubtedly the most spectacular flowers of the season.

The favourite garden hellebore is the Christmas rose itself, *Helleborus niger*, with white, saucer-shaped flowers, often tinted pink on the outside, and containing a central cluster of golden stamens. Unfortunately, the stalks of the ordinary species tend to be rather short, so that the flowers get splashed with mud, but the subspecies *macranthus* (sometimes known as *altifolius*) has longer stems which hold the flowers well above the foliage. There are also several excellent named cultivars.

In order to secure the best for your garden from such a wide choice, it is a good idea to see plants at nurseries or garden centres.

The flowers of the Christmas rose may not open punctually at Christmas but may wait till the New Year. However, once they do appear they are among the longest lasting of all flowers. Another of the genus, *Helleborus corsicus*, pictured here, may bloom a week or two earlier; its lovely cup-shaped flowers, of the palest green, are perfectly hardy but are at their best if given some protection from the icy winds which are commonly experienced at this time of year. The hellebores are splendid for home decoration if the flowers are cut when just open.

Apart from *Iris unguicularis* (*stylosa*), which opens its blooms during mild spells, few flowers will be found among border plants. The appearance of bareness may, however, be avoided by the presence of some evergreen perennials (see the list on page 35) which retain their foliage through the winter.

Also valuable in filling otherwise bare patches are many sub-shrubs, such as grey-leaved *Ballota pseudodictamnus* and *Hebe pinguifolia* 'Pagei', silvery *Santolina*, and varieties of sage (*Salvia*) and thyme (*Thymus*).

Above *Erica carnea* (now *herbacea*), one of the most valuable of all dwarf shrubs, has many superb cultivars which produce a display of flowers in shades of pink and rosy red throughout the winter and into the spring. In the background is the bright foliage of *Thuja plicata* 'Cuprea' and the silvery *Abies lasiocarpa* 'Compacta'.

Left *Helleborus corsicus*, a lovely hellebore from Corsica, is a Mediterranean species closely related to the popular Christmas rose *Helleborus niger*, and displays its long-lasting, pale green flowers on stout stems above its magnificent greyish evergreen foliage.

Bulbs and Corms

Depending upon the season, some of the species listed in the November notes on page 164 may carry their flowers into December.

Additional species of crocus may come into flower, among them *Crocus imperati* and *C. laevigatus*. Two snowdrops, *Galanthus caucasicus* var. *hiemalis* and *G. rizehensis*, from the Caspian coast and Turkey, may produce some early flowers before the common snowdrop, *G. nivalis*, comes into bloom.

Rock Gardens and Pools

There is little to be seen in flower in the rock garden, though among the many species and varieties of *Primula* and *Viola* the occasional bloom may appear.

In the water garden the chief interest still lies in the foliage plants round the margin, including many of the ferns that revel in damp places.

Lawns

Now that the mower has been put away for the winter, the best treatment for a lawn is to admire it from a distance and give it a rest from trampling feet. If lawns have to be walked across, those that survive the winter looking their best are the ones provided with something to walk upon, such as stone slabs set into the turf.

Fruit

If carefully picked and stored, apples and pears of the finest cultivars will now be reaching perfection and may be enjoyed at their best.

Vegetables

Apart from those kinds already harvested and available from store, including onions, potatoes and beetroot, it should still be possible to dig Jerusalem artichokes, carrots, celery, leeks, parsnips, winter radishes, salsify, scorzonera and swedes, especially if a good layer of straw or litter has been placed along the rows to prevent the ground from freezing hard.

Among the vegetables above ground which can be gathered are brussels sprouts, cabbage, chicory, savoy, spinach beet and seakale beet (swiss chard).

Greenhouses

There is a wide choice of beautiful plants, with colourful flowers, fruits and foliage, to provide plenty of variety in the greenhouse during December. Many of them are the same as those included in the notes for November (see page 165). Others that may be added include the silvery leaved *Primula × kewensis*, with sulphur-yellow flowers, the dainty *Primula malacoides*, pictured here, and the popular cineraria, with flowers of many colours.

House Plants

To the brief selection given on page 165 under this heading must be added the many flowering pot-plants which are given as presents at Christmas time. Among the most attractive are those known as indian azaleas, smothered with dazzling flowers, mainly in glowing shades of pink and red, and the african violet (*Saintpaulia*), now available in a large number of variants, some with single and some with double flowers, in many colours, including blues, purples, pinks and whites.

Above *Primula malacoides*, the fairy primula, has been developed from a species native to south-west China, with small mauve blooms, into one of our most magnificent winter-flowering plants for cool greenhouses. It has larger flowers of much greater substance in an assortment of colours, including many different shades of rose, pink, salmon and purple, as well as cream and white. In the foreground is an example of the many attractive cultivars of the common ivy, *Hedera helix*.

What to do in December

Trees and Shrubs

Planting may still be carried out when the weather allows and the ground is in the right state (see pages 198–199). Otherwise, heel the plants in (page 199) or put them in a frostproof place till things improve; there is nothing to be gained by undue haste if conditions are wrong.

Many shrubs that are perfectly hardy when mature are somewhat tender in their early stages. When severe cold threatens, it is therefore wise to give some protection to newly planted ones in exposed places.

The force of cutting winds can be greatly reduced by erecting a screen of sacking, woven wattle hurdles, pea or bean sticks or even netting strung between posts. A good mulch of straw, compost or similar material (see page 183) spread over the ground can prevent damage from frost to young roots, which may be killed by temperatures that leave stems above ground unscathed.

Snow should be shaken or brushed from trees, shrubs and hedges, before its weight can cause damage.

Patio shrubs grown in tubs, such as hydrangeas and fuchsias, should be brought into a shed, garage or cold greenhouse if severe weather threatens.

Climbers and Wall-plants

Though the shelter of the wall itself usually gives protection enough, some of the more tender kinds are safer with a certain amount of extra protection during severe weather. Often all that is needed is a length of sacking hung in front of the plant.

A more protective method is to fix some wire-netting to the wall around the plant and fill this with bracken, straw or something similar while the cold lasts. It is important, though, not to pack the protective material together too tightly, or stagnant air and dampness will not be able to escape, and disease may result.

Roses

Most leaves will have fallen by now, and should be gathered up and put on the compost heap (see page 183) if they appear clean and healthy. Those that look diseased – in particular any showing signs of black spot (see page 235) are best burnt, to prevent the infection from being carried over.

Planting may still be carried out if the ground is not too hard or wet (see page 199). If any long shoots on bushes and standards have not yet been attended to, shorten them as soon as possible to two feet (sixty cm) or so to prevent wind damage. Often a few last flower-buds will be found, and if these are cut off and brought indoors they may open and make a cheerful display.

If the surface of the rose-bed has become compacted during the season, it should be freshened by pricking it over with a fork, and if possible adding a mulch of organic matter, such as garden compost to prevent it from being beaten down again by the winter rains.

Borders and Beds

Most of the herbaceous border perennials can stand a great deal of cold, especially if the soil has been well mulched. Some of the less hardy kinds, however, may benefit from a rather thicker protection from severe frost. A well-tried method is to lay a piece of wire-netting over the plant, pile a good thick layer of straw, bracken or dry leaves on top, cover it all with another piece of wire-netting, and keep it in place by pegging it down at the corners. It can then be easily removed at the end of the winter.

Biennials in the open continue to grow, however slowly, through the winter, and should therefore always be kept from being smothered by fallen leaves, which will not only impede growth but may lead to rotting.

Many borders are backed by hedges, the roots of which are likely to invade the border soil, robbing it of nourishment and moisture. Now is a good time, while tidying and digging, to prune those roots hard back.

Though the Christmas rose (*Helleborus niger*) is a perfectly hardy plant, its flowers can be spoiled by heavy rain and splashes of mud unless it is given some protection. A frame light, or a pane of glass, resting on bricks at the corners, will serve the purpose, or a cloche will do. If you cut a bloom or two just as they are opening and bring them indoors, they will last for weeks in a vase of water.

Bulbs and Corms

Weed seeds that were brought to the surface during the planting of tulips and other bulbs put in late in the season are likely to germinate during mild spells. Hoeing or hand-weeding while they are still seedlings will save a good deal of work and trouble later on; or you can spray with a suitable herbicide (see pages 230–231).

Rock Gardens and Pools

The seeds of many favourite alpines are not able to germinate successfully unless they are exposed to a period of freezing in order to break their dormancy, as happens in their native habitats, where they may be covered with snow for weeks or months on end.

The seed should be sown as soon as possible, if that has not already been done, so as to give as long a period of exposure as possible. Sow in pans or boxes containing a good seed compost (see page 219), and after the sowing is completed cover the surface of the compost with a sprinkling of grit or sharp sand. Then place the pans or boxes in the open with no protection from the weather – though it may be wise to cover the pans or boxes with some wire netting to foil seed-eating birds.

Garden pools, especially the popular small ones, can very quickly become frozen solid in hard weather. It is best to try to keep at least one part of the pool unfrozen in order to allow noxious gases to escape. If allowed to remain, they can cause considerable harm or even kill both fish and plant life.

Matting, or even an old blanket, draped over the surface of the pool, can be used for protection, but if the surface should after all be frozen a can of boiling water stood on the ice will melt a hole. Since the sides of the pool may be damaged by the expansion of ice, it is worth while to try floating rubber balls in the pool when freezing weather threatens. By yielding to the expansion of the ice, they can reduce the pressure on the sides of the pool.

Lawns
If the ground is not wet or sticky, spiking (page 208) can still be carried out to improve aeration and drainage. In mild weather, digging and other soil operations (shown on pages 184–5) are still possible in preparation for sowing next spring, but must be completed soon if the soil is to gain the benefit of exposure to the winter.

Mowers should be cleaned and overhauled if they have not already been attended to. Make arrangements for repairs and maintenance now, and so avoid the frustration of having to wait your turn next spring, when service engineers have their busiest time.

Leatherjackets may be controlled by treating infested lawns with a suitable pesticide (see page 237). Ground freshly dug in preparation for new lawns should have its pest population greatly reduced by hungry birds, so chemical control will not normally be needed unless you find that damage occurs next season.

Fruit
In favourable weather, hardy fruit trees and bushes of all kinds may still be planted, so long as the soil is in the right condition (see pages 198–9).

They may also all be pruned now, except for the stone fruits – cherries, plums and peaches – which are best left to the spring, if pruned at all. (For step-by-step details, see pages 216–217.)

Healthy young shoots of currants, gooseberries and vines removed during pruning may be used as hardwood cuttings (page 192) to raise new plants.

Old canes of raspberries, blackberries and loganberries should be removed, if this has not already been done, and the new ones tied in (see page 201).

Grape vines under glass need plenty of fresh air, so ventilators should be opened wide. Vines are very hardy, and frost will do them no harm while dormant; indeed, it is thought to make for vigorous bud-burst when spring comes.

Vegetables
Try to get your seed order sent off before Christmas. Then it will receive prompt attention, instead of having to take its place among the flood of new year's orders, and you are likely to get the kinds you ordered, instead of finding them sold out.

Some vegetables in the open ground will benefit from a little protection against being spoiled by frost. Late cauliflowers may be saved from discoloration and damage by breaking a large outer leaf over the head to protect it as it develops. Celery can be reduced to a slimy mass both by severe frost and by heavy rain, but it may be saved if, when foul weather is forecast, the ridge is covered with dry straw. Peg down some wire-netting over the straw to stop it being snatched away by the wind.

If you have any vegetables in store, it is a good plan to examine them regularly so that any which show signs of disease may be removed. If they are left they are likely to contaminate the rest. Should the disease not have spread too far, the bad patches can be cut out and the vegetable used immediately.

Greenhouse and Frame
Light is of supreme importance during the winter, so if you have not yet thoroughly cleaned the glass it is best to do so at once. If your greenhouse has not been insulated, now is the ideal time to do so, when the benefits are greatest. An efficient system (see page 229) need not cost much, and with the savings in heating bills it could pay for itself remarkably soon.

Towards the end of the month it should be possible to start propagating chrysanthemums from basal cuttings; how to do so is shown on page 194. Carnations may also be raised from side shoots as they become available throughout the winter.

House Plants
Many plants in pots are given as presents during the festive season. With modern packaging and transport, they are mostly in excellent shape when bought, but they need helping to adjust to new surroundings and to settle in after their travels. Keep them away from draughts, and freshen up the leaves by very gently removing the dust of the journey with a soft cloth or sponge and tepid water.

Be careful not to water too much. It is all too easy to make the compost in pots soggy, so that roots lack sufficient air.

Practical Gardening Techniques

The following pages give step-by-step details of tried and proved methods by which the garden may be successfully managed, with as much opportunity for enjoyment, and as little likelihood of disappointment, as is within the gardener's control.

From the first page of this section to the last, no previous knowledge of gardening is assumed. Even at the beginning of the section, dealing with the nature of soils and methods of cultivation and improvement, no experience of digging is taken for granted, but the process is clearly demonstrated in simple pictures and accompanying instructions, in order to reduce the amount of effort required and produce the most effective results.

With the vast experience of the Royal Horticultural Society to draw upon, this section represents a combination of firmly established gardening practices and up-to-date findings of research by plant scientists directed towards constant improvement both of the plants available for growing in gardens and of the methods by which they are raised and grown.

The purpose of this section is to provide a guide to the full range of gardening operations. It should be used in conjunction with the reminders at the end of each set of monthly notes. The reminders show when the various operations should be carried out; the section that now follows shows how to do so.

Hand tools

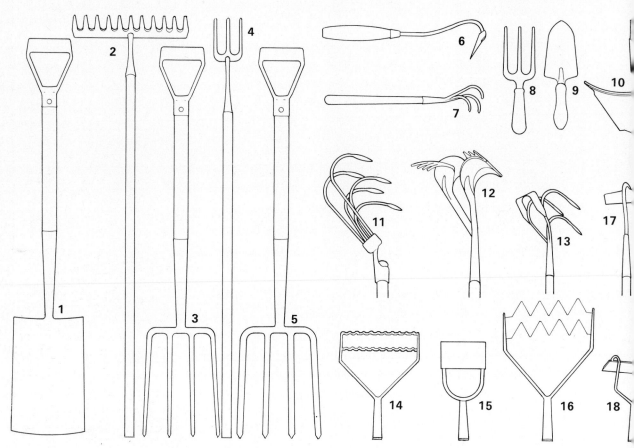

There is such a vast range of garden tools available that it is sometimes difficult to decide what to buy.

The first thing to bear in mind is that the cheapest tools very often turn out to be the most expensive in the long run. They are liable to have a short and unsatisfactory life and soon need replacing. They are also apt to be expensive in the amount of effort required to use them.

It is best therefore to start off with a few essential tools, of the best quality that you can afford. More can be added later as optional extras.

The importance of looking after tools properly can hardly be overstressed. They should never be put away with any dirt adhering to them. Even after a tiring day's digging or hoeing a few extra minutes should always be devoted to cleaning the blades. Scrape off as much dirt as possible (a piece of wood may be used for the purpose), then wash the blade clean, dry it and finish by wiping with an oily rag.

Spades

Compare several before buying and choose one that suits you, particularly in weight and in length of shaft. The wrong spade will not only be uncomfortable to use but will make digging arduous.

Stainless steel spades, though expensive to buy, are extremely durable and make digging much easier.

Forks

The fork is another essential digging tool, particularly in stony ground where a spade is difficult to use. It may also be used for breaking up soil in readiness for surface cultivation. The usual type has four tines, square in cross-section; there is also the flat-tined type, designed for lifting potatoes.

Choose a size that you find comfortable. A stainless one will give excellent service.

Small forks for weeding include long-handled models which are designed to avoid stooping and stretching.

Hoes

There are many types of hoe.

Dutch hoes are skimmed backwards and forwards just below the surface, severing weeds; the user walks backwards and so does not tread on the hoed ground. Newer versions with serrated or zigzag edges can penetrate a hard surface more easily.

Draw hoes are used with a chopping motion, while walking forwards. They are also used for earthing up potatoes and drawing seed drills. A short-handled version, the onion hoe, is used at close quarters with one hand. Small grubbers, with prongs instead of blades, are used in the same way.

Other designs include strengthened blades for heavy work. The double hoe has a blade on one side and two prongs on the other.

Cultivators of several kinds, with curved prongs, sometimes combined with blades, may be used to break up the soil.

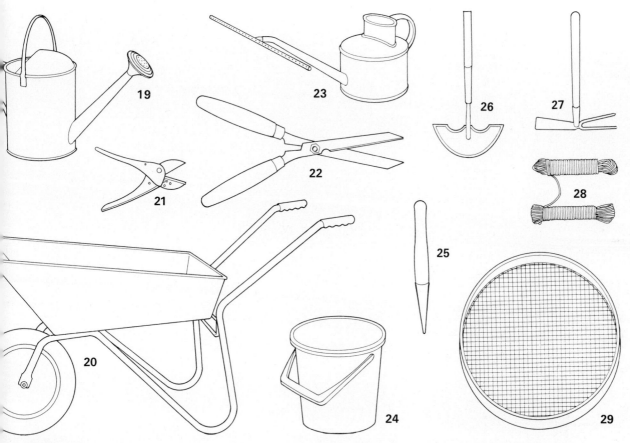

Rakes

The basic garden rake has steel teeth, which crumble the soil into a tilth when used as shown on pages 190–1.

Spring-tined rakes for the lawn have flexible tines of steel, rubber or bamboo.

Hand forks, Trowels and Dibbers

The hand fork is useful for weeding and for preparing the soil for planting. It is often sold as a set with a trowel, which is an essential planting tool. Make sure both are strong enough not to bend or break.

Dibbers of various kinds are used to plant out seedlings and insert cutting.

Secateurs and Shears

Modern secateurs are of two main types: those with a scissor action and those that cut against a soft metal anvil. Both can be excellent if kept sharp, clean and oiled.

Modern lightweight shears are excellent too; notched blades are useful for cutting thicker stems than normal.

The most generally useful watering can is the two gallon (nine litre) size with two detachable roses, coarse and fine. For applying liquid herbicides a separate can with a dribble bar will be needed. A plastic bucket is useful for mixing chemicals.

A wheelbarrow will make gardening easier, especially where there is much compost, manure or earth to be shifted.

A garden line will be needed for making drills, especially in vegetable gardens. It can be a length of cord stretched between sticks, but is easier to use if wound on a reel, with the free end tied to a spike.

Edging irons, usually of half-moon shape, are used for trimming edges of lawns and grass verges.

A garden sieve is very useful for sifting soil and compost to get rid of stones and lumps. A half-inch (one cm) mesh size is best for general purposes.

Many other gardening aids may be added, according to requirements.

KEY TO ILLUSTRATIONS

1 Spade. **2** Rake. **3** Digging fork.
4 Long-handled weeding fork.
5 Potato fork. **6** Onion hoe.
7 Pronged grubber. **8** Hand fork.
9 Trowel. **10** Ridging tool.
11 Five-pronged cultivator.
12, 13 Combined hoe-cultivators.
14 Push-pull hoe, serrated blade.
15 Traditional dutch or push hoe.
16 Push-pull hoe, zigzag blade.
17 Draw hoe, single-mounted blade.
18 Draw hoe, double-mounted blade.
19 Watering can, detachable rose.
20 Wheelbarrow, metal-framed.
21 Secateurs, anvil pattern.
22 Shears, with notched blade.
23 Watering can, sprinkler bar.
24 Bucket, plastic, medium size.
25 Dibber, metal pointed.
26 Edging iron for lawn trimming.
27 Double hoe, blade and prongs.
28 Garden line, of nylon cord.
29 Garden sieve for sifting soil.

Power tools

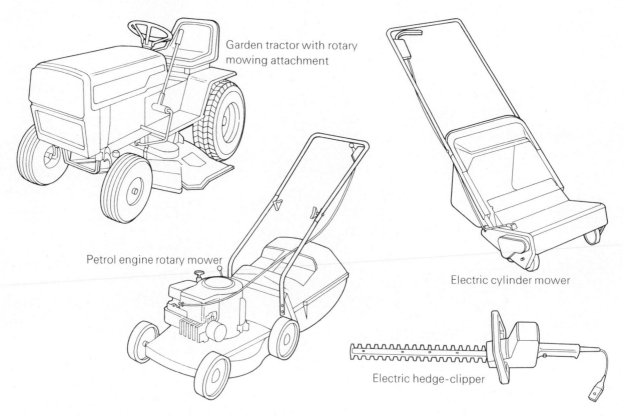

Garden tractor with rotary mowing attachment

Petrol engine rotary mower

Electric cylinder mower

Electric hedge-clipper

During recent years more and more gardeners have been investing in various kinds of power tools and machines, reducing the need for muscular exertion and bringing the garden into line with the well-equipped home.

Before money is spent on garden machinery, however, the first consideration must be how much it is going to be used. There is no point in buying expensive equipment if it is going to spend most of its time idle.

Apart from the initial cost and the running expenses, there is the cost of maintenance to be considered; no machine can be expected to give good service unless it is regularly serviced itself. There must also be adequate storage space.

Most power tools and machines are available in either petrol or electric models. With petrol-driven ones safe storage must be provided for highly inflammable fuel; with most electric models great care must be taken not to tangle, or worse still to sever, the cable that carries the power.

Lawn Mowers

Cylinder models are built on the same principle as most hand-propelled mowers, which are still widely used on small lawns, where the expense of a motor mower can hardly be justified. Revolving blades slice the grass against a fixed lower blade, leaving a fine, even surface.

Those with side wheels are cheapest, but they cannot mow over lawn edges, for which models with a relatively large rear roller are needed.

Powered versions are of two kinds: those that have power-driven cutters but still need to be pushed, and others that are driven forward as well.

Rotary mowers operate by means of horizontal blades spinning round at high speed beneath a protective hood. They do not give the same smooth finish as cylinder mowers do on level lawns, but they are excellent for cutting long grass.

Grassboxes are available with cylinder mowers and many rotary ones. The general opinion is that grass cuttings should be removed except in dry summer weather.

Hover mowers cut grass on the same basic principle as rotary ones, but instead of resting on wheels they are supported on a cushion of air. They are particularly useful on grass banks.

Trimmers

Powered edge trimmers save a great deal of time and effort in giving the edges of lawns a tidy appearance after the grass has been mown. Using shears – even the special long-handled ones – to clip all the way round even a moderate-sized lawn, can be a long and tiring job, but a powered trimmer enables it to be done at a slow walking pace. There are several makes, all based on a toothed blade rotating vertically at the end of a long handle.

Spin trimmers are instruments for severing weeds at ground level in awkward places. They operate by spinning a short length of nylon cord at very high speed. The nylon slices through soft plant growth but does not harm tree-trunks, fences or posts, and so can be used close up to them.

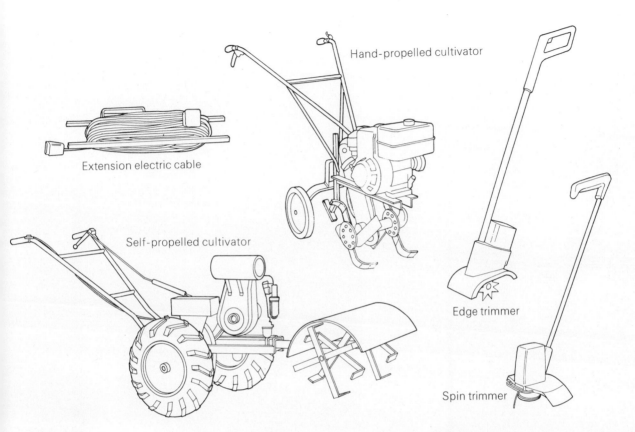

Hand-propelled cultivator

Extension electric cable

Self-propelled cultivator

Edge trimmer

Spin trimmer

Hedge Clippers

In a small garden, where there is only a limited amount of hedge to be kept in trim, a good pair of hand shears – particularly of the modern lightweight type (see page 179) should be more than adequate for the job. It is indeed generally agreed that nothing can beat hand shears for the best results.

However, where there is a considerable amount of hedge to be trimmed, particularly if it is tall, a powered hedge trimmer of the reciprocating type can be a great boon in lightening the task.

Most of these hedge-clippers are powered by electricity through a cable, and it is most important that they should be properly insulated to prevent shocks if the cable should be accidentally cut. To lessen this possibility it is best to take the cable over the user's shoulder, so that it cannot touch the blades.

The easiest and most effective method of use is to pass the clipper backwards and forwards across the hedge in a series of short sweeps, to give an even trim.

Cultivators

There are many different models of powered cultivators available, all working on the same principle: they turn the soil over by means of steel blades mounted on a rotating central shaft.

Powered cultivators are of two different kinds. With the first, the engine drives only the blades, which pull the machine forwards as they rotate, the user assisting from behind. The second type has driven wheels; some have front-mounted and others rear-mounted blades.

Such machines are regularly used by people who cultivate sizeable areas for purposes such as growing vegetables. They can be of great value for the initial breaking up of new ground, for which it is usually possible to hire one.

Garden Tractors

Small tractors now on sale are comfortable to operate and have many interchangeable attachments, such as rotary mowing units and cultivators. They are mainly suitable for larger properties.

Electric Cable

Electrically driven power tools and machines have several advantages in terms of convenience over many of those powered by petrol engines. In addition to not requiring the storage of fuel, electric devices are usually quieter in operation and are often easier and quicker to start.

They do, however, have the limitation that the cable with which they are supplied is often not long enough to allow them to be operated at any distance from the house without an extension cable.

It is extremely important that this cable should not only be of a suitable rating for the machinery it supplies but should also be equipped with the right plug and socket. In addition it should have some kind of spool on which it can be neatly wound so that it does not get tangled with itself or the operator or foul the machine.

It is also of the utmost importance that the electrical installation should have been carried out by a qualified electrician who is aware of the purpose of such an installation and the machinery it will supply.

181

Soil

Soil Types

Soils may be divided into six types, though few garden soils match them exactly.

Stony soils

The action of weather and other natural forces on the original rock has not gone very far, so the proportion of soil to rock is rather low. A disadvantage of stony soils is the amount of effort they need. An advantage is that they are usually well drained.

Clayey soils

These are at the other extreme. The particles of rock have become so finely ground over the years that they have reached a state that scientists call colloidal and gardeners call sticky. In wet weather clay soils cling to the spade; in dry weather they set hard. They are difficult to work and usually badly drained but have high potential fertility.

Sandy soils

The rock particles have been broken down more than those of stony soils but not as much as those of clay ones. Sandy soils are commonly light in colour as well as in texture. Their chief disadvantage is that they fail to hold moisture and plant foods but they are easy to work.

Limy soils

These are of two kinds: shallow, with more or less solid chalk below, and deeper, with the lime content mixed with other material; so there are various kinds of limy soil, from light to heavy. A disadvantage of such soils is that plants known as lime-haters will not thrive in them.

Peaty soils

These are formed from old vegetation which has been subjected to conditions that have left it in a state of partial decomposition. They are commonly dark in colour and poorly drained, and they tend to be both acid and deficient in nutrients. For most garden purposes they need improved drainage, reduction of acidity and the addition of suitable plant foods.

Loamy soils

These provide the best growing conditions for the majority of cultivated plants. They consist of a balanced mixture of fine and coarse particles, including clay and sand, together with organic matter and a supply of plant foods. Loams work easily and drain well, but they also hold on to moisture and nutrients.

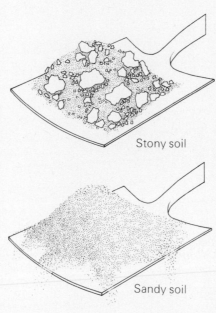

Stony soil

Sandy soil

Clay soil

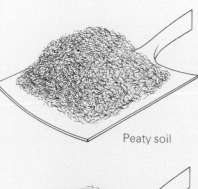

Peaty soil

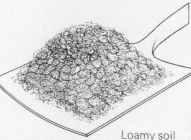

Loamy soil

Improving Soil

A vitally important requirement for healthy and vigorous plant growth is that the roots should have access to a readily available supply of moisture and air.

Shortage of water is a problem particularly associated with light, sandy soils, which drain very quickly. Such soils benefit from the addition of plenty of bulky organic matter such as garden compost (see opposite page).

Shortage of air, on the other hand, is a problem particularly associated with soils from which water does not drain quickly enough. Generally that means heavy clay soils, in which the particles are bound so tightly together that it is difficult for anything to work its way through them.

In some cases, especially where the ground has been repeatedly cultivated, the trouble may be caused by the formation of a hard, impervious pan some way below the surface. Very often such conditions can be remedied by thorough digging in which the subsoil is broken up and organic material added (see pages 184–5). The incorporation of coarse sand or grit may help greatly in opening up heavy soil.

If such methods are not enough, it may be necessary to dig drainage trenches, two to three feet (60–90 cm) deep with a fall of one in forty and leading to a ditch or a soakaway containing broken bricks or other rubble. Lay earthenware drainpipes along the trenches and cover with coarse gravel before filling in. A cheaper way is to omit the drainpipes and use rubble or shingle, as shown below.

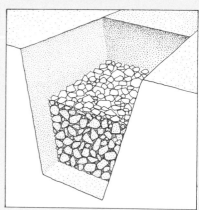

Rubble drains, constructed as explained above, may be used to rid small areas of surplus water.

In addition to the visible ingredients of soil, there are – or should be – millions of living things invisible to the naked eye. These micro-organisms break down complex food substances into simpler forms that can be absorbed by roots. To provide conditions in which these micro-organisms can thrive, soil needs humus, the dark, crumbly substance resulting from the decomposition of plant and animal remains.

The more the soil is cultivated, the quicker humus is exhausted. To replace it, added organic material is needed, such as manure, leaf-mould, peat, spent hops or garden compost, made as shown on the right. Nearly all soils are improved by humus-forming material; it helps to bind light soils and to open up heavy ones. (Peaty soils probably do not need added organic matter; they tend to be badly drained and deficient in nutrients and so need draining and the addition of sand or grit and suitable fertilizers.)

As well as organic matter, which varies greatly in nutrient value, there are many inorganic fertilizers available which are easy to apply and contain stated amounts of plant food. The commonly used fertilizers supply nitrogen (N), phosphoric acid (P_2O_5) and potash (K_2O), either singly or mixed to make compound fertilizers.

Growmore, containing 7%N, 7%P_2O_5, and 7% K_2O, has equal amounts of all three, and rates of use are given on the packet.

A soil's acidity is indicated by its pH, easily measured by a simple testing outfit. Neutral pH is 7; below that figure the soil is acid and above it alkaline. Most garden plants do well in slightly acid soil, with a pH about 6.5. If tests give a lower figure, showing greater acidity, this may be reduced by adding lime.

Ground limestone, applied at a rate of $\frac{1}{2}$ lb per square yard (270 g/m²) for sandy soil, one lb per square yard (550 g/m²) for loamy soil, or $1\frac{1}{2}$ lb per square yard (800 g/m²) to heavy or peaty soil, will correct moderately over-acid soil.

Never let lime come in contact with manure, or valuable nitrogen will be lost.

Excessive alkalinity is rarer and more difficult to correct. Adding acid peat may be tried, or applying powdered sulphur at 4 ounces per square yard (130 g/m²).

Garden Compost

An excellent source of organic material, particularly now that animal manure is scarce and expensive, is a compost heap, which turns garden and kitchen waste into a dark, crumbly substance of great value in improving the soil. Among materials that can be used are annual weeds, mowings, tea leaves, potato peel and other vegetable trimmings, dead flowers, hedge trimmings and damp, shredded newspaper.

This can simply be built up in layers, each sprinkled with earth, and finished with a covering of soil (see top right illustration). Such compost may not be ready for over a year and even then may contain undecomposed portions.

Better results are obtained by using a bin and putting in substantial amounts at a time, if necessary accumulating material in plastic sacks till there is enough. Heat generated in the heap will speed the process, kill weed seeds and harmful organisms and give an improved product.

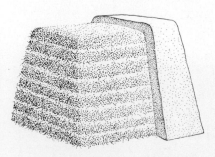

A simple compost heap may be built up of successive layers of garden and kitchen waste covered with soil. The material may be slow to break down, and the resulting compost may tend to be cold and heavy.

Sulphate of ammonia may be scattered over completed layers at the rate of one ounce per square yard (35 g/m²) to assist the microbial action that turns waste into compost. Many gardeners use proprietary brands of activator, which should be applied as instructed.

Compost Containers

For easy removal of finished compost, the wooden bin (top right) has removable boards in front. The plastic bin (below left) has grooved sections which slide up and down, and the one made of wire mesh (below right) has a side that hinges forward.

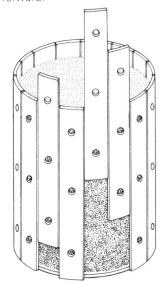

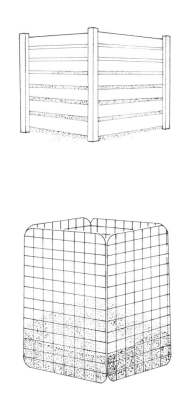

Digging

Single Digging

This is the simplest form of digging and means turning the earth over to a single spade's depth. It is usually all that is needed to bring most types of soil into workable condition for sowing. To make the operation as effortless as possible and to avoid backache and strained muscles, three rules should be obeyed. First, do not attempt to dig when the soil is either hard or wet and sticky; it should be just moist enough to allow the spade to go in easily. The best time is the autumn, to enable winter frosts to get into the newly turned ground and break it up, so that it crumbles easily under the rake when the time arrives for cultivating the surface the following spring in order to produce the even tilth on which sowing and germination depend.

Secondly, do not take thick spadefuls of earth, in the mistaken belief that decreasing the number of rows to be dug will also decrease the time the job takes. Thick clods are not only unnecessarily tiring to dig but slow the process down. *Two thin rows are quicker to dig than one thick one.* Make each slice of earth no more than four or five inches (ten–twelve cm) thick, at any rate to begin with, and never go beyond six inches (fifteen cm).

Thirdly, let the weight of your body do as much of the work as possible. The spadefuls of earth, called 'spits', should not be lifted (lifting places undue strain on the arm muscles) but simply turned over, the spade always being kept close to the ground while it is loaded with soil, and not raised again until it is empty.

There are five movements in handling a spade properly. First, take the top of the handle in the right hand, palm towards you. Then, holding the lower part of the shaft lightly in the left hand, lift it, bending the elbow till your left forearm is horizontal. Second, bring the spade down, letting the shaft slide through the fingers of the left hand. As soon as the blade enters the soil, put your left foot on its shoulder. Third, using the whole weight of your body, drive it in to its full depth. Fourth, take your left foot from the spade and pull the handle backwards till the end nearly touches the ground. This will lever the spit free. Fifth, sway forward, giving a twist of the wrist to turn the spit over. (These instructions are for right-handed people: reverse them for the left-handed.)

1 Start each spit with a cross cut at a distance of a spade's width from the previous spit.

2 Keep the spade upright as it enters the soil and place the left foot firmly on the blade.

3 Throwing the whole weight of the body on to the spade, drive it into the soil to its full depth.

4 Pull the handle backwards with the right hand so as to lever up the spadeful of soil.

5 With a twist of the wrist, turn the spit of soil over and throw it forwards, leaving a shallow trench.

6 A layer of garden compost or manure placed at the bottom of each trench will enrich the soil.

Double Digging

In some conditions it may be best to dig the ground to a depth of two spits. It may be that the soil is badly drained, so that after rain the water cannot get away. The result is that roots of plants attempting to grow in such soil are in danger of being drowned. In many cases such conditions can be greatly improved by breaking up the subsoil so that the water can escape. This is often all that is needed with ground that has been shallowly cultivated for some time, so that an impervious crust has been formed just beneath the surface. If the problem lies deeper, and is caused by the nature of the land, it may be necessary to install special drainage, by means of unglazed clay drainpipes leading either to a soakaway or a ditch.

Other conditions that call for double digging may occur with ground which has not been cultivated before and in which the topsoil forms a shallow layer. Here, the spade cannot be driven in to its full depth before it meets hard, resistant subsoil. In such conditions, roots cannot penetrate the lower levels in search of moisture, and so plants tend to suffer in dry weather, when watering may be forbidden.

Light soil which lacks body and is deficient both in plant foods and in moisture-holding capacity may often be greatly improved by double digging. It helps if there is plenty of organic material, such as garden compost or manure, available for incorporating in the soil during the process.

The first step is to divide the plot lengthwise into two halves. Dig out a trench a spade's depth and two feet (60 cm) wide across half the plot at one end and place the excavated soil beside the other half. Next break up the bottom of the trench to the full depth of the garden fork. Spread compost or manure over this and fork it in. Then dig a second trench, throwing the topsoil forward to fill in the first. Break up the bottom, and continue in this way up one side of the plot and down the other. Finish by filling in the last trench with the topsoil from the first. When double digging grassland, skim off the turf before digging each trench, chop it up and put it in the bottom of the previous trench, where it will rot down and add organic matter to the soil.

1 After digging a trench halfway across the plot, break up the bottom to a full fork's depth.

2 Cover in with topsoil sliced from another strip next to the first, to make a second trench.

3 Transfer loose soil from each trench to the one before, to ensure that depth of cultivation is even.

4 Break up the bottom of the trench before adding organic material to improve the soil.

5 Spread compost or manure, or use chopped-up turf placed upside-down in the trench.

6 After adding organic matter to the last trench, cover it in with topsoil from the first.

Construction

Paths

The cheapest and quickest paths to lay are those of gravel, but later on a great deal of time and effort will need to be spent in weeding, mending and rolling them if they are to be well maintained. Concrete paths take more time and effort at first, but will need little or no further work.

Mark out the edges with pegs and cord, then dig out the soil to a depth of nine inches (twenty-three cm); if it is good topsoil it can be used to improve and deepen beds and borders. Fill the bottom six inches (fifteen cm) with hard rubble such as broken bricks or stones and ram it down well. Peg lengths of wooden board along each side of the path, so that the top edge is three inches (seven cm) above the surface of the rubble.

Make sure that the boards are level, both with each other and along their length, and spread between them a concrete mixture made up of one part cement, two parts of sand and three parts of shingle, with water to make a stiff paste.

Finish by levelling the surface of the concrete with a piece of board. Place this across the lengths of wood and move it to and fro while drawing it from one end of the section to the other.

At the end of the section fix a cross-piece of wood between the side-pieces and level with them. Bring the concrete flush with this; any surplus can be thrown into the foundation of the next section. Cover the surface with some sacking or plastic sheet to prevent it from setting too quickly. When the concrete has set, the boards can be moved along and the next section laid.

While concrete is ideal for utilitarian paths such as those in the vegetable garden, many people find it unattractive, especially near the house. Among more pleasing materials are bricks, which may be laid on edge in many different patterns, and stone (natural or artificial) either formally arranged in rectangular slabs or less formally laid in irregular pieces as crazy-paving.

Patios

These may be constructed from any of the same materials as paths, alone or in combination. Concrete is the least attractive for patios or terraces, though there are coloured powders which can be mixed with it before adding the water, in order to make it look a little more attractive. It is also possible to make the surface both more interesting in texture and less slippery in the rain by waiting till the concrete is nearly dry and then raking it with a light rake or brushing it with a stiff broom.

There is little doubt, however, that for most people a terrace of stone or brick is much more appealing. It offers unlimited scope for different patterns and may be given added interest by the introduction of plants, both in containers and in pockets of soil left in the paving.

A selection of suitable carpeting plants will be available at your local garden centre; those with aromatic leaves such as creeping thymes are particularly attractive.

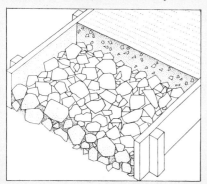

Above Concrete paths are laid in sections, between boards, on a firm foundation of well-rammed broken rubble or hardcore.

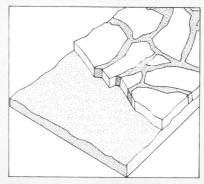

Above Crazy-paving, popular for informal paths, is made of irregular slabs of stone bedded firmly on a layer of sand to prevent wobbling.

Above Paved areas may be brightened and given added interest by leaving pockets of soil between the stones. These spaces can be planted with suitable hardy trailing and carpeting plants such as prostrate thymes and dwarf varieties of pinks. Less hardy subjects may be grown in tubs and brought under cover for the winter.

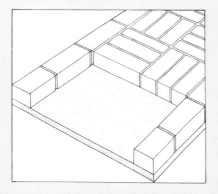

Left Bricks laid on edge give the opportunity for many different patterns and make paths that are both attractive and durable.

Steps

Where the garden is on a sloping site, different levels can be created, connected with each other by steps. These may be constructed of concrete, mixed and laid as described for paths on the opposite page. Most gardeners, however, will probably prefer to use more attractive-looking materials such as bricks or stone.

Whatever materials are used, there are certain principles of design and construction which should be observed. In the first place steps, like paths, should be wide enough to enable two people to walk along them side-by-side in comfort.

Secondly, each tread should measure at the very least twelve inches (thirty cm), or better still sixteen inches (forty cm), from front to back, to give adequate foot room.

Thirdly, each step should be of the same height, which should not be more than six or seven inches (fifteen–eighteen cm) so that the very young and the elderly can manage them without difficulty. Some experts recommend that each step should slope very slightly downwards from front to back, so as to give greater strength, since any settlement that occurs will tend to consolidate the structure.

It is important that all paving, whether steps, terraces or paths, should be made absolutely firm. Even if only one brick or stone wobbles when trodden on it can lead to a nasty accident. A foundation of six inches of well-rammed rubble or hardcore is needed under steps and terraces, and also under main paths which are going to have to bear the weight not only of people but of loaded wheelbarrows.

Paths which are not going to be subjected to much traffic may have the hardcore omitted, so long as the soil is completely firm and will not sink. Spread a layer of sand, three inches (seven cm) deep, over the hardcore or earth, rake it level and bed the bricks or stone slabs on it, tapping them firmly into position so that they do not rock. Scoop away sand or add to it as necessary to allow for irregularities; this will need to be done more often with natural stone than with precast slabs, which are uniform in thickness.

If slabs are laid close to each other, weeds will appear in the crevices. To avoid this, they may be laid half an inch (one cm) apart and the joints filled with mortar.

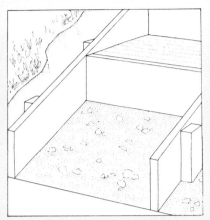

Above Concrete steps, made of the same mixture as concrete paths and laid in the same way, are very hard-wearing and suitable for those parts of the garden where appearance is not of first importance.

Above Risers of bricks set in mortar are attractive in appearance and provide a firm support for the treads, which may be of concrete or of stone, either natural or in the form of precast slabs.

For making mortar joints between paving blocks, thoroughly mix one part of cement and five parts of sand. Do not add water. It is quicker, easier and less messy, and it gives better results, if the mixture is used dry. Simply brush it over the surface of the paving with a stiff brush so that it completely fills the joints. Be careful to sweep away all surplus mortar from the surface, so as not to discolour the slabs.

Within a short time rain and moisture from the ground and the atmosphere will have been absorbed by the dry mixture and caused it to set firmly.

Walls

Where there is a difference in ground level, a simple and pleasing way of dealing with it is to build a retaining wall of stonework. One method is to set the stone in cement mortar. That will, however, look rather bare and will rob you of the chance of growing the attractive plants which are suitable for walls.

To grow such plants, the wall is built without mortar, a process known as dry-walling. As the weight of earth to be held in place may be considerable, particularly after rain, the wall should not be vertical or it may topple forwards. It must be built with a backward slope from base to top.

Start by digging a trench about nine inches (twenty-five cm) deep and somewhat wider than the blocks of stone to be used. Fill this trench with hard rubble and ram it down. Lay the first course of stones, cover with an inch or so (2.5 cm) of soil, then lay a second course, with the joints coming above the middles of the stones below; this makes a stronger job than if the joints are directly above each other. Continue in this way, and finish with a top layer rather wider than the rest from back to front, so that rain will be directed back into the earth instead of running down the inside of the wall and weakening it by washing away the soil.

Above A dry-stone retaining wall between different levels in the garden offers the opportunity to grow a wide variety of the many attractive plants which are particularly well suited to such situations.

Rock Gardens

Ground that slopes naturally from one level to another may make an excellent site for a rock garden. On the other hand, a garden that is entirely level can be contoured so as to add interest to an otherwise rather flat scene by the creation of artificial mounds of soil with slabs of stone embedded in them. Here a vast range of alpine plants may be grown which enjoy such surroundings and look their best in them.

The most widely used types of rock are limestone and sandstone. If available, local stone is usually best, both because it blends with its surroundings and because it is likely to be cheaper; delivery charges from a distant quarry may be more than the cost of the stone itself. Not a great deal is needed, however.

Using too many rocks is not only unnecessarily expensive but tends to produce a fussy and unnatural effect. All that is needed is enough stone to give the effect of a few rocky outcrops protruding above the soil.

The site for the rock garden should be an open one. Though a hedge, fence or trees a short distance away may be useful as a windbreak, avoid constant shade.

Having established the desired contour of the ground, either from a natural slope or by digging out and mounding up the soil, place a large rock at one corner, tilting it slightly backwards. Continue with a line of rocks, diminishing in size, similarly tilted and so arranged that their strata all run in the same direction, the last one being half buried. Then place a similar line at right angles to the first. If enough stones are available, another layer can be built further up the slope, and perhaps a third. Take care to lay them with their strata all running the same way, so that they look as if they are part of the same underlying rock formation.

Fill in between the rocks with soil, making sure that no air pockets are left. If the soil is at all heavy, mix in plenty of coarse sand or grit so as to improve the drainage.

There is a very wide range of different types of plant to choose from for the rock garden, from small upright conifers and dwarf shrubs to creeping plants that cascade over the rocks, and from brightly flowered rock-roses to the succulent rosette-forming plants such as stonecrops and houseleeks.

The plants are available in containers, so they can be transplanted at any time with the minimum of root disturbance. The best times, however, are early autumn in mild districts and spring in colder areas; summer planting may cause problems through drought before new roots have developed. Using a trowel or hand-fork, dig a hole big enough for the plant's roots, and fill this with water; also water the plant in its pot so that it comes out easily. When the water has drained away put in the plant and firm the soil round it, making sure that no air-pockets are left. A layer of grit round the plant will prevent surface waterlogging, which may cause rot.

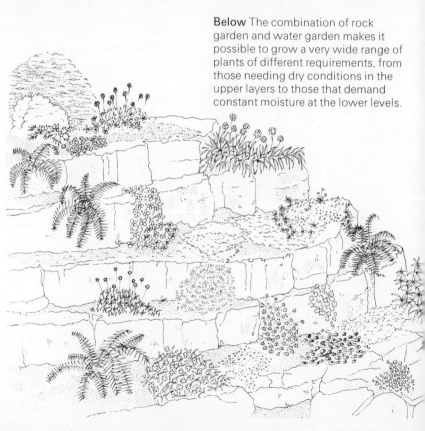

Below The combination of rock garden and water garden makes it possible to grow a very wide range of plants of different requirements, from those needing dry conditions in the upper layers to those that demand constant moisture at the lower levels.

Above To start construction, place a large rock at the corner and smaller ones to form two lines branching out from it at right-angles. Fill in with gritty soil to ensure rapid drainage.

Above Additional tiers of stone may be built, according to the material available and the height desired. The strata should all lie in the same direction, and the stones given a slight tilt so that rainwater runs into the soil, not down the slope.

Pools

Rock gardens and pools are often associated with each other as garden features. The reason is simple. Where the site is a naturally sloping one, the upper levels tend to drain rapidly after rain and so provide a suitable environment for rock plants, which dislike constant wetness.

The lower levels, however, tend to remain damp, and so provide the right conditions for plants which thrive in and around water. Where the site is naturally flat and soil has been artificially banked up to make a rock garden, the hollow from which that soil was dug will already have the makings of a pool.

The site, like that of the rock garden, should be sheltered from strong winds, but should not be overhung by trees. Fallen leaves are a nuisance to remove, but if left in the pond they decompose, polluting the water and endangering the health of fish and plants. Besides, deep shade encourages weak growth and poor flowering.

A pool should never be less than fifteen inches (about forty cm) deep, and preferably more. It should also be reasonably large, not only because a bigger surface area looks better than a smaller one but because the greater volume of water the slower it is to heat up and cool down. A small, shallow pool can become overheated or frozen solid very quickly.

The shape of a pool should always be kept simple. Pools with complicated outlines not only look fussy and unnatural but are more difficult to construct and maintain. The most popular shape for small gardens is a curved one. An easy way to achieve a pleasing outline is to lay out a length of hosepipe or stout rope roughly to shape where the pool is to be. This can then be adjusted till the result is satisfactory, and the final position fixed with wooden pegs driven into the ground to serve as a guide for the spade in cutting the outline into the earth. When excavating the soil, leave a shelf along the side for growing marginal plants.

The easiest and generally most satisfactory lining for a pool is plastic sheet specially made for the purpose. Ordinary PVC or polythene perishes too quickly, but nylon-reinforced sheeting sold specially for pools can be expected to last for ten years, and butyl rubber longer still.

To find the size of sheet required, add twice the maximum depth of the pool to the length and to the breadth. After removing all stones from the excavation, and lining it with a layer of sand to give smoothness, spread the sheeting over it and hold this down round the edges with bricks or stones. Run water into the pool slowly through a hosepipe.

When the pool is full, surplus sheeting may be cut off, so as to leave an overlap of about eight inches (twenty cm) all round. Finish by covering the edge with paving or rock-garden stone, slightly overhanging the pool, both to hold the lining in place and to hide it. Always keep the pool filled; sunlight shining direct on to the plastic may cause deterioration.

Below A fountain in the pool not only gives a decorative effect but aerates the water, increasing its oxygen content and improving the living conditions for plants and fish. A submersible electric pump, connected by waterproof cable to a mains point installed by a qualified electrician, circulates water from the pool itself, not from a tap, drawing it in at the base and sending it up through a nozzle which produces a jet.

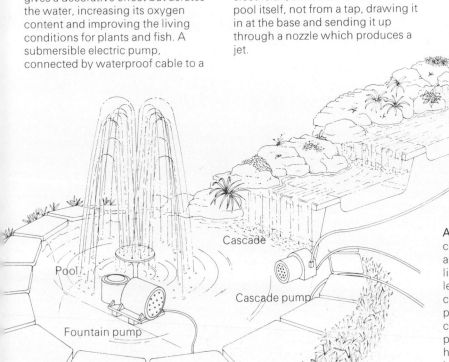

Cascade

Pool

Fountain pump

Cascade pump

Above The cascade shown here in cross-section is made up of a channel arranged in a series of waterfalls and lined with plastic sheeting to prevent leakage. A submersible pump concealed below the surface of the pool at the bottom keeps the water continuously in circulation by pumping it up through tubing to the highest point of the channel and letting it flow down by the force of gravity.

Surface Preparation

Producing a Tilth

After the ground has been dug (see pages 184–5), preferably in the autumn, it should be left rough through the winter so that frost can penetrate the clods of earth. After several months of exposure to freezing and thawing, these should readily break down when drying winds get to work on them in the spring. Then it should be a simple and relatively effortless matter to produce a good surface, known as *tilth*, when sowing time comes.

Choose a day when the soil is dry enough not to cling to the feet, but moist enough to be worked easily. First it will be necessary to cultivate the top six inches (fifteen cm) or so of soil with a garden fork or pronged cultivator to break down the clods and make the ground more or less level. Do not go any deeper, or you may bring to the surface the weeds, manure or other organic matter that was buried during digging, together with lumps of unweathered soil which will not crumble and should remain well buried. Cultivate thoroughly enough to break up all clods, but do not overdo things to the extent that the ground becomes compacted and the benefits of opening up the soil are lost.

Fertilizer may be incorporated with the soil during cultivation; if the amount is small, mix it with dry sand to ensure even distribution. At the same time, any weeds that have made their appearance should be removed, together with large stones.

It is a good idea to have two buckets or other receptacles with you, one for the stones and the other for the weeds, which if annual can go on the compost heap (see page 183) and if perennial are best burnt. Do not overdo the removal of stones; a certain proportion of smaller ones helps to keep the soil open, so that rain can both enter and drain away easily.

To get rid of any remaining lumps and make the surface even, the customary method is to tread over the bed with a shuffling movement, as illustrated on the right. This may be useful on light soils, so long as the ground is not wet and the treading is done very lightly.

Where the soil is heavy, however, treading can seriously damage the soil structure and result in poor germination and growth. In such conditions, therefore, it is best not to tread the soil in order to break up lumps but to use a rake.

Light soils may be trodden to make the surface even before raking. Heavy soil is best not trodden; to do so may seriously damage its structure.

Raking is done with a light back and forth movement, the teeth of the rake just entering the surface and moving as little soil as possible.

To make a drill, stretch a line along the row and draw a pointed stick or hoe along it to produce a furrow of suitable depth for the type of seed.

Sow seeds as thinly as possible along the drill. This avoids overcrowded, weak seedlings and reduces the amount of thinning needed later.

After the initial cultivation has been completed, the seed-bed will be ready for its final raking in preparation for sowing. Raking is a simple operation, and the results should be satisfactory if three things are borne in mind. First, the surface should be in the right state, not too wet and not too dry. Secondly, the ground should not be walked on more than necessary; make it a rule not to tread on any part again once it has been raked. Begin at one end and work backwards, so that you do not have to retrace your steps. Thirdly, do not attempt to rake too deeply, only the top inch or two (three–five cm).

For right-handed people, the best way to use a rake is to hold the upper end of the handle with the right hand, palm downwards, and the lower part of the handle with the left hand, palm upwards. For left-handed people, the position of the arms should be reversed. Bend slightly forwards, with the arms extended so that the handle is as near to the horizontal as possible. This will ensure that the teeth of the rake enter the ground at the correct angle. Then, by moving your arms comfortably to and fro, you will find that the rake sweeps backwards and forwards, reducing the surface to the required tilth with the minimum of effort.

The surface should not be made any finer than is required by the nature of the seed to be sown. Large seeds, such as peas and beans, need only a fairly coarse tilth, while small seeds need a finer one. The fineness of the surface should not, however, be taken too far, especially with soils composed of clay or silt. With these, the microscopic particles may cake together after rain and then dry into a hard surface crust, known as a *cap*, through which emerging seedlings may find it difficult, or even impossible, to force their way.

In addition, too dense a surface may prevent air from reaching the roots of young plants, where it is needed for strong, healthy growth. The supply of water, too, may be inadequate where a cap has formed. Rain, unable to penetrate the hard crust, may either run off or stay on the surface till it evaporates, and the roots receive no benefit from it.

Where the soil is so fine that it is difficult to prevent a crust from forming, a sprinkling of sharp sand or grit raked into the surface may improve matters.

Sowing

After a satisfactory tilth has been produced, it is important not to spoil the surface by undue trampling on it during the process of sowing. Where flower beds are concerned, it is very often possible to stand on a path or grass verge and reach across to do the sowing, without putting a foot on the soil. This is usual when sowing annuals in the front of the border.

Vegetable plots, however, are usually too wide for this. In such cases one way to overcome the problem is to place a length of board beside the row and stand on it while sowing. The board will distribute your weight and avoid leaving footprints. Since even with this method the soil under the board is bound to become compacted to some extent, there is a trend towards dividing the vegetable garden into separate beds about four feet (120 cm) wide, narrow enough for the middle to be within reach of the pathways between; sowing and further operations such as thinning and weeding can then be carried out without treading on the beds at all. It is claimed that yield may be improved, and cultivation made easier, by this method.

There are two ways of sowing in the garden. The first is to broadcast it, and that is the method generally used for lawns and for annuals. Rake the ground lightly in one direction so that the teeth leave shallow furrows. Scatter the seeds thinly over the treated area and finish with a light raking at right angles to the first.

The second way to sow seeds is in rows, and this is the method most often used in the vegetable garden. Furrows, known as drills, are produced by stretching a garden line across the bed and drawing the blade of a hoe or a pointed stick along it so as to make a depression in the surface of the soil. Sow the seed along the bottom of the drill, taking a pinch at a time and letting it trickle out as thinly as possible between thumb and forefinger.

Sowing thinly saves seed, reduces the need for thinning later, lessens overcrowding and makes for sturdier plants. After sowing, cover the drill with a light raking of soil, working along the row, not across it, so as not to displace seed.

The soil should be moist (but not wet) to help germination. If necessary, water before sowing, using a fine rose and being careful not to cause the surface to cake.

Bird Protection

Most birds are among the gardener's best friends for most of the time, devouring large numbers of insects, grubs and other pests during the course of the season, together with vast quantities of weed seeds. They can, however, become major pests at sowing time. Not only do many of them enjoy the seeds of cultivated plants as well as weeds but they find seed-beds ideal for taking dust-baths.

Bird scarers made of bright metal foil or plastic may work for a time, but the birds quickly become used to them. The best way is to prevent the birds from getting at the seeds by means of a barrier such as wire-netting tunnels placed over the rows. Where seed has been broadcast, an effective method is to stretch black thread across the bed, just above the surface. The invisible strands will pluck at the birds and frighten them away.

Above Seeds sown in rows may be protected from birds by means of fine-mesh wire netting.

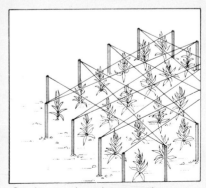

Seeds sown broadcast may be protected by black thread stretched between wooden pegs.

Propagation

CUTTINGS

A wide range of garden plants can be readily grown from cuttings, a method of propagation of particular importance for the large number of cultivars which can be increased only by vegetative means.

Cuttings may be taken from several different parts of the plant and at different stages of maturity; rooting is quickest with soft young material. The process consists of choosing the right material and giving it the right conditions for rooting.

In a great many cases the cuttings are detached from the parent plant before rooting takes place. In other cases it may be necessary, or safer and more reliable, to induce the cutting material to form roots before detaching it completely.

Hardwood Cuttings

With many woody plants, these are the easiest of all cuttings to propagate successfully. Because they are taken from deciduous trees and shrubs during the leafless dormant period, they do not run the same risk of shrivelling through loss of moisture by transpiration as leafy cuttings do.

Though hardwood cuttings may be taken at any time during the dormant season, generally it is considered that they will have the best capacity for rooting if taken just when the leaves fall in the autumn. The next best time is just before bud-burst in the spring, but then protection may be needed to reduce water loss from unfolding leaves before roots form.

Choice of wood is of the utmost importance. The best chance of success is with vigorous shoots that are one season old. The most effective way of ensuring that there is an ample supply of such wood when required is to prune the parent plant hard back during the previous dormant season.

Remove the cutting with the whole of the year's growth. Using a sharp pair of secateurs, cut the stem right back to where it joins the old branch, leaving no snag. Though some plants will root readily from any part of the stem, generally it is the part at the base that roots best. The tip, if it roots at all, is likely to produce an inferior plant.

Even a leafless cutting loses some moisture to the air. To prevent it from drying out, do not allow too much to protrude above the ground. Generally the best length for most hardwood cuttings is about six inches (fifteen cm). Cut the base straight across; it is advisable to do so just below a bud where cuttings with soft pith are concerned, and many experts consider it best to do with others too. Cut the top end off with a slanting cut above a bud.

The prepared cuttings may either be planted straight out in the ground or kept for the time being in a box of sand with just their tips exposed.

Before inserting, the bases of the cuttings may be dipped in a hormone rooting product. Make a slit in the soil about five inches (12 cm) deep with a spade and insert the cuttings in this about four inches (ten cm) apart. If the soil is heavy, add some sand; cuttings need air in order to root. After inserting the cuttings, firm the soil round them so that the top inch or so (twenty-five mm) is above the surface. Red currants and gooseberries – usually grown on a single stem – should have all buds but the top three removed before insertion.

Trees and shrubs that may be propagated from hardwood cuttings include the following:

Black currants	*Populus* (poplar)
Cornus (some)	*Prunus* (some)
Cotoneaster (many)	Red currants
Deutzia	*Ribes* (flowering)
Forsythia	Roses (many)
Gooseberries	*Salix* (willow)
Kerria	*Spiraea* (many)
Leycesteria	*Viburnum*
Philadelphus	(deciduous)
	Weigela

1 Take hardwood cuttings by removing the whole of the season's growth, using a sharp pair of secateurs. Cut right back to the new stem's junction with the older branch from which it grew.

2 Trim the stem by cutting the base straight across and making a sloping cut at the top end, just above a bud. Rapid and vigorous rooting may be stimulated by dipping the base of the cutting in a hormone rooting product.

3 Make a slit in well-cultivated soil, adding sand if it is heavy, and insert the prepared cuttings vertically in this. Firm the soil round the cuttings, leaving about an inch (twenty-five mm) above the surface.

Semi-ripe Cuttings

Several trees and shrubs may be successfully propagated by means of what are known as semi-ripe cuttings. These are taken in the latter part of the summer from the current season's shoots, which have slowed down in growth and become firm, though not fully hardened, at the base, while the tip is still green.

Cut the shoot right back to its junction with the old stem from which is has grown. Trim it cleanly across at the base and remove the soft upper part, making a slanting cut slightly above a bud.

The usual length for cuttings of this type is from four to six inches (ten–fifteen cm). Remove all the leaves from the lower two inches (five cm), cutting them off flush with the stem. To complete the preparation, the base of the cutting may be dipped in a rooting hormone.

To prevent the cuttings from drying out some form of closed frame is generally used. Good results may be obtained from a cold frame, containing well cultivated soil with plenty of peat and sand mixed in. Make holes in this one and a half inches (four cm) deep, insert the cuttings, water through a fine rose to settle the soil.

Several deciduous plants may be raised from both semi-ripe and hardwood cuttings (see list opposite). Among suitable evergreens are many from the following genera:

Abelia	*Escallonia*
Aucuba	*Hebe*
Ceanothus	*Hypericum*
Choisya	*Lavandula*
Daphne	*Magnolia*
Elaeagnus	*Pyracantha*

Heeled Cuttings

In many cases, especially among evergreens, semi-ripe cuttings are found to root more readily if they are taken with what is know as a *heel*. Some, such as *Pyracantha* and evergreen *Ceanothus*, may be difficult to root without it. What makes a cutting of this type is the inclusion at its base of a small piece of the parent stem. This may be obtained by pulling off the shoot so as to bring a strip of old wood with it, or by slicing off the shoot with a sharp knife, taking a sliver of the parent stem as well. Trim away any ragged tail left on the heel. After this the heeled cutting may be dipped in rooting hormone and inserted in the usual way.

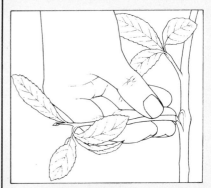

1 To make a heeled cutting, pull the shoot off at its base so that it brings with it a thin piece of old wood from the parent stem. To trim the cutting ready for planting, cut off any tail pulled away with the heel.

1 Remove a semi-ripe shoot with all its current season's growth. Take off any soft wood towards the tip.

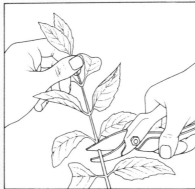

2 Trim the cutting to four to six inches (ten–fifteen cm) and remove all leaves from the bottom two inches (five cm).

3 To encourage rapid and vigorous rooting the base of the cutting may be dipped in rooting hormone.

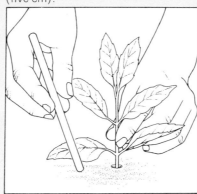

4 Insert cuttings 1½ inches (four cm) deep in sandy soil. Water through fine rose before covering.

2 After trimming the shoot by cutting off soft growth from its top end, removing all leaves from the lower portion and dipping the heeled base into rooting hormone, insert it into prepared soil and water it in.

Softwood Cuttings

These are taken from the tips of new stems while they are in active growth and before they have started to harden. Since their tissues are soft and their leaves immature, they are liable to collapse rapidly. On the other hand, because they come from the most vigorously growing part of the plant they have the greatest potential for producing roots in the right conditions.

It is extremely important that softwood cuttings should not be allowed to wilt. For this reason some gardeners take them early in the morning, before they have time to suffer water loss as the day advances. Once taken, they should never be exposed to drying conditions; if they cannot be planted at once, place them in water or in a polythene bag, for the time being, and be careful to keep them out of direct sunlight.

The time to take softwood cuttings of outdoor plants is spring or early summer, as soon as young shoots are long enough.

With indoor plants, many of which are commonly propagated by this means, softwood cuttings can be obtained later in the season by forcing the plants into rapid growth through increased heat. Pruning hard will usually provide added stimulus.

Softwood cuttings are usually made two to four inches (five–ten cm) long, but excellent results can often be obtained from shorter lengths of some easily-rooted plants such as fuchsias. Leave the tip intact, cut the base cleanly across just below a leaf joint and remove the leaves from the bottom third. To prevent rot, dip the base in a fungicide. A combined rooting hormone and fungicide is often used, but if so it must be of softwood strength.

Insert the cuttings to about a third of their length in pots or boxes of suitable compost and treat as semi-ripe cuttings (see page 193). A very large number of herbaceous perennials and greenhouse plants are raised in this way.

Root Cuttings

Propagation by means of root cuttings can be highly successful with certain plants.

The time to take such cuttings is when the parent plant is fully dormant. Lift the plant and wash away the soil so that the root system can be clearly seen. Choose for propagation only plump young roots that have grown during the past season.

The cuttings must be thick enough to have ample food reserves, both to initiate new buds and shoots and to keep themselves alive till the resulting new plants are in full growth. In general, root cuttings propagated in a frame or greenhouse may be from two to three inches long (five–eight cm), but those in the open, which may take twice as long, will need to be at least four inches (ten cm).

To distinguish one end of the cutting from the other slice the top straight across and the bottom with a sloping cut.

To reduce the danger of rotting it is wise to treat the cuttings with a fungicidal powder; those containing captan are suitable. A simple way is to shake the cuttings and powder together in a polythene bag.

Though it is possible to insert the cuttings outside in well-drained soil, a box or pot of compost containing loam, peat and sand placed in a frame is likely to prove quicker and better. The results will also be easier to transplant, without damage. Make holes with a dibber or stick and insert the cuttings, right side up, with their tops at surface level. Cover with a sprinkling of sharp sand. If the compost was moist no watering will be needed till shoots appear.

With thin-rooted plants, such as some phloxes and primulas, the cuttings are not buried by laid flat on the surface.

Among plants propagated by root cuttings are many belonging to the following genera:

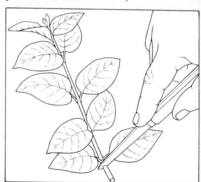

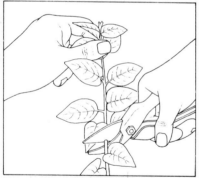

1 Cut off the top part of an actively growing young stem early in the season, before it turns woody.

2 Leaving the tip intact, trim to a suitable length (see text above), cutting just below a leaf joint.

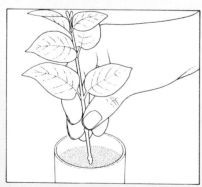

3 Remove lower leaves and dip the base in fungicide powder, alone or combined with rooting hormone.

4 Make holes in compost with a dibber and insert the cuttings. Water through a fine rose.

Acanthus	*Eryngium*
Aesculus	*Limonium*
Anchusa	*Papaver*
Anemone	*Pulsatilla*
Aralia	*Rhus*
Arnebia	*Robinia*
Catalpa	*Romneya*
Chaenomeles	*Rubus*
Clerodendron	*Spiraea*
Erodium	*Verbascum*

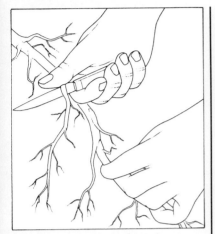

1 Sever a young root close to the parent plant and cut the top square across. Trim off all fibrous roots.

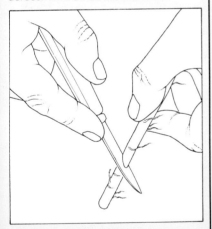

2 To distinguish the two ends, remove the lower part with a slanting cut to a suitable length (see text).

3 After powdering the cuts with fungicide, insert cuttings with their tops level with the compost.

Leaf Cuttings

Some plants may be propagated from leaves, including several house plants.

While methods vary, all plants propagated in this way share certain basic requirements for success. First, the leaf should be healthy and undamaged. Secondly, though it should be young it should also have reached full size; if not, it will use up time and energy in trying to develop rather than producing new plants. Thirdly, the compost should be open enough to admit plenty of air; a mixture of half peat and half grit is suitable. Fourthly, to prevent the leaf from drying out it must be propagated in a closed case of some kind. A domed propagator is ideal, but an inflated polythene bag supported over a flower pot will do.

The easiest cutting consists of a whole leaf complete with its stalk. Since a bruised stalk is likely to rot, the end should be cut with a sharp knife or razor-blade, using as little pressure as possible. Make a shallow hole in the compost and insert the stalk. New plantlets should appear at the end of the stalk within a few weeks, and when developed can be potted separately. Plants that may be propagated in this way include some species of *Begonia* and *Peperomia*, also *Saintpaulia* (african violet).

Another method consists of inducing the development of plantlets from leaf wounds. Lay the leaf upside down and make cuts with a razor-blade at several places across veins. Then lay the slashed leaf – top side up – on the surface of a tray of compost and peg it down. Plants propagated in this way include *Begonia rex* and *Streptocarpus*.

1 Cut a young but full-grown leaf and stalk from the parent plant. Trim off the end of the stalk.

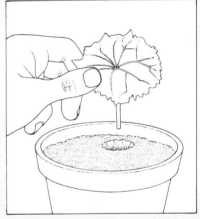

2 Make a hole in the surface of the compost, insert the stalk and firm gently. Cover to prevent drying out.

Leaf Slashing

Prepare the leaf by turning it upside down and cutting through the veins in several places, as indicated by thick lines in the drawing. Fill a tray with lightly moistened compost, lay the leaf, top side up, on the surface and peg it down with a piece of bent wire. Cover to prevent drying out. Resulting plantlets may be detached when developed enough, and potted up separately.

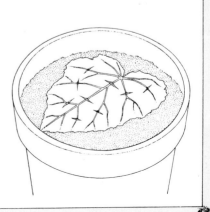

LAYERING

A very useful way of propagating many woody plants without an enclosed frame is the method known as layering, in which roots are produced before the stem is severed from the parent plant.

The process, which occurs frequently in nature, consists of the development of roots at a point where a stem is brought into contact with the soil or some other suitable medium combining moisture-holding capacity with an open texture.

The advantage of layering is that there is no danger of dehydration, as with the usual cuttings. Ordinary layering, however, calls for shoots pliable enough to reach the ground. Plants with rigid stems may need air-layering.

Simple Layering

Shoots selected for this type of layering should be young and vigorous; those produced by hard pruning at the end of the previous season are ideal. The operation is usually performed in early spring, so that the shoot has a whole season in which to develop a strong root system.

Bend the stem to the ground, and about nine inches (twenty-five cm) from its tip mix peat and sand into the soil. Make a hole four inches (ten cm) deep, with a sloping side towards the plant and a vertical side away from it. After removing sideshoots and leaves from the shoot where it reaches the hole, peg it down with wire, bending the tip end upwards against the vertical side. Wounding the base by slitting or twisting is often found to assist rooting.

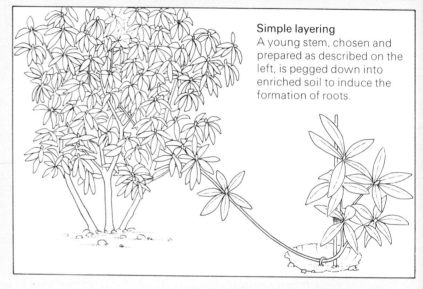

Simple layering
A young stem, chosen and prepared as described on the left, is pegged down into enriched soil to induce the formation of roots.

Air Layering

This method is not so widely used, but can be tried with stems that are too rigid or too high to be brought down to soil level. The operation is usually performed during the spring on wood of the previous season's growth, but it can also be carried out in late summer on shoots that have grown during the current season and are beginning to harden.

Starting about six inches (fifteen cm) behind the tip of the stem, remove leaves and sideshoots for a length of four or five inches (ten–twelve cm). To encourage rooting, wound this part by removing a ring of bark a quarter of an inch (five mm) wide or by making an upward slice halfway towards the centre of the stem; then treat with rooting hormone. The medium into which the roots will grow

must hold plenty of moisture; sphagnum moss is ideal, but peat will do.

Thoroughly moisten the moss or peat and place a good handful round the prepared stem, holding it in position with a square of black polythene. Bind this tightly to the stem top and bottom by means of sticky tape. When well rooted the stem may be cut off from the parent and potted up.

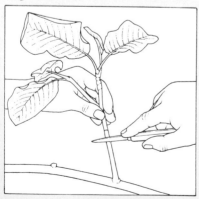

1 Trim leaves from part of the stem and wound with a knife. Treat the cut portion with rooting hormone.

2 Place moist moss or peat round the stem and cover with black polythene, bound top and bottom with tape.

3 When well rooted remove the covering and sever from the parent plant. Pot up into good compost.

DIVISION

The easiest way to increase most herbaceous perennials is by dividing them, a method much used for choice cultivars which will not come true from seed.

Young plants with fibrous crowns can usually be pulled apart by hand, and the pieces planted separately. Older clumps with tough crowns may have to be prised apart with a garden fork. If they are very hard it may be best to cut through the crown with a sharp knife and then disentangle the roots. The woody middle part of the clump is usually too old to replant; discard it and plant only young and vigorous outer portions.

Do not let the roots become dry but plant immediately, at the same depth as before. After planting give a thorough watering to settle the soil round the roots.

When dividing clumps with tough crowns it may be necessary to use a sharp knife. Replant only vigorous outer portions with good roots.

Tuber Division

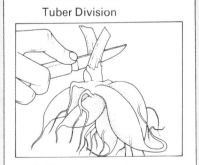

In dividing tubers such as dahlias it is important that each piece for planting should carry at least one good bud.

BULB SCALES

Lilies, and certain of their relatives such as *Nomocharis*, have bulbs surrounded by thickened scale leaves which can be used for propagation. The best time is the autumn, after flowering. With established lilies in the garden, simply scrape away enough soil to expose the bulb. Snap off some plump, undamaged scales at the base and replace the soil.

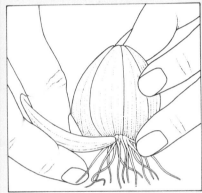

1 Snap off plump, undamaged scales at the base, treat with fungicide and place them in a mixture of peat and grit in a plastic bag.

OFFSETS

Species of several families, including houseleeks and other succulents, sword-leaved plants such as yuccas, bromeliads and many more greenhouse subjects, produce plantlets, called offsets, as side growths. These may be carefully split or cut away from the parent plant and either planted out in the open or potted up.

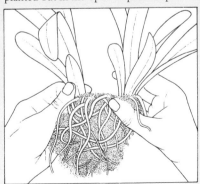

New plants appearing as sidegrowths, known as offsets, at the base of the parent plant may be removed and planted separately.

To prevent rotting, treat the scales with a fungicide powder; a simple way is to shake them with it in a bag. Then place them in a mixture of moist peat and grit in a polythene bag, inflate it and tie the neck. In a warm place, such as an airing cupboard, they will soon develop bulblets; some need a short period of cold first. Pot the bulblets and grow them on in light and warmth.

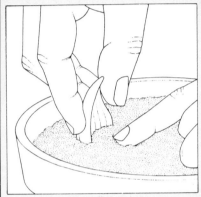

2 When bulblets have developed from the broken base, plant in pots of compost and grow in warmth at first. Next season harden off and plant out.

RUNNERS

Many plants, including strawberries and such indoor favourites as *Chlorophytum comosum* and *Saxifraga sarmentosa*, produce plantlets along runners. Peg these down with wire into pots of soil or compost so that they root into it. When the new plants are well established and growing strongly they can be severed from the parent.

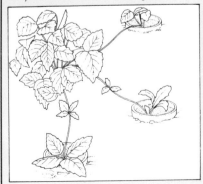

Strawberry runners may be pegged with wire into pots of soil sunk in the ground. The new plants can later be transplanted without root injury.

Planting

Planting out Seedlings

Many plants are not sown in their final quarters but transplanted as seedlings. Some hardy ones, such as cabbages and leeks, are sown in a seed-bed in the open, so as to make the best use of limited space. More tender ones are sown under glass and planted out in the open when the danger of frost is over; these include outdoor tomatoes and half-hardy annuals such as french marigolds, nemesias and petunias. Still others, too tender to go outdoors in our climate, are grown as pot-plants in the greenhouse or home.

Fill trays or pots with seed compost and firm it down gently so that the surface comes just below the rim. Scatter the seed thinly, cover lightly with compost (very small seeds may be left bare), water through a fine rose, and lay a sheet of glass covered with newspaper over the container. Remove the covering when the seedlings appear, and transplant them when they are big enough to be handled; if left they will soon become overcrowded, spindly and liable to disease. The process, illustrated below, is known as pricking out. It will give the seedlings room to develop into sturdy plants.

Bedding plants are commonly grown without further disturbance till the time comes to plant them out; meanwhile they are hardened off by gradual exposure to cooler and airier conditions. After a good watering, the plants are carefully lifted, gently separated, planted and watered in.

Newer types of container for seedlings, designed to reduce injury to roots when transplanting, include trays divided into compartments, giving each seedling a self-contained root system, and plastic channels, in which large numbers of bedding plants are now produced. Many people now use soil-blocks, moulded from special compost to form self-supporting units in which individual seedlings are raised.

Seedlings grown in pots may either be pricked out into them or sown direct; it is usual to sow three or four seeds to a pot and remove all but the strongest of the resulting seedlings. Never use too large a pot. Start with the smallest size, and as the plant grows bigger move it into larger pots one size at a time.

Planting Bulbs and Corms

With the vast range offered by nurseries and garden centres to choose from, it is possible to have bulbs and corms in flower throughout the year. (For information on what may be expected to be in flower, see the monthly chapters in the first part of the book.)

In general, the best time to plant spring-flowering bulbs and corms is in the autumn, when they are dormant. Notable exceptions to this general rule are the snowdrops and snowflakes, which settle into their new quarters more readily and give better results the following year if they are transplanted while in flower.

Most summer-flowering bulbs are usually planted in spring, when hard frosts are over and the soil is in a workable condition; but lilies are planted in October. Autumn-flowering bulbs may be planted in the summer.

Most bulbs will grow satisfactorily in any reasonably good soil, provided that it is well drained. Adding sand will help; if the soil does not contain enough, put some in the holes before planting the bulbs.

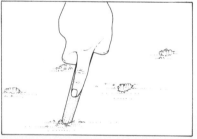

1 Prepare a second tray of compost to receive the seedlings by making holes in the surface, two inches (5 cm) apart, with a small dibber.

2 Carefully lift a batch of seedlings from one end of the tray and gently separate them, holding them by a leaf, not by the stem.

1 Make planting holes twice the depth of the bulbs (shallower in heavy soils) and place them on the bottom with their tips uppermost.

3 Lower seedlings carefully into the holes, firming each one into position by gently pressing the compost round it with the dibber.

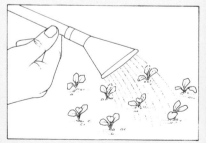

4 After pricking-out has been completed, settle the seedlings in their new quarters by watering them in through a fine rose.

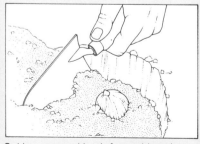

2 Use a trowel both for making the hole and for filling in the soil after planting. Take care to fill in thoroughly, leaving no pockets.

In medium to light soils bulbs are generally planted at about twice their own depth. In heavy soils it is wise to plant somewhat nearer the surface, where the soil dries out more readily after rain than it does further down. This will reduce the risk to the well-being of the bulbs that is always present if they are allowed to stand in wet conditions for long periods.

When preparing holes for planting bulbs it is always best to use a trowel rather than a dibber, so as to ensure that each hole is wide enough for the bulb to rest firmly on the bottom, with no air-pocket.

Bulbs and corms of suitable kinds may be planted in almost every part of the garden: in beds and borders, among trees and shrubs, in the rock garden, in spaces left in paving and in tubs and window boxes. Many are particularly suitable for naturalizing in grass, where once they are established they will continue to flower year after year with little attention. Special planting tools are available which cut out neat cylinders of turf and soil, but a sharp spade will do. Shown below is a method of planting with little disturbance.

1 Cut a capital H in the grass with an edging iron or sharp spade; then slice under the turf in each direction from the cross-cut to make two flaps.

2 Fold the flaps back to expose the soil, loosen it with a fork, plant the bulbs in an irregular group, and then replace the flaps as they were.

Planting Trees and Shrubs

Always make planting holes wide enough to take the roots of trees and shrubs without cramming them in. The depth should be just enough to ensure that when planting has been completed the old soil-mark at the base of the tree or shrub comes level with the surface of the ground. A simple way is to lay a cane across the hole and adjust the depth till the soil-mark coincides with the cane.

Fork over the bottom of the hole and work in plenty of organic matter, such as well rotted manure, garden compost or damp peat. Spread out the roots of plants lifted from the ground; keep the soil intact round the roots of container-grown ones. Fill in the hole and tread down firmly.

Planting should never be attempted if the ground is wet and sticky or frozen hard. If conditions are unfavourable when the plants arrive they can be heeled in till things improve by placing the roots in a shallow trench and covering them with soil. Trees and tall shrubs are usually heeled in at an angle to prevent them from being blown over.

The soil-mark on the tree should come level with a cane laid across the hole. When filling in, shake the tree to settle the soil round the roots.

Planting Roses

The most widely grown bush roses are propagated by budding. In this process, the named variety is grown on the roots of a suitable wild rose. The point at which the two join, known as the bud union, can be seen as a swelling where the brown rootstock and the green stems meet.

The planting hole should be deep enough to allow the bud union to come just below the surface of the ground. Mound up soil to the necessary height in the centre of the hole, sit the bush on this, spread out the roots and start filling in the hole. Shake the plant gently to work the soil round the roots and tread it down lightly but firmly.

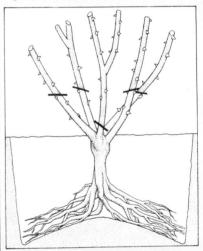

Mound up soil in the centre of the planting hole so that the bud-union of the rose bush to be planted comes just below the surface of the soil.

Growing Bags

Large plastic bags filled with special compost may be used to grow vegetables prone to root troubles, such as tomatoes.

Supporting

Supporting Flowers

It is important that those plants which need support are given it as early as possible. If the task is postponed, a heavy downpour of rain, a sudden gust of wind, or even the sheer weight of new growth, may cause a plant to collapse. Even if the stem is not snapped, it may be badly kinked, and once this has happened it is difficult, if not impossible, to restore the health and appearance of the plant. It will certainly take considerably more work to do so than if the necessary support had been given in good time.

As a general rule, herbaceous perennials in the front of the border are low-growing and do not need any support. Those in the middle of the border include many that are sturdy enough to stand up by themselves, but there are several that must be given support if they are to grow well and look their best. In a large number of cases all that is needed is a few twiggy pea sticks pushed into the ground between the new shoots when they appear in the spring.

Plants that make taller clumps may need more support. An effective method is to fix strong wide-meshed netting, stretched between stout canes, above the clump, about eight inches (twenty cm) from ground level. If this is done while the shoots are small, they will grow up through the netting and hide it from view.

There are many other methods of supporting those clumps with stems that are too slender in relation to their height to support themselves; some examples are shown below.

For those plants that bear their flowers in tall spikes, such as delphiniums and hollyhocks, it is best to support each spike with a separate cane, to which it should be tied as it grows. When full-grown, the spike should come above its supporting cane.

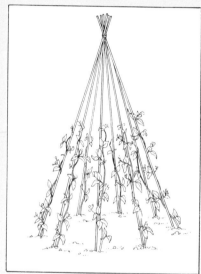

A circle of canes arranged like a Red Indian tepee provides a practical and attractive support for sweet peas in a limited space.

Trees

It is always best to stake trees at the time of planting. Until they have developed extensive enough root systems to anchor themselves securely into the surrounding soil, there is always the danger that they will be blown over by strong winds. Even if that does not happen, they may be so badly rocked about in their new quarters that they suffer damage from which they never fully recover. The better the support a tree is given at the time of transplanting, the sooner it will be able to support itself later on.

Stakes should be strong, durable and preferably new; old ones may have become brittle and liable to snap. Drive the stake into the bottom of the hole before starting to plant (see page 199), and as soon as the planting is completed tie the tree to it.

Many different types of tie may be used for the purpose, ranging from cord to the various plastic and rubber kinds on sale at garden centres and stores. Some examples are shown below. Whatever method is used, it should be one that prevents the tree from rubbing against the stake, or injury may result.

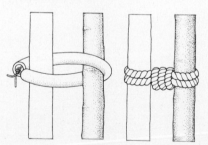

Hose and wire tie   Cord or rope tie

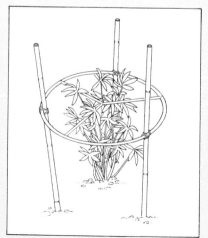

Strong support for herbaceous plants is given by this metal ring, which is soon hidden by foliage, together with its supporting canes.

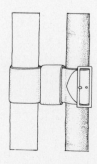

Plastic tie with buckle and spacer

A triangle of outward-sloping canes, with twine tied round them at suitable levels, provides unobtrusive support for plants with slender stems.

Fruit Trees

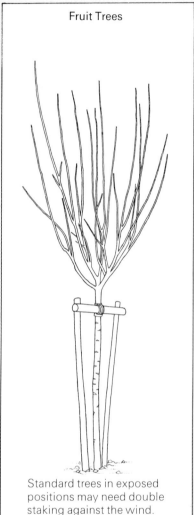

Standard trees in exposed positions may need double staking against the wind.

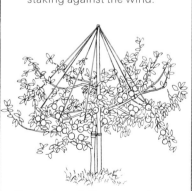

Supports radiating maypole-like from a central stake hold up heavily laden branches.

Raspberries

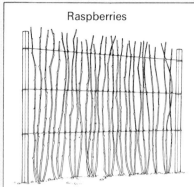

Raspberry canes are trained on wires between posts. Remove old canes after fruiting and tie new ones in their place.

Peas and Beans

The long-established method of supporting traditional varieties of garden pea is by means of twiggy sticks pushed into the ground beside the rows of plants. In recent years, however, pea-sticks have become difficult to obtain, and plastic netting, strung between posts alongside the row, is now widely used instead.

Runner beans reach a considerable height, as do climbing french beans, and when grown in a continuous row they need a very stable supporting structure which can withstand strong winds without being blown down. Many gardeners grow them up circles of canes tied together at the top like tepees, which stand up to the wind better and look decorative.

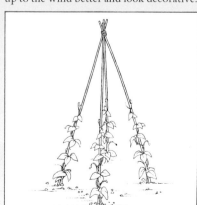

In limited space, and for decorative effect, beans may be grown up stout canes arranged like a tepee.

Peas

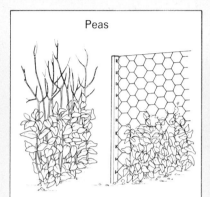

Peasticks (left) are becoming scarce, and netting fixed to posts (right) is now widely used as an effective support.

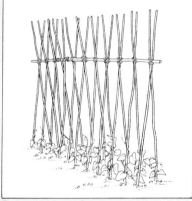

Poles or canes, fixed to a cross-piece towards the top, provide secure support for runner beans.

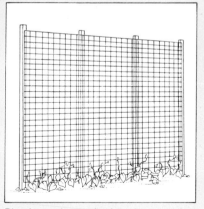

Plastic mesh attached to stout posts makes a useful and pleasing support for twining and other climbing plants.

Training

Climbers

True climbers are those plants that have some means of supporting themselves. Though there are many different ones for the gardener to choose from, they all belong to one of three basic kinds.

The first kind consists of those plants that are able to cling to walls and other vertical surfaces by themselves. They include the ivies, which cling by means of special aerial roots, and the Virginia creeper, which clings by means of sucker pads. Once they have attached themselves, they need no additional support, but a temporary cane in the early stages may help them to make a good start.

The second kind consists of plants that climb by means of twining. Some, such as honeysuckle, twine with their whole stems, others, such as vines, with their tendrils, and still others, such as clematis, with their leaf-stalks.

The third kind consists of plants that do not cling or twine but scramble over anything within reach of their vigorous, supple stems. For plants that do not cling by themselves, a wall or other flat surface is not enough. There must be projecting supports of some kind, round which stems or other parts of the plants can twine, or to which non-twining plants can be tied.

Several different systems of support for use on walls are illustrated below. The simplest and least obtrusive method is to stretch wires an inch (2.5 cm) or so in front of the wall. Do not use ordinary nails to hold the wires; they soon rust and break. Galvanized vine-eyes, which can be either hammered or screwed into the wall, will give many years of trouble-free service. A widely used method of support, which can be an attractive feature in itself, particularly when the plants are leafless, is a panel of trellis. This can be made cheaply and easily at home from wooden laths, or bought ready-made from a garden centre, where other versions made of plastic or wire mesh may also be available.

Wall Shrubs

In addition to climbers, there are many other shrubs which are particularly suitable for growing against walls and fences. The first group of these consists of shrubs originating from warmer climates and rather too tender to be grown in the open ground; they are described in catalogues as 'not reliably hardy without wall protection'. Many are evergreens, tolerant of cold but needing shelter from wind.

The second group of non-climbing wall shrubs consists of those which are quite hardy in the open and are placed against a wall not to protect them from the weather but to enable them to be grown within a limited space. Many strong-growing hardy shrubs such as the forsythias may soon become too big for the small garden, but trained against a wall can be kept within bounds.

Two points need careful attention. First, the plants should be suited to the aspect; it is no use putting a sun-lover against a north wall. Secondly, always leave at least nine inches (twenty-three cm) between the base of the plant and the wall, where the soil tends to be very dry.

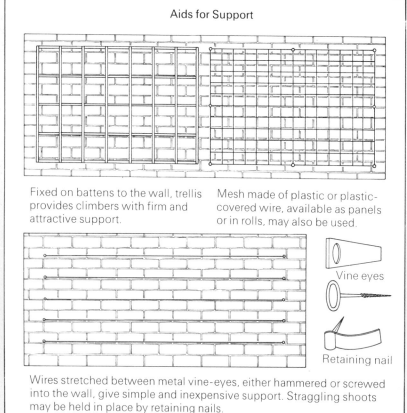

Aids for Support

Fixed on battens to the wall, trellis provides climbers with firm and attractive support.

Mesh made of plastic or plastic-covered wire, available as panels or in rolls, may also be used.

Vine eyes

Retaining nail

Wires stretched between metal vine-eyes, either hammered or screwed into the wall, give simple and inexpensive support. Straggling shoots may be held in place by retaining nails.

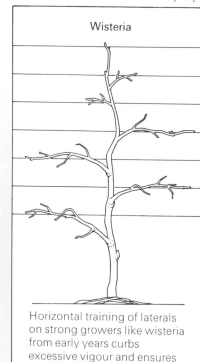

Wisteria

Horizontal training of laterals on strong growers like wisteria from early years curbs excessive vigour and ensures even spacing over the wall.

Roses

It is important when growing roses against walls, fences, screens and similar structures to train the main shoots as far as possible into a horizontal position. This makes for more balanced and easily managed growth and results in a better display of flowers.

When choosing roses for walls, bear in mind the area to be covered. Ramblers and other strong growers which produce vigorous annual replacement shoots and need severe pruning (see page 216) may be too rampant for small spaces. Climbing sports of modern hybrids are popular for such situations: they take up less room, need little pruning except dead-heading, and are mostly repeat-flowering.

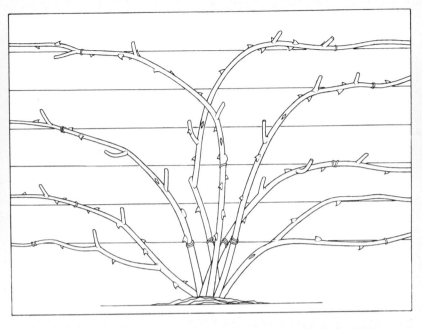

Right New season's canes of ramblers are trained in to replace last year's, which are cut out at the base after they have finished flowering.

Training Cordons

Where space is too limited for apples and pears to be grown as standards or bushes, they can still be grown as cordons. To control vigour the single main stem, grafted on a dwarfing rootstock, is fixed to wires at an angle of 45 degrees. Summer pruning of laterals to three leaves and sub-laterals to one or two leaves leads to the formation of fruiting spurs.

Training Espaliers

Espalier apples and pears consist of a main vertical stem carrying branches in horizontal tiers, usually about fifteen inches (forty cm) apart. They are ideally suited to growing on walls or fences, where the added protection may save them from the spring frosts which sometimes destroy the blossoms of fruit trees grown in the open. Espaliers may also be grown alongside paths or as both attractive and productive screens between vegetable and fruit plots and the rest of the garden. Espaliers are usually sold with three or four tiers. A well produced espalier is the result of a considerable outlay of time and skill, and needs further time and skill from the gardener if it is to be kept shapely and productive. For the purposes of training and pruning each branch is treated as a cordon. Since considerable weight of fruit may be produced, each branch must be securely fixed to a stout wire. Examine ties regularly to see they are not too tight.

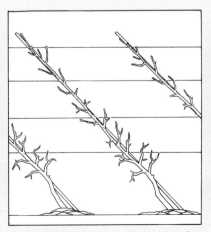

High quality apples and pears can be produced in a limited space on cordons, trained on wires and hard-pruned in summer.

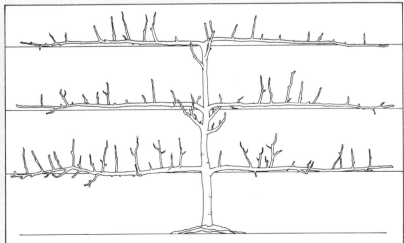

Espalier apples and pears, trained on wires either against a wall or to form separating screens, are useful and pleasingly formal.

Watering

The first and most important rule is never to give water to plants except when they can make use of it. If they cannot, the water will not merely be wasted but may do harm. This is particularly true of plants in pots; more houseplants, it is said, are killed by overwatering than by underwatering. Roots – except for those of water-plants and bog-plants – cease to function properly if kept constantly wet, and may rot; the plant is then unable to take up water.

During most of the year there should be enough moisture in reasonably good garden soil for watering to be unnecessary; and the more compost or other organic matter there is in the soil to hold moisture in store, the longer that period of adequacy will last.

However, there often comes a time in late spring and summer when soil moisture runs low, and if water is not applied plants may wilt. That leads to the second rule: water plants in good time; if allowed to flag they may never fully recover.

The third rule is to water thoroughly. If only enough water is given to wet the surface layer, and the soil beneath remains dry, the result will be that the lower roots will tend to shrivel and surface roots develop instead. The plant will then be vulnerable to drought when the surface dries out, which may coincide with an official ban on watering gardens.

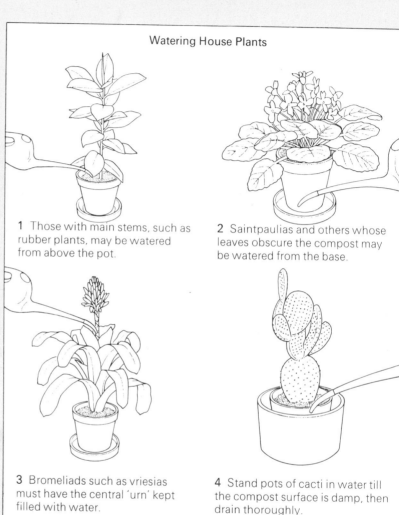

Watering House Plants

1 Those with main stems, such as rubber plants, may be watered from above the pot.

2 Saintpaulias and others whose leaves obscure the compost may be watered from the base.

3 Bromeliads such as vriesias must have the central 'urn' kept filled with water.

4 Stand pots of cacti in water till the compost surface is damp, then drain thoroughly.

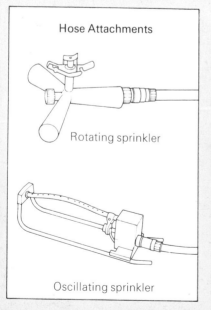

Hose Attachments

Rotating sprinkler

Oscillating sprinkler

There are several different ways of watering. The easiest is by means of a can. The two-gallon (nine litre) size is the most commonly used for general garden purposes; bigger ones are heavy and awkward, and smaller ones take too many journeys to and from the tap. (A small one is, however, useful for house-plants.) The can should have a long spout and a detachable fine rose.

A hosepipe from an outside tap will save many journeys. Buy the reinforced kind; cheap hoses kink and spring leaks. For watering an area, perforated flat hose may be used, but its continuous spray tends to saturate the ground. Better are sprinklers, either rotating ones or the oscillating kind, which waters a rectangular area.

The fourth rule is never to water so vigorously that the surface of the ground becomes beaten down. This is particularly important where seed-beds are concerned; a surface that has been battered may harden into a crust through which seedlings cannot force their way.

Particular care needs to be taken with seed-trays, where heavy watering will not only compact the surface but may wash seed and seedlings away. Using a fine rose, start by directing the water not on to the tray but to one side of it; pass the can steadily across the tray and finish on the other side of it. This will save the seed and seedlings from a sudden rush of water when pouring starts and stops.

Lawns

New Lawn Construction

Among the first considerations when a new lawn is planned is what it is intended for. Is it primarily to be looked at or to be used? On the answer to that question depends not only its design (covered in the Garden Planning section between pages 8 and 25) but the choice of the grass. If the purpose of the lawn is simply to give visual pleasure, a mixture exclusively of fine-leaved fescue and bent may be grown, which will give a velvety sward but will not stand up to hard wear. If, on the other hand, the lawn is intended to be constantly played on by growing children, it will need the addition of tougher species such as perennial rye-grass. Decide what is best suited to your needs.

The site for a lawn should be an open one with plenty of sunshine for at least some of the day. Heavy shade from trees should be avoided, not only because lawn grasses need light but because the soil in such places tends to become too dry for them to survive. On the other hand, ground that is constantly wet should also be avoided. Unless it can be made suitable by draining, it is best used for plants that prefer damp conditions.

The lawn is an important feature of most gardens. Properly constructed and maintained, it will give many years of pleasure.

Levelling a Sloping Site

1 Remove the topsoil to a spade's depth from the whole of the slope and pile it in a heap to one side for later replacement.
2 Dig out the exposed subsoil (**A**) from the upper half of the slope and transfer it to the lower half (**B**). Make it level and firm.
3 After the levelling of the slope has been completed, spread the topsoil evenly over the whole area.

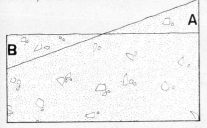

Levelling

Besides being attractive to the eye, a level lawn has the practical advantage that it is better for walking and playing games on, and very much easier to maintain.

The site for a new lawn is often strewn with bricks and rubble. Before levelling can start these must be removed. If the surface consists of rough grass and weeds, strip off the top inch (2.5 cm).

The first rule in levelling is to make all major adjustments to the subsoil, keeping the topsoil to be spread over the surface when the levelling has been completed. To level a sloping site, start at the lowest point. Dig out the top spit of soil and place it in a heap to one side. Continue up the slope, removing the topsoil and adding it to the heap; moving it downhill like this requires the least effort. Next, dig out a spit of subsoil from the top of the slope, piling it in a wheelbarrow. Wheel this down the slope and place it on the subsoil that was exposed when the first lot of topsoil was removed.

Continue working down the slope in this way, lowering and filling, till the ground is roughly level. It may be necessary to build retaining walls (see page 187) above and below the lawn. If the slope is a steep one, it is possible to have more than one lawn, or a combination of lawns and paved areas, at different levels.

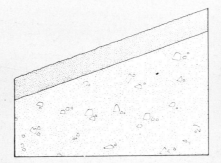

Preparing the Surface

Thorough preparation is necessary to ensure that the surface is truly level and that all bumps and hollows are eliminated. The time and effort involved will be more than repaid not only in the superior quality of the resulting lawn but in its greater durability and ease of maintenance. The equipment needed is a spirit-level, a piece of board about seven feet (2.1 metres) long and some wooden pegs, about eight inches (twenty cm) long, marked clearly with a line round the middle.

Having removed the topsoil, hammer in a peg as far as the mark. Then position other pegs round it, six feet (1.8 metres) apart, to form a grid. Lay the board across from the first peg to the others in turn, hammering them in till their tops come level with that of the first, shown by a spirit-level placed on the board. Add or remove soil till the surface comes flush with the mark on each peg. Continue in this way across the whole site.

It is important that lawns should be well drained; if they remain wet for long, the finer lawn grasses will suffer and may die, leaving patches which either remain bare or become invaded by weeds. If the drainage is poor, the opportunity can be taken to remedy matters after levelling by spreading a layer of broken brick, clinker or other hard rubble over the subsoil before replacing the topsoil. If that is not enough, it may be necessary to install a soakaway or a system of drainpipes.

The ground should always be given several weeks to settle down before turfing or sowing are carried out; then any irregularities that appear during settlement can be adjusted. To have the ground ready for autumn sowing or winter turfing, work should start in summer.

Since the ground should not only be well drained but able to retain moisture during dry weather, organic matter such as compost or well rotted manure may be added to the soil, especially if it is on the light side. Keep the organic material below the surface so that it does not impede the final cultivation; it is best placed just below the top spit, by spreading it over the subsoil before returning the topsoil if that was removed for levelling, or by forking it in during digging (see page 184). The final cultivation to create a firm and even surface is as described on page 190.

Turfing v Sowing

The two usual methods of making a lawn are from turf and from seed. Before deciding which method to use, it is as well to consider the arguments for and against each.

Of the things that can be said in favour of turf, the chief one is that it can be used to create a more or less instant lawn. There is no long period of waiting for the grass to germinate and grow to a fit state to be used and enjoyed. There are also no problems with birds pecking up the seed and dust-bathing, or with cats and dogs ruining a carefully prepared and sown surface by rolling about on it. Also, turf is best laid during late autumn and winter, when there are not too many other urgent things to be done.

The disadvantages of turf are that it is expensive and takes considerable time, work and skill to lay properly.

One of the main advantages of seed is that it is a good deal cheaper to buy. It is also quicker, easier and less laborious to sow seed than to lay turf. There is more choice, too: mixtures of seed are available to suit different conditions and requirements.

The disadvantages of seed are that the grass takes longer to establish, needs more preparation, and is more at the mercy in its early stages not only of birds and animals but of the weather and of weed seeds, for which the prepared surface offers ideal conditions.

Laying Turf

Turf should always be examined carefully, not only before buying it but when it is delivered, to make sure it is of good quality. Inferior turf will never make a good lawn. Points to watch for are the composition and condition not only of the surface of the turf but of the roots below and the soil between. First, the turves should be uniform in size and thickness; the usual size is three feet by one foot (ninety × thirty cm) and the thickness an inch or a little more (three cm).

Secondly, the grass should be uniform in texture, with no coarse species, and free, or practically free, from weeds. Thirdly, the roots should be firm, not limp or shrivelled. Fourthly, the soil should be loamy, with a fair proportion of organic matter; lack of this makes turf liable to break when handled.

The best time for laying turf is from late autumn to early spring, when there is little risk of hot sunshine or drying winds before it becomes rooted into its new site. The turves are usually rolled when they are delivered. If they are to be laid within the next two or three days, they can be stacked in that condition; if not, they should be laid out flat in a spot shaded from the sun and watered to keep them moist. In any case, they should be laid as soon as possible, though not when the ground is frozen or wet.

A few days before laying the turf, a dressing of superphosphate may be raked into the surface of the soil to encourage rooting; or a general-purpose mixed fertilizer may be used. When the surface is finally ready, the boundaries of the lawn can be marked out on the prepared ground. It is always best to have more turf than is strictly necessary to cover the exact area of the intended lawn. Then the turves can be laid so that they extend two inches (five cm) or so beyond the boundary in each direction. Later, when the turf has become established, it can be trimmed.

Start by stretching a garden line tightly across the site. Lay the first row of turves against this, placing each one tight against the next to make sure there are no gaps. Never walk on the surface of the prepared ground. Stand on a wooden board; this will distribute your weight and avoid leaving footprints to form depressions.

Next, lay a second row of turves close up against the first. Stagger the joints so that they do not coincide with those of the first row but come at the middle of the turves already laid. Proceed to lay rows in this way till the whole area is covered. Have a bucket of soil and a trowel with you so that irregularities can be adjusted by scooping out or packing in under turves that come high or low.

When laying has been completed, rolling the turf with a light garden roller will help to settle it in place and make it even. Finish by spreading a mixture of sifted soil and sand along the joints, and work it well in with a broom or the back of the rake.

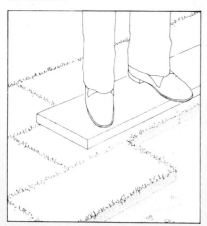

When laying turf never stand directly on the surface but on a board, to distribute the weight and avoid making indentations with the feet.

After laying has been completed, a rolling with a light garden roller will settle the turves in place to make an even and level surface.

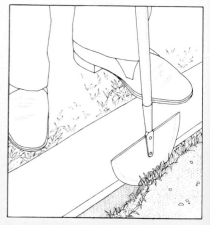

To trim the edge of the lawn neatly and accurately, use a board as a guide to the edging iron. A spade with a sharp blade may be used instead.

Lawn from Seed

There are two seasons suitable for sowing lawns; early autumn and spring. Of the two, early autumn is probably better. The soil is still warm enough for the seed to germinate rapidly, usually within a week to ten days, and the young grass will have time to establish itself before the frosts; but with the days becoming shorter and the weather cooler, top growth will not be too vigorous, so that after an initial topping the new lawn may not need mowing again till after the winter.

If sowing has to be done during the spring, it should be carried out in April, when the soil is warming up and conditions are favourable for germination. This will, however, be slower than during the autumn, and may take two or three weeks. There is also the risk that the weather will turn dry, to the detriment of germination and of the emerging seedlings, so that watering is needed.

The choice of seed will be governed by conditions and requirements (degree of wear, shade etc.). There are several mixtures designed for different purposes. The amount of seed required will depend on the mixture; the finer grasses are usually sown at the rate of one and a half ounces to the square yard (fifty gm/sq metre) and the tougher ones at one ounce to the square yard (thirty-three gm/sq metre). Most packets will have recommended rates of sowing printed on them so that the amount needed can be calculated.

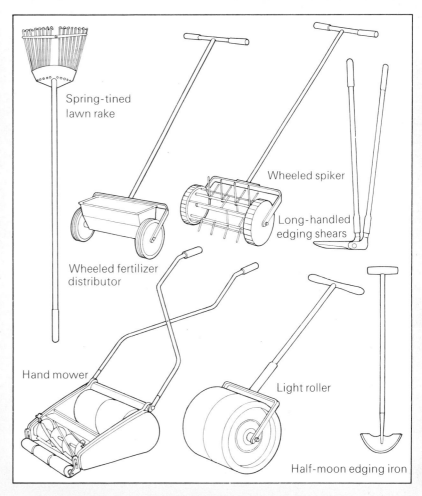

Spring-tined lawn rake

Wheeled spiker

Long-handled edging shears

Wheeled fertilizer distributor

Hand mower

Light roller

Half-moon edging iron

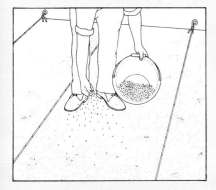

To make sure that the seed is evenly distributed, the site may be divided into a number of equal strips. Divide the seed into the same number of equal portions and use one of those portions to sow each strip of ground.

Never sow the seed more thickly than at the recommended rate in the mistaken belief that by doing so you will produce a denser sward more quickly. In fact, the opposite is more probable. Overcrowded seedlings are likely to be weak and drawn and prone to disease, in particular damping-off.

Choose a calm, fine day for sowing, when the surface of the soil is dry but there is moisture just beneath. Rake lightly to produce a crumbly surface. If the area of the lawn is small, divide the seed into two equal parts and sow one half up and down the site and the other half across it, so as to ensure even distribution. A large site is best divided into a number of equal strips. The seed is divided into a similar number of equal portions and sown at the rate of one portion to each strip.

It is also possible to sow by means of a wheeled fertilizer distributor, which can be adjusted to deliver seed.

After sowing, rake the seed in lightly and evenly. Do not overdo this; if the seed is covered too deeply it may fail to germinate.

Seed-eating and dust-bathing birds may be kept at bay by black thread stretched over the surface (see page 191), or twiggy brushwood strewn over the seedbed.

When the seedlings are about two inches (five cm) high, roll the bed with the back roller of the mower to firm the surface, which may have been lifted during germination. Two or three days later, when the grass is standing erect again, it should be given its first mowing. Set the mower blades high, so that the grass is only topped.

Mowing

There are several reasons for mowing. Apart from giving the lawn a neat appearance, it favours the growth of the more desirable grasses at the expense of the coarser grasses and weeds, which cannot survive continual cutting back.

Mowing should be done regularly through the season, from March to October. A light topping may also be needed in mild winter spells. The height of the cut grass should be about half an inch (twelve mm) on the finest lawns and one inch (twenty-five mm) on hard-wearing ones. Frequency of mowing should be such as to keep the grass at those heights. When growth is fastest, from May to July, this may mean two or three times a week. In general, mowings should be removed by collecting them in a grass-box attached to the mower.

Feeding

In many gardens the lawn tends to be neglected where feeding is concerned. Yet it usually needs feeding more than many other parts of the garden. A considerable quantity of mowings will be removed from it during the season, and with them the nutrients which the grass has taken from the soil. If food is not replaced, the finer grasses will be at a disadvantage compared with coarser kinds, as well as weeds and mosses, which are better able to survive conditions of near starvation.

A dressing of lawn fertilizer, applied in the spring when the grass is bursting into growth, will in many cases be all that is needed for the whole season. While it is possible for the gardener to make up a mixture from different ingredients, it is generally easier, more satisfactory and little if any more expensive to buy one of the many excellent ready-mixed fertilizers sold under brand names and carrying instructions on the rate of use. Some contain peat, to help distribution and improve the soil surface. The fertilizer may also be mixed with six to eight times its own weight of sand and/or dry sifted soil to make it easier to apply.

If weeds are troublesome, it may be worth using one of the proprietary mixtures which also contain a selective weed-killer. Applying the fertilizer by hand is satisfactory so long as it is done evenly; or a wheeled distributor may be used.

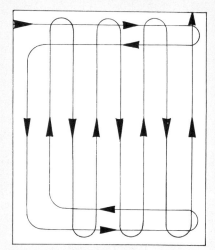

For parallel stripes, mow along the arrowed line. Make each mowing at right angles to the previous one.

In the summer, if growth flags and the colour is poor, more fertilizer may be applied, or sulphate of ammonia at a rate of half an ounce per square yard (sixteen gm/sq metre), may be made. Do not use sulphate of ammonia after mid-August; it will cause soft growth, liable to disease. If a late application of fertilizer is needed, use an autumn fertilizer low in nitrogen.

Maintenance

By autumn, the surface may have become compacted through use and constant mowing. It can be improved by spiking to let in air. Special spikers are available, such as the wheeled version shown on page 207, but in small areas a garden fork pushed into the surface at intervals of nine inches (twenty cm) is perfectly satisfactory.

Before the winter, go over the surface with a flexible rake very thoroughly to remove the matted layer which tends to form during the season. This will improve the appearance and encourage denser turf.

After spiking and raking, the lawn can be brought into first-rate condition by top dressing the surface with bulky material. A suitable mixture is one part of sphagnum peat, four of good sifted loam and two of sharp sand. With heavy soils increase the proportion of sand, and with light soils decrease it. Worked well in with a broom, the top dressing will improve the texture and help to level surface irregularities.

Lawn repairs

The edge of a lawn can easily be damaged by a careless step, or simply by wear and tear. Not only are such damaged edges unsightly but they make mowing more difficult and invite weeds. The easiest way to repair the edge is to cut out a square of turf containing the broken part and move it forward till the damaged portion is outside the lawn. Lay a board across the turf, line it up with the edge on each side and use it as a guide to trim off the damaged piece. This will leave a gap behind the turf which was moved forward; fill this with another turf cut to size or fill the gap with soil and sow it.

A bare patch in the lawn caused by the unwanted attentions of cats or dogs should not simply be raked and reseeded; better cut out the affected patch and returf it or replace with fresh soil and sow new seed.

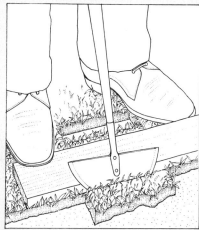

Above: To repair a broken edge, bring the broken piece forward and trim it, using the board as a guide.

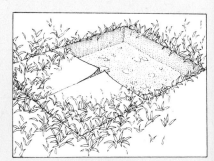

To renovate bare patches, remove a piece of turf and replace, or fill with fresh soil and re-sow.

Pruning

Pruning Tools

The most important pruning tool for most gardeners is a good pair of secateurs. Of the three basic types, one has two blades, which cut like scissors. The others each have a single blade, which cuts in one case on to a soft metal strip and in the other against a curved bar.

A pair of shears is needed, not only for clipping hedges but for trimming back clumps of heather and similar plants. There are many excellent makes available, strong and durable yet light and comfortable to handle.

Long-handled pruners will cut stems too thick for ordinary secateurs. There are also extra-long pruners for dealing with branches otherwise out of reach.

For cutting thick branches, a pruning saw is needed. One with a tapering blade can be used in narrow spaces; some have coarse teeth on one side and finer teeth on the other. Grecian saws have curved blades and teeth which cut on the backward stroke.

Pruning knives require great skill in use, and for most pruning jobs have largely given way to secateurs. They are, however, used to pare large cuts to make them smooth, and so help the healing process.

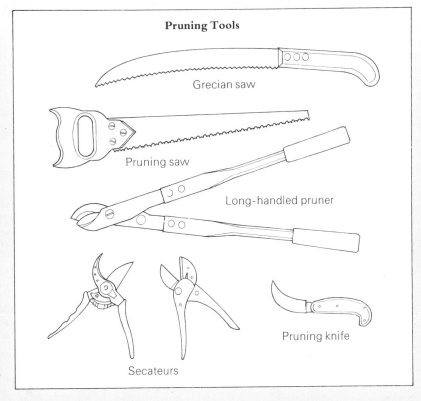

Pruning Tools

Grecian saw

Pruning saw

Long-handled pruner

Pruning knife

Secateurs

Reasons for Pruning

Ways of pruning vary considerably, according to the nature of the plant and the methods and requirements of the gardener. Reasons for pruning, however, are basically the same in all cases. To quote from the authoritative Royal Horticultural Society's *Dictionary of Gardening*, 'Pruning consists in the removal of any part of a tree or shrub, either stem, branches or roots. The term might be extended to apply to all operations in gardening which entail the cutting away of part of a plant, for the general effect will be the same: the direction of the energies of growth into channels desired by the cultivator'.

Pinching out the tips of herbaceous plants to make them grow bushy, or removing old flower-heads to encourage more to develop, may be called pruning, but the term is usually applied only to trees and shrubs, and that is how it is used here.

Never prune a tree or shrub unless there is a good reason for doing so. It is not always an annual necessity. The purposes of pruning may be summed up as follows: to keep the plant healthy; to maintain shape and balance; to produce the best decorative effect and/or crop.

Pruning to keep a tree or shrub healthy consists mainly of removing shoots or branches that are dead, diseased or damaged (easily remembered as the three Ds) as soon as they are noticed. If left, dead and diseased shoots may spread infection to the rest of the plant, and damaged ones provide an easy point of access for infection from outside.

In addition, shoots that cross or rub against each other should be removed, together with weak and overcrowded ones, particularly in the centre of the tree or shrub, where impeded air and light may lead to feeble, disease-prone growth.

A great many trees and shrubs – after, as appropriate, initial training to establish a framework – need no other pruning than the occasional removal of unsound wood. Apart from that, such trees and shrubs should be left to develop in their own way, according to their characteristic habits of growth.

It is better not to prune at all than to mutilate a plant by savage cutting through a misguided desire for neatness or because its size and nature are unsuited to its location.

All trees and shrubs have a natural size to which they will eventually grow. From the vast range available at nurseries and garden centres it should be possible to choose ones whose height and spread by the time they are full-grown will fit into the allotted space, so there will be no need for constant drastic cutting back of shoots and branches in an attempt to keep them within bounds.

Some pruning operations, however, go beyond the occasional removal of wood that is faulty, overcrowded or out of place. These are the operations which are performed – generally as an annual routine or even more frequently – to control growth for a variety of purposes.

The most obvious examples are formal hedges and pieces of topiary trimmed into artificial shapes. These need regular clipping from an early age if they are to be dense in growth.

Basic pruning techniques

Though there are various reasons for pruning, and many different methods of carrying it out, certain basic rules should always be obeyed in order to make the operation as easy and effortless as possible and give it the greatest chance of success. All pruning is a form of surgery, and precautions need to be taken to promote healing and prevent infection of the cuts.

First, always make clean cuts, without bruising or ragged edges. To achieve this result, use only tools of good quality and keep them in good condition. Always find time to clean and oil them before putting them away after use. Keep them free not only from rust but from sap, which if not cleaned away will dry hard and become difficult to remove. If left it will clog the blades of secateurs and saws and reduce both their efficiency and their ease of operation.

Always make sure that pruning tools are sharp before using them; blunt ones not only give unsatisfactory results but make the work a great deal harder.

Secondly, never try to cut wood that is too thick for the tool being used. The attempt will risk not only damaging the wood but straining the tool and reducing its efficiency. Resist the temptation to twist the tool while cutting, in order to force it through a thick branch. This will certainly result in a ragged cut and may put the tool permanently out of alignment. If the cut cannot be made easily with secateurs, use a pruning saw.

Thirdly, never leave any snags of wood which are bound to die back after pruning. If a branch has to be removed, do not allow a stub – commonly called a hat-peg – to remain. It will not grow, and any wood that will not grow must eventually decay. The trouble is that the decay may spread into the live wood and carry infection to other parts of the tree or shrub.

Any branch to be removed should be cut off flush at its point of origin, leaving no stump of wood to prevent the wound from healing over.

The same principle also applies to the more usual pruning process of cutting back a shoot to a chosen bud to stimulate it into growth. If the cut is made at a point some distances beyond the bud, a piece of useless wood will be left, which will die

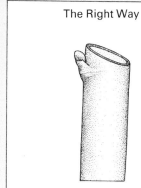

The Wrong Way

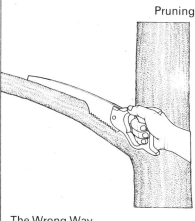

Left to right Cut too near bud; cut too far from bud and sloping the wrong way; bad cut with jagged edges.

The Right Way

The cut shown here is just beyond the bud, slopes the right way and has been made with a clean, sharp tool.

Pruning Branches

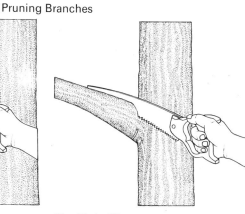

The Wrong Way

Cutting off a branch at the point shown will leave a snag which will die back, impede healing and may become infected.

The Right Way

After undercutting a short way to prevent tearing, the branch is sawn off flush with the trunk, leaving no stump.

back and could provide entry for diseases.

When removing dead and diseased wood it is very important to cut back to healthy tissue. If there is a brown stain in the wood where it has been cut, this means that there is an infection at that point. The stem must therefore be cut back still farther, if necessary again and again, till a point is reached where the wood is clean and shows no sign of staining. Only then can you be confident that all affected tissue has been removed.

It is a sensible precaution to collect up and burn all prunings, instead of leaving them lying around as a possible source of further infection.

Pare sawn surfaces with a sharp knife until they are smooth and jagged edges have been removed.

As an additional precaution it is wise to make it a general rule to protect all wounds more than an inch (25 mm) across with a sealing compound. There are several bituminous paints and similar products specially made for the purpose. They are easily painted over cut surfaces to prevent the entry of disease spores, wood-boring insects and rain.

Trees and Most Shrubs

Usually, ornamental trees need little or no regular pruning. They may, however, benefit from formative pruning in their early stages to establish a framework and to remove surplus, weak or ill-placed shoots. In most cases this early training will have been carried out by the time they leave the nursery. Subsequently, although regular pruning of them is usually unnecessary and undesirable, occasional pruning may be needed.

Sometimes thinning may be required to relieve overcrowding, particularly towards the centre of the tree. Remove unwanted shoots entirely, cutting them back either to a branch or a well-placed sideshoot. If they are merely shortened they will make matters worse by producing several new growths.

Another condition that can be corrected by timely pruning is that which arises when a branch grows too vigorously, making the tree lopsided. Shorten it back to a less vigorous sideshoot growing in the same direction. If a leading shoot forks at the apex, spoiling the shape, remove one of the competing leaders entirely.

Most shrubs need only occasional pruning, to remove defective, overcrowded or badly-placed shoots. Some groups of shrubs, however, give better displays when regularly pruned, and these groups are dealt with in the following pages.

Thinning Out a Tree

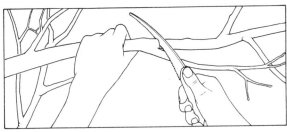

Tree before thinning

Removal of inward growing sideshoots improves appearance and allows in light and air.

Tree after thinning

Cut out completely any stems that cross and rub against others before they cause damage.

Competing Leaders

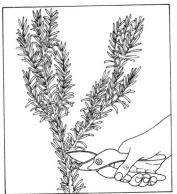

If a competing leader is spoiling the appearance, cut it out completely, right back to its point of origin.

Shaping a Tree

Sometimes an excessively vigorous branch will appear, distorting the outline and giving the tree a lopsided appearance, as shown on the left (a). To restore the desired outline (b), the over-vigorous branch must be removed entirely. Cut it back by at least two-thirds of its length to a less vigorous side-shoot, as shown above. Use a pruning-saw, not secateurs, for thick wood, and paint the cut with a sealing compound.

SHRUBS PRUNED HARD IN EARLY SPRING

For flowering on current year's growth

The first group of shrubs that give their best display if they are regularly pruned are those that flower in the summer and autumn on new wood that has been produced during the same year. With shrubs of this kind, wood is already too old to flower by the following year, so pruning consists of cutting out in early spring as much as possible of the old growth so that a fresh array of vigorous new shoots is produced. If left unpruned, these shrubs degenerate into untidy bushes crowded with useless, twiggy stems.

It is important with this group that they are pruned as soon as growth starts in early spring, so as to give the new shoots as long as possible to grow and develop before they flower. Where the habit of growth permits – as with the hardy fuchsias whose top growth is killed back during the winter – pruning may simply take the form of cutting all stems down to ground level. With many other species, such as *Buddleja davidii*, the previous season's flowering shoots are cut back each year to one or two pairs of buds above a basal framework of branches.

After such hard pruning, the new shoots can grow very rapidly. Some of the strongest growers of the group may reach a height of seven feet or more (over two metres) by flowering time. In such cases it may be wise, particularly in exposed places, to prune lightly in the autumn as well, cutting off the top third or so of the tallest stems to reduce the risk of wind damage.

A list of popular shrubs in this group is given on the right. Be sure of the correct species before pruning. Sometimes species within the same genus differ in their requirements: for instance, *Buddleja alternifolia*, which blooms on the previous year's growth, would produce no flowers if pruned like *Buddleja davidii*.

In the addition to those which flower on the current year's growth, a few shrubs such as *Prunus triloba*, which flower early in the year on wood produced during the previous season, may be pruned hard back after flowering, to make new shoots which will blossom the following spring.

For Flowering on Current Year's Growth

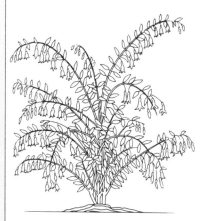

1 Pictured above is a well-grown fuchsia in full flower during the late summer, when growth is at its maximum.

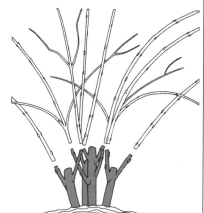

2 Early the following spring the flowered stems are cut hard back to one or two pairs of buds from their points of origin.

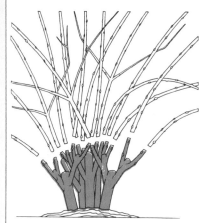

3 Next spring the new shoots which arose from the retained buds and flowered during the summer are cut hard in their turn.

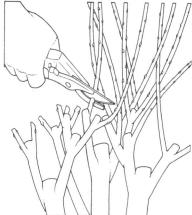

4 In later years the cutting back is repeated. If basal stems become congested, cut some right out at ground level.

Shrubs pruned in this way include the following:

Buddleja davidii
Caryopteris
Ceanothus (deciduous)
Ceratostigma
Fuchsia (hardy)
Hydrangea paniculata
Perovskia

Prunus glandulosa
Prunus triloba
Romneya
Spiraea x bumalda
Spiraea douglasii
Spiraea japonica

For Stem and Foliage Effects

Hard pruning in early spring may be used not only to improve the flowering performance of certain shrubs but also to intensify the decorative effect of coloured bark and foliage in suitable cases. The method of pruning is very much the same as that described on the opposite page, but the object is entirely different. Most of the shrubs in this group would flower on the previous season's wood if allowed to do so, but by being cut back severely in early spring they will produce instead vigorous, unbranched young shoots.

Outstanding for the vivid colour of its bare stems after the leaves have fallen is the red-barked dogwood, *Cornus alba*, which if planted where it can be seen from the house will make a cheerful sight throughout the winter when there is little else to attract the eye. The colour of the young shoots produced by hard spring pruning is much richer than that of older wood.

Another popular dogwood, *Cornus stolonifera* 'Flaviramea', is also pruned hard in the spring and produces yellow to olive-green young shoots, particularly effective beside the red-stemmed kinds.

Several other shrubs may be pruned in the same way to provide highly decorative young stems of various colours for winter effect. Among them are some species of willow, such as *Salix alba*, with orange-scarlet and golden varieties, the violet-coloured *S. daphnoides*, and *S. irrorata*, whose purple stems are covered with a striking white bloom. Other species which respond well to hard spring pruning are the white-stemmed brambles *Rubus biflorus* and *R. cockburnianus*.

Some shrubs with handsome foliage may be treated in the same way to increase the size and decorative value of their leaves. Among them are the variegated dogwoods *Cornus alba* 'Elegantissima' and 'Spaethii', the purple-leaved smokebush *Cotinus coggygria* 'Foliis Purpureis', the golden, purple and variegated elders, and the purple hazel, *Corylus maxima* 'Purpurea'.

The height of the framework which carries the new season's shoots will in most cases be decided so as to show the coloured stems or foliage to the best advantage. Some, such as the brambles, make no framework of branches at the base and old stems should be cut down to ground level.

For Producing Coloured Stems

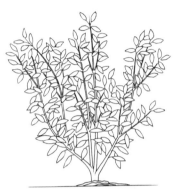

1 The red-barked dogwood *Cornus alba* produces more handsome foliage and more richly coloured stems if pruned hard in early spring.

2 After their winter display the past season's shoots are cut back to one or two pairs of buds from the basal framework.

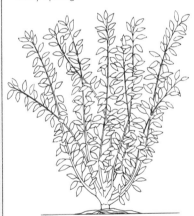

3 By the season's end vigorous new unbranched shoots will have grown from the buds, with leaves that show rich autumn colour.

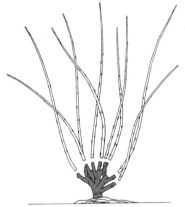

4 The following spring the bright red stems are cut back again, to produce another season's crop of strong young shoots.

Shrubs pruned this way:	
For coloured stems	For foliage
Cornus alba	*Cornus alba* 'Elegantissima'
Cornus stolonifera	*Cornus alba* 'Spaethii'
Salix alba	*Cotinus coggygria* 'Foliis
Salix daphnoides	Purpureis'
Salix irrorata	*Sambucus nigra* 'Albovariegata'
Rubus biflorus	*Sambucus nigra* 'Aurea'
Rubus cockburnianus	*Sambucus nigra* 'Aureomarginata'
	Corylus maxima 'Purpurea'

PRUNING AFTER FLOWERING

Many of the most popular deciduous flowering shrubs bear their flowers in spring or early summer on shoots produced during the previous growing season. These flowers appear either on the last year's wood, as with *Forsythia*, or on laterals produced from it, as with *Deutzia* and the early-flowering spiraeas.

Shrubs in this group are pruned as soon as flowering is over by removing the one-year-old stems which have carried the flowers. The object is to channel the plant's energy into the young growths at the base of the older wood, so that during the rest of the year they can develop into strong replacement shoots for flowering the following season.

When several new shoots appear at the base of a stem, it is generally best to cut back to the lowest, which is usually also the strongest, so long as this does not spoil the balance of the shrub.

After several years of regular pruning in this way, it may happen that the main stems forming the framework at the base of the shrub become overcrowded. It is then best to cut out some completely.

Shrubs in this group include:

Buddleja	*Kolkwitzia*
alternifolia	*Neillia*
Cytisus scoparius	*Philadelphus*
Deutzia	*Ribes sanguineum*
Dipelta	*Spiraea x arguta*
Forsythia	*Spiraea thunbergii*
Hydrangea x	*Stephanandra*
macrophylla	*Tamarix* (spring)
Kerria	*Weigela*

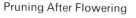
Pruning After Flowering

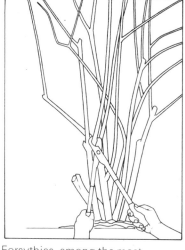

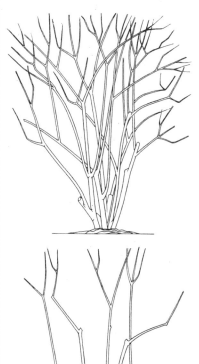

Forsythias, among the most popular of this group, are pruned in spring as soon as the flowers fade. The rather crowded specimen shown top left should have its old branches shortened, as above, to their junctions with younger shoots, so as to remove useless wood and retain the vigorous new stems which will flower the following spring.

By this replacement pruning a more shapely specimen is produced (below left), with as much flowering growth for the future and as little played-out wood from the past as possible.

PRUNING EVERGREENS

Most of the evergreen shrubs in our gardens have a naturally compact habit of growth. So long as they have enough room to develop they usually require little or no pruning except for the removal of faded flowers and the occasional dead, diseased, damaged or misplaced shoot.

Evergreen shrubs should be pruned at the right time of year. If pruning is done too early there is a considerable risk of damage by frost and cold winds. If, however, it is done too late it will produce soft growth, unlikely to stand the winter. The best time is generally from late April to May.

Nearly all the broad-leaved evergreen shrubs which are now established were introduced into our gardens from countries with milder climates. During a hard winter many suffer frost and wind damage, which often takes some time to become apparent. An advantage of late spring pruning is that the extent of the damage can then be seen.

A few low-growing evergreens respond well to hard pruning in order to keep them compact. *Hypericum calycinum*, the rose of Sharon, and *Mahonia aquifolium* make excellent ground cover with a spring shearing of old growth. Cotton lavender (*Santolina*) may be kept as a mound of grey, finely divided foliage if cut nearly to ground level each spring.

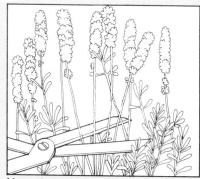

Above Lavender may be kept compact by clipping off an inch or so (twenty-five mm) of the previous year's growth in April.

CLIMBERS AND WALL PLANTS

In general, the basic principles of pruning plants grown on or against a wall are the same as those for plants grown in the open. All dead, diseased and damaged wood should be removed as soon as it is seen. Those plants that flower after midsummer on the current year's growth, such as *Ceanothus × burkwoodii*, *Ceanothus* 'Gloire de Versailles' and *Clematis × jackmanii*, may be pruned early in the year; those that flower before mudsummer on the previous season's wood, such as the spring-flowering *Ceanothus impressus*, *Forsythia suspensa* and *Clematis macropetala* may be pruned as soon as flowering is over.

The tendency of many wall plants is to produce vigorous shoots directed away from the wall, and pruning – particularly in the early stages – is largely devoted to overcoming this tendency. The breast-wood, as these growths directed away from the wall are called, is removed, and shoots directed sideways are trained against the wall to form a framework.

Some very vigorous shrubs benefit from summer pruning to keep them within bounds and to curb their tendency to produce an excessive amount of shoot growth at the expense of flowers. Among those which respond well to this treatment is that favourite climber *Wisteria*, pictured on the right. In July or August the new seaon's lateral shoots are shortened back to four or five leaves to divert energy into the formation of flower buds on these spurred-back growths. During the following winter the resulting spurs are cut back further, to leave two or three buds.

HEDGES

Several flowering shrubs such as fuchsias, roses and *Berberis × stenophylla* make good informal hedges. Those that bloom on the current year's wood are pruned in early spring, and those that bloom on old wood are pruned when flowering is over.

Formal hedges need pruning sufficiently in their early stages to develop a dense base without gaps. Clipping is best done from the base upwards. The sides should taper inwards towards the top. This not only makes for a more attractive appearance but lessens the danger that heavy falls of snow and gusty winds might damage the hedge and break it apart, making it unsightly.

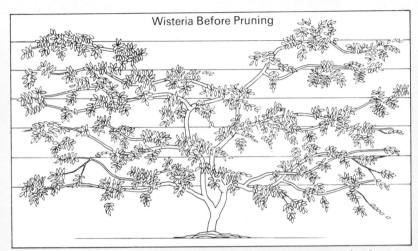

Wisteria Before Pruning

To control growth and induce flower-bud formation, summer pruning is needed. Lateral shoots should be cut back to four or five leaves.

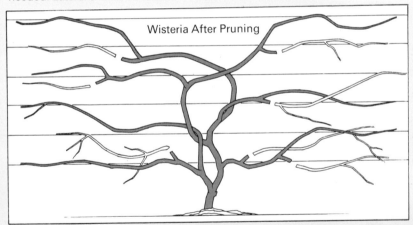

Wisteria After Pruning

During the following winter the resulting spurs are cut hard back to leave two or three buds to a shoot.

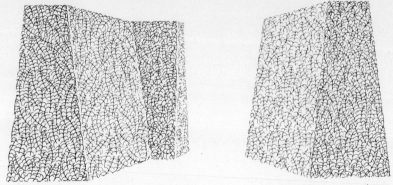

Above A formal hedge that is trimmed to taper inwards from the base to the top not only looks attractive but is less liable than a parallel-sided one to damage from the weight of snow or from boisterous winds.

ROSES

Bush Types

The most widely-grown garden roses are the hybrid teas and floribundas. Both flower on the current year's growth and are best pruned in late February or March, according to district and weather. The ideal time is when the buds are starting to swell. In all cases remove dead and diseased wood, also weak stems and any that cross or grow inwards.

In the spring after planting, cut back the shoots of Hybrid Teas (and Hybrid Perpetuals) to two to four buds, and those of Floribundas to three to five buds; the stronger the shoot the less severely it should be pruned. In subsequent years cut back the stems of Hybrid Teas to between two and six buds according to their vigour. Floribundas, which usually grow more vigorously and flower more freely, are pruned rather less severely. New shoots from the base are shortened by a third and older wood to between two and five buds.

Standard roses are pruned in a similar way to those grown as bushes.

Summer pruning consists of the regular removal of flower heads as they fade. Always cut back to a strong bud or shoot, and do not remove more foliage than necessary or growth will be adversely affected.

A certain amount of autumn pruning may be needed in exposed places to prevent strong winds from rocking tall bushes in the ground. Shorten long stems by about a quarter during November.

Miniatures and polyantha pompons are mostly similar in their habit of growth and of flowering to the hybrid teas, and are pruned in the same way.

Ramblers and Climbers

Those that flower on laterals from the previous year's canes include true ramblers, which send up new shoots from the base each year, and strong growers whose new canes appear mainly from old stems. As much old wood as possible is removed after flowering and new shoots tied in.

Climbers that flower on the current year's growth are summer pruned by cutting back laterals as the flowers fade. During the dormant period cut laterals to three or four buds and tie in new wood.

Pruning Bush Roses

1 All dead and diseased stems must be removed completely. Cut back to clean, unstained wood.

2 Thin, weak and damaged stems should also be cut out, to give strong shoots room to develop.

3 Remove all stems that cross, rub or grow inwards. Keep the centre of the bush open and uncrowded.

Ramblers are pruned after flowering by cutting out the flowered wood and replacing it with the new season's canes, tying them in horizontally. Cut back laterals to two or three buds.

FRUIT

For pruning purposes it is useful to consider both tree and soft fruits as belonging to four groups.

The first group consists of apples, pears, sweet cherries and red currants, which bear fruit mainly on wood two-years old and more. The second consists of peaches, morello cherries, black currants, blackberries, loganberries and summer-fruiting raspberries, which bear fruit mainly on one-year old wood. The third consists of plums, damsons and gooseberries, which fruit on one-year old and older wood. The fourth consists of autumn-fruiting raspberries, which fruit on the current season's shoots.

In group one, apples and pears (except restricted forms) are winter pruned by shortening laterals to from three to six buds and leaders by up to a third. Sweet cherries need little but removal in early summer of crowded shoots. Wall-trained ones are kept in shape by pinching back laterals not needed to fill space. Red currants are dealt with below.

In group two, raspberries and black currants are also dealt with below. Blackberries and loganberries have the fruited canes cut out and the new ones tied in to replace them. Morello cherries and peaches in bush form have overcrowded growth thinned out in early summer and branches carrying little young wood shortened to induce fresh growth. Those trained as fans are pruned by replacing fruited shoots with fresh ones each year.

In group three, plums and damsons are treated in the same way as sweet cherries. Gooseberry bushes are pruned in winter. Thin overcrowded growth; shorten strong laterals by half, tip medium ones and leave short ones intact.

Autumn-fruiting raspberries have all canes cut to the ground in February.

Restricted forms such as cordons and espaliers are summer pruned by shortening young laterals to three or four good leaves above the basal cluster. In winter, the summer-pruned laterals are cut back to encourage spur formation.

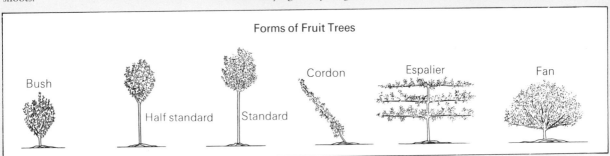

Forms of Fruit Trees

Bush Half standard Standard Cordon Espalier Fan

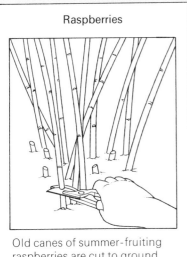

Raspberries

Old canes of summer-fruiting raspberries are cut to ground level when the fruit has been picked. New canes are tied in to replace them. Autumn-fruiting ones should have all canes removed in February; fruit will be borne on the current season's growth.

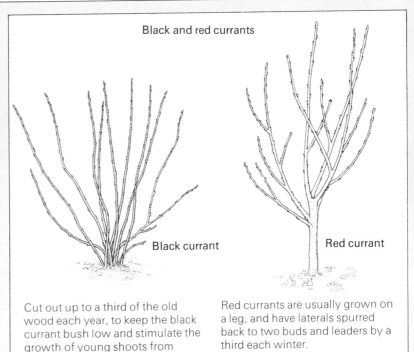

Black and red currants

Black currant

Red currant

Cut out up to a third of the old wood each year, to keep the black currant bush low and stimulate the growth of young shoots from below.

Red currants are usually grown on a leg, and have laterals spurred back to two buds and leaders by a third each winter.

Pots and Containers

Containers make it possible to grow and enjoy a wide variety of plants in places where gardening would otherwise be out of the question. Many apartment dwellers nowadays have no garden at all, yet they manage to enjoy the beauty of plants in their homes; a thriving business has developed to supply them with house-plants of all kinds, not only through florists and garden centres but increasingly through supermarkets and department stores.

The majority of these house-plants are sold in standard plastic pots, but there is a large selection of decorative containers, in a wide range of materials, in which the plants can be placed to show them off to the best advantage.

Outside the home, too, there are many places such as walls, windowsills, balconies, steps and patios that can be brightened and made more attractive with a container-grown plant or two.

Even people with gardens can add greatly to the range of their pleasures with containers on terraces and beside paths, where they act as focal points and allow plants to be admired more closely. There are practical advantages too: a container can hide a drain cover, and plants too tender for the open can be grown in containers and brought under cover during cold spells.

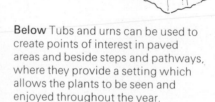

Below Tubs and urns can be used to create points of interest in paved areas and beside steps and pathways, where they provide a setting which allows the plants to be seen and enjoyed throughout the year.

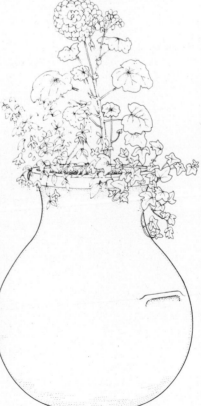

Above A stone trough enables a wide variety of rock plants to be grown together, forming an alpine landscape in miniature.

There are containers to suit every situation and taste, from the strictly utilitarian to the more elaborate. As a general rule an unobtrusive colour is to be preferred.

The range of materials from which containers are made is wide and varied, and each has its advantages and disadvantages. Among the most enduringly attractive are the old-fashioned stone urns, with or without pedestals, often elaborately decorated with designs of flowers and fruit, and with fluted and scalloped sides. These have now become much prized and expensive collector's items, but replicas are available at reasonable prices in artificial stoneware and plastic materials such as polystyrene, which has the advantage of being light and easy to move.

There is also a large selection of elegant replicas made of fibreglass and finished to resemble weathered stone, marble and lead. They are weatherproof and immune to damage by frost.

Wooden tubs make handsome containers. The larger ones can be used to grow sizeable shrubs, or even small trees, and look particularly attractive beside doorways. Many are made from old beer barrels and wine casks sawn in half.

Some firms make tubs specially for plants, with modern weatherproof finishes. Those made from old barrels should be treated with a wood preservative before use; do not plant too soon after such treatment.

The most basic containers are those used for raising plants from seed and potting them on, either for planting in the garden or for growing as pot plants in greenhouses and frames or in the home. Though many people still prefer clay pots for their appearance, the majority of flower-pots are now made of plastic, which is lighter and easier to handle and clean.

The diameter ranges from two inches (fifty mm) to ten inches (254 mm), the most popular sizes being from three inches (seventy-six mm) to eight inches (203 mm). Because plastic is more retentive of moisture, good drainage is essential. For that reason most plastic pots have several holes in the bottom.

For sowing small amounts of seed, round pans are suitable. For larger amounts plastic seed-trays, usually measuring fourteen by eight by two inches ($355 \times 215 \times 55$ mm), are available, with or without clear covers to assist germination and help seedlings in their early stages.

To give plants in containers the best possible conditions to enable them to thrive, it is important that the compost in which they are grown should be of the right composition and contain the correct amount of the right plant foods. For nearly fifty years the seed and potting composts formulated by the John Innes Institute have been used by professionals and amateurs alike.

John Innes seed compost consists of two parts sterilized loam, one part peat and one part sand, to which is added $1\frac{1}{2}$ oz of superphosphate and $\frac{3}{4}$ oz of chalk per bushel (forty-eight gm superphosphate and twenty-four gm chalk per forty litres).

John Innes potting compost No. 1 (JIP 1) consists of seven parts sterilized loam, three parts peat and two parts sand, to which is added four oz John Innes base (two parts by weight hoof and horn, two parts superphosphate and one part sulphate of potash) and $\frac{3}{4}$ oz chalk per bushel (126 gm base and twenty-four gm chalk per forty litres).

The loam is sterilized – more correctly

partially sterilized – to destroy weed seeds and harmful organisms. This may be done by heating it in a wide container in an oven at 180°F (80°C) for half an hour.

Ideally the loam should come from rotted-down turves. Garden soil will do, but is less satisfactory. Peat should be passed through a quarter inch (six mm) sieve and lightly but thoroughly moistened before mixing; it is difficult to do so later. Sand should be sharp and lime-free.

In addition to JIP 1 – used largely for rooted cuttings and seedlings – there are two further versions of John Innes potting compost: JIP 2, which contains twice the quantity of base fertilizer and lime, is ideal for most pot plants after their early stages. JIP 3, which contains three times as much base and chalk, is suitable for strong growers in large pots. For lime-hating plants the chalk is omitted.

John Innes composts may be bought ready prepared. To be sure that the quality is up to standard, look for the seal of the John Innes Manufacturers' Association.

In recent years soil-less composts have been increasing in popularity. Originally developed because of increasing difficulty in finding good quality loam, they consist mainly of peat, with various additives. They are clean and light and can give excellent results. They do, however, need attention to make sure they never dry out; once that happens they are difficult to moisten again.

While the compost in containers must

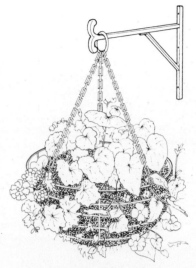

Hanging baskets, lined with sphagnum moss or perforated black polythene to hold in compost, display trailing plants like fuchsias to perfection.

be kept moist, particularly during summer when it can dry out rapidly, it should never be allowed to remain waterlogged. For that reason drainage holes must be adequate to allow surplus water to escape. The problem then may be to prevent compost from escaping too. A good layer of crocks (pieces of flower-pot) or stones placed over the bottom, particularly of containers with large drainage holes such as window-boxes, will prevent the compost from being washed through.

Window-boxes, of wood, plastic or fibreglass, may be planted with foliage and flowering subjects to provide year-round interest.

Vegetables

Planning a Vegetable Plot

There are several very good reasons for devoting at least part of the garden to the growing of vegetables. First, fresh produce eaten within an hour or two of being gathered usually has a taste and a texture that shop-bought vegetables cannot match. Secondly, the gardener, unlike the commercial grower, can allow certain crops to develop their full flavour. Shop tomatoes, for instance, are almost always picked unripe and can never approach the flavour of those allowed to mature on the plant. Thirdly, home-grown vegetables can save money.

For successful results, the site for the vegetable plot must be an open one which gets plenty of sun. Avoid sites which are shaded by trees and tall buildings. Not only do such positions discourage vigorous growth but they increase the risk of a build-up of diseases and pests.

If there is no suitable open site available, it is better to give up the idea of growing vegetables, and so save disappointment.

On the other hand, sites that are exposed to strong winds are likely to give much diminished crops. It has been demonstrated by research that protection against even moderate winds can increase yields by as much as a third. What is needed is not a solid barrier, which may make matters worse by creating violent air turbulence, but a screen that allows the wind through but reduces its force.

The effectiveness of a windbreak extends to a distance of between six and ten times its height: so one that is three feet (ninety cm) high will reduce wind force for a distance of from eighteen to thirty feet (5.5 to nine metres).

The windbreak may be a living hedge, which will take some time to grow and needs work to maintain it, or an artificial construction such as a lath screen or one of the manufactured mesh products.

In most gardens the vegetable patch will be situated across the far end of the plot from the house, and the aspect will be fixed accordingly. If, however, there is a choice, the rows of vegetables should run north and south. This arrangement will ensure that each crop receives its share of light – an important consideration with tall-growing plants such as runner beans, which if running east and west would keep crops to their north in shadow.

Crop Rotation

Generally speaking it is unwise to grow the same, or closely related, vegetable crops on the same piece of ground in successive years. The chief reason for this is that to do so is to run the risk of building up a concentration of pests and diseases.

Nearly all pests and diseases are only able to attack a single crop or a narrow range of related crops. If they are provided year after year with the 'host' plants on which they live, they will multiply and may reach epidemic proportions. If, however, they are denied their 'host' plants, the danger of a harmful build-up will be considerably reduced.

There are other reasons, too, why crop rotation is practised. Different vegetables may have different nutritional needs.

A simple system of crop rotation is based on a three-year cycle. The plot is divided into three sections – labelled A, B and C in the top illustration opposite – which represents the first year of the rotation.

Section A has plenty of organic material such as well-rotted manure or garden compost incorporated with the soil during digging. It is used for crops that thrive in rich soil, such as peas, beans, celery and celeriac, onions, leeks, shallots and garlic, lettuces, spinach, spinach beet and seakale beet (swiss chard) and tomatoes.

Section B is given a dressing of fertilizer and if necessary lime (see page 183). It is used to grow brassica crops: cabbages, brussels sprouts, broccoli and calabrese, cauliflowers, chinese cabbage, kale, swedes, radishes and turnips.

Section C is given a dressing of fertilizer and is used to grow potatoes and root vegetables, including carrots, beetroots, parsnips, salsify and scorzonera.

In the second year, the part that was Section A during the first season becomes Section B; it is dressed with fertilizer, limed if necessary and used for growing brassica crops. The first year's Section B becomes Section C and is dressed with fertilizer and used for potatoes and root crops. The first year's Section C becomes Section A, is enriched with manure or compost and is used for growing peas, beans etc. In the third year B becomes C, C becomes A and A becomes B. In the fourth year the first year's layout is repeated, and so on in future years.

First Year

At the start of the three-year rotation shown here, incorporate plenty of organic material such as manure or garden compost with the soil of Section A during digging, and grow peas, beans and other crops that need newly-enriched soil (listed in the previous column). Give Section B a dressing of fertilizer, lime it if necessary and use it to grow brassica crops such as cabbages (also listed in the previous column). Apply a dressing of fertilizer only to Section C, and use this section to grow potatoes and root vegetables such as carrots and parsnips.

Second Year

The first part of the plot, which was Section A during the previous year, now becomes Section B. It is not manured but given a dressing of fertilizer, limed if necessary and used for growing brassica crops.

The middle part, which was Section B during the previous year, now becomes Section C. It is given a dressing of fertilizer only and used for growing potatoes and root vegetables.

The third part, which was Section C the previous year, now becomes Section A. Manure, compost or other organic material is incorporated during digging and peas, beans etc are grown.

Third Year

The first part, which was Section B the previous year, now becomes Section C. It is given a dressing of fertilizer and used for growing potatoes and root vegetables.

The middle part, which was Section C the previous year, now becomes Section A. Organic material such as manure or compost is incorporated with the soil and peas, beans etc are grown.

The third part, which was Section A the previous year, now becomes Section B. It is given a dressing of fertilizer, limed if necessary and used for growing brassica crops.

In the fourth year, the layout becomes the same as in the first year.

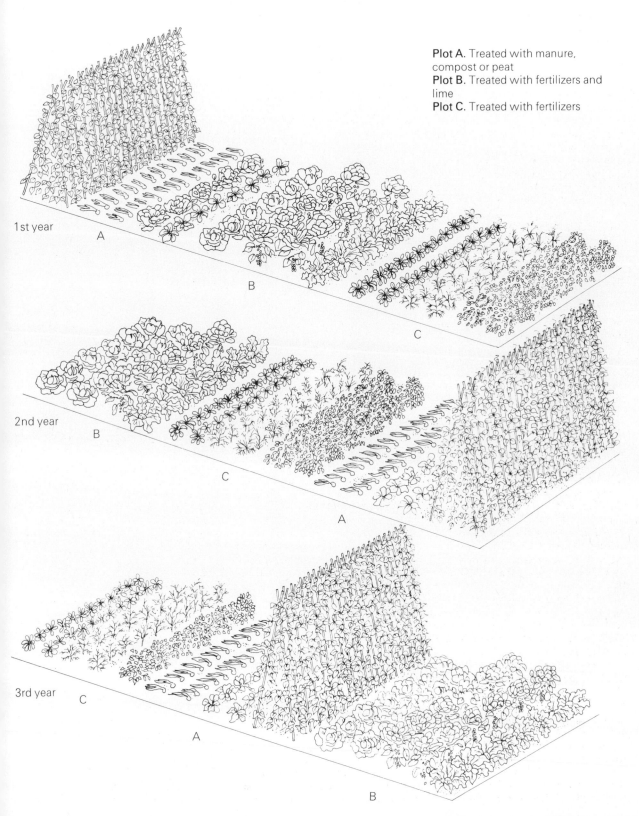

Plot A. Treated with manure, compost or peat
Plot B. Treated with fertilizers and lime
Plot C. Treated with fertilizers

1st year

A

B

C

2nd year

B

C

A

3rd year

C

A

B

Some of the most rewarding vegetables suitable for the home garden cannot be fitted into a rotation plan because they are grown as permanent crops and do not give their best yields until they are several years old. Perhaps the most highly esteemed of these is asparagus, which when bought in the shops is usually expensive and often tasteless, but when home-grown probably gives a higher return for the original outlay than any other vegetable. A well-grown bed of asparagus may continue to yield excellent crops every year for twenty years or more, with little attention except a dressing of fertilizer in the spring and an occasional weeding.

Another rewarding permanent crop is the globe artichoke, which although grown for the edible fleshy parts of its flower-heads has handsome foliage.

These permanent crops are usually grown in a special bed at the end of the vegetable plot, where they may remain undisturbed, together with rhubarb.

Most of the popular herbs used in cooking are also permanent or semi-permanent plants. Many people prefer to grow them not in the vegetable garden but near the kitchen door, where they are handy for picking as needed. A useful collection of perennial herbs might include mint, sage, thyme, chives, pot marjoram, rosemary and winter savory. Parsley, the most widely grown herb of all, needs to be raised from seed each season.

With the majority of vegetables, which occupy the ground for a limited period of a few weeks or a few months, it is often difficult to follow exactly the same pattern of crop rotation from one season to the next, particularly in a small garden where there may not be room to grow more than a few vegetables. Plans can only be guidelines and may have to be modified. Try, however, to keep to the general principal of never following a crop with another from the same group on the same piece of ground for at least two years.

Some gardeners make an exception in the case of onions, which they grow in the same place year after year with excellent results. Whatever plan is followed, it is important to watch out for signs of any serious build-up of diseases or pests. If that should happen, similar crops must not be grown in the same place for several years.

Where the amount of ground available

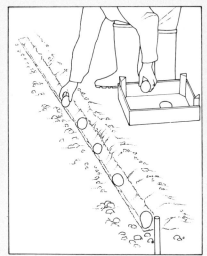

Early potatoes give an excellent return. Plant fifteen inches (thirty-eight cm) apart in drills four inches (ten cm) deep.

for the cultivation of vegetables is limited, the immediate question is what kinds to grow. A first consideration must be personal taste, so that what is grown is liked — or at least not disliked — by all, or at any rate most, of the family.

What to Grow

An important aim is to produce vegetables which are expensive to buy. This often means early crops, which may call for protected cultivation (see page 226). There is great satisfaction in eating newly-gathered early potatoes and carrots when bought ones are dear and have lost their freshness. It is, however, hardly worth while in a limited space to grow maincrop potatoes.

It is also possible to grow cultivars which are difficult to find in the shops. Most commercial producers are obliged to grow cultivars specially developed for their resistance to travel, so that they reach the market without being bruised or broken. Home gardeners, who do not have the problem of sending their produce to market, can select the cultivars they grow for qualities such as flavour.

Another consideration is the return on the work involved. For instance, the effort needed to grow earthed-up trench celery in heavy soil is unlikely to be justified by results. It would probably be better to grow self-blanching celery, which needs no earthing-up, or the turnip-rooted celeriac, which is hardier and less susceptible to attack by pests and diseases.

Trenching

Celery planted in trenches and later earthed-up is fullest flavoured, but needs well drained soil for good results.

Asparagus will give good crops for many years. When planting, spread roots on each side of soil mounded along the trench.

Earth-up potatoes when nine inches (twenty cm) tall. Draw soil halfway up the plants, to prevent tubers from being exposed and turning green and poisonous.

Cultivation

Most vegetables are raised from seed sown directly into the ground where the crop is to grow until it is harvested. Details of how to prepare the surface of the soil are given on page 190, and the method of sowing is explained on page 191. The majority of seeds are sown in V-shaped drills half to three-quarter inches deep (12–20 mm); the smaller the seed the shallower the drill. Large seeds, such as beans and peas, are sown about one and a half inches deep (forty mm).

Weeding should be started as soon as the crop is visible. The weeds *between* the rows pose the biggest threat, so deal with them first; those *along* the rows matter less.

Thinning should be avoided as far as possible by sowing sparingly. If thinning is needed, do it as soon as the plants are big enough to handle. In order to cause as little disturbance as possible, the ground should be moist. If necessary water it some time beforehand. Make the soil firm round the seedlings that are left, and remove all the thinnings so that they do not attract pests.

During recent years increasing use has been made of chemical weedkillers, particularly by commercial growers; details

can be found on page 230. For the home gardener with a small vegetable plot, however, these herbicides are of limited use at present. Most people prefer hand-weeding or hoeing, for which the dutch or push hoe is widely used. It is slid under the surface to avoid damaging roots or bringing up weed seeds.

Earthing-up is done with a draw hoe. The object with potatoes is to prevent tubers from being exposed to light and turning green and poisonous. The plants are earthed-up once when they are nine inches (twenty cm) high. Trench celery is earthed three or four times during the season to blanch the stems; always leave the green leaves at the top uncovered.

Though most vegetables are sown in their final positions, some are usually transplanted. There are two reasons for this. The first is to lengthen the growing period of somewhat tender crops such as tomatoes and sweet peppers by sowing them early under glass so that when it is safe to plant them out they will already be well developed. For details of raising such plants see page 198. They can usually be bought from nurserymen and garden centres at planting-out time.

The second reason for transplanting is to save space by sowing some hardy crops such as brassicas in a seed-bed and planting them in their final quarters as ground falls vacant.

Increasing Yields

Where space is limited, several methods may be used to make that space yield as much produce as possible.

Successional sowing is the most practical way of overcoming the common problem of gluts followed by shortages. Sow such crops as lettuce, radish, carrot and beetroot in short rows regularly every two or three weeks throughout the growing season. Then you will be able to enjoy a continuous supply of tender young produce, instead of seeing much of it wasted by running to seed or becoming tough and unpalatable.

Intersowing is another useful technique for getting the most out of a limited area. It consists of sowing a quick-growing crop such as radishes or a small lettuce like 'Little Gem' in the same row as a slow grower such as parsnips. The quick crop will appear first and be gathered before the slow crop needs the full space. Intercropping is a similar space-saving method, but in this case the fast-maturing crop is grown between rows of slower-maturing ones. For instance, spinach may be grown between rows of leeks.

Increasing yields does not only apply to produce grown for immediate consumption but to that grown to be used from store. Beans – runner, french and broad – crop heavily and freeze well. Several root crops may be stored for winter use.

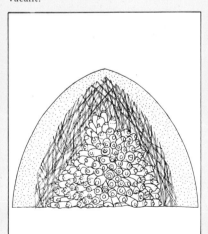

Carrots, turnips, swedes and potatoes may be stored for the winter in clamps, outdoors or under cover. Surround them with straw and cover with six inches (fifteen cm) of earth.

Beetroot and other root vegetables may be stored under cover between layers of slightly damp sand or peat in any available container, such as a barrel or a large box.

Fruit

Most present-day gardens have only a limited amount of space for growing fruit. Everything possible should be done, therefore, to make sure that what space there is available is used to the full.

The most important considerations when planning a fruit garden are these:

1 If you are going to grow fruit, set aside a part of the garden for that purpose and that purpose only. Mixing fruit with other things makes it more difficult to manage and is unlikely to give good results. However, an exception is usually made in the case of strawberries, which lose vigour and crop poorly if allowed to occupy the same site for more than three or four years at the most. They are therefore best grown in the vegetable plot.

2 The site should be open enough to ensure that there is plenty of light to assist growth and ripening and that there is a good air flow to prevent dank conditions which encourage disease. Exposure to violent winds is, however, to be avoided. If necessary, construct or plant a wind-break. Frost pockets should also be avoided, since blossoms may be so severely damaged by spring frosts that there is a reduced crop – or no crop at all. The ideal site is one from which cold air readily drains. Sometimes low-lying positions can be improved by making a gap in the hedge or other boundary at the lowest end of the site. This allows cold air to escape as it flows down the slope.

3 In deciding how much of the area to give to soft fruit and how much to tree fruit, personal preference plays a large part. The smaller the available space, however, the more reason to grow only, or mainly, soft fruit; not only does it take up less room but it is much better picked fresh from the garden; tree fruit can usually be bought from the shops in excellent condition.

4 It is generally best to group the same kinds of fruit together. Not only does this produce a much neater and more attractive appearance than mixing them up, but it makes cultivation and other gardening operations such as spraying, pruning and applying manure and fertilizer much easier.

5 Plant only sound, healthy material from a reputable supplier. Wherever possible with soft fruit buy Certified Stock inspected under the Ministry of Agriculture scheme.

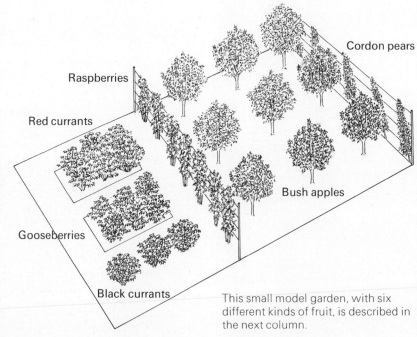

Raspberries

Red currants

Gooseberries

Black currants

Cordon pears

Bush apples

This small model garden, with six different kinds of fruit, is described in the next column.

When well grown, using healthy stock of good modern cultivars, strawberries produce a heavier yield for a given area than any other soft fruit. In addition to the traditional summer-fruiting ones, there are now so-called perpetual cultivars which continue to produce fruit until the autumn frosts. Set the plants eighteen inches (forty-five cm) apart, in rows three feet (ninety cm) apart, in a well manured section of the vegetable garden free from perennial weeds. Planting between July and mid-September will give a good crop the following year. Do not let plants occupy the same ground for more than three or four years.

Another crop usually grown in the vegetable garden is rhubarb. Though the part that is eaten is not fruit but leaf-stalk, it is usually served as the sweet course.

Rhubarb is grown from divisions of the root-stock, carrying at least one good bud and planted three feet (seventy-five cm) apart in fertile, well drained soil enriched with plenty of manure or compost and free from perennial weeds. Planting may be done at any time during the dormant period, from October to early March. A thick mulch will help to conserve the moisture that rhubarb needs for good growth. For early, tender stalks, forcing may be used, as shown below.

To keep strawberries clean, use a layer of straw or specially made mats, as shown above.

Rhubarb can be forced under special pots, as shown here, or boxes, surrounded with straw or leaves.

The principles of planning a productive and easily-managed fruit garden in limited space are demonstrated by the fruit garden plots in the Royal Horticultural Society's garden at Wisley. Pictured at the top of the previous page is the layout of the smallest of these gardens, showing how six different kinds of fruit can be produced from a plot sixty feet by thirty feet (eighteen × nine metres).

At the eastern boundary is a row of twelve cordon pears planted two feet six inches (seventy-five cm) apart. Next come nine bush apples, grown on a dwarfing rootstock to keep them within the allotted space, planted ten feet (three metres) apart in rows twelve feet (3.5 metres) apart.

A row of twenty raspberries, planted eighteen inches (forty-five cm) apart across the plot, begins the soft fruit section. Small groups of black currants, red currants and gooseberries, planted five to six·feet (1.5 to 1.8 metres) apart, complete this section.

Placing the soft fruit together in this way makes it possible to surround the whole section with a cage of wood or metal posts and rails enclosed in netting to keep out birds.

Grouping similar fruits together also makes it easier to feed them according to their individual needs. While all the usual kinds do best in a deep, well cultivated soil with plenty of organic matter and slightly on the acid side – with a pH of about 6.5 (see page 183) – their nutrient requirements vary. Black currants and pears, for instance, benefit from heavy dressings of nitrogen, but apples and raspberries if given large amounts of nitrogen may produce too much vigorous growth and bear a diminished amount of fruit.

Where space and conditions allow, the size of the fruit garden may be increased, together with the range of fruits grown. There is not the same range of dwarfing rootstocks for the stone fruits as there is for apples and pears, so they tend to take up a considerable amount of space when grown as trees, and to cast too much shadow unless planted at the north end of the fruit garden. It is, however, possible to obtain fan-trained cherries, plums, peaches and nectarines on suitable rootstocks and grow them successfully against a warm wall or fence, though it takes time and patience.

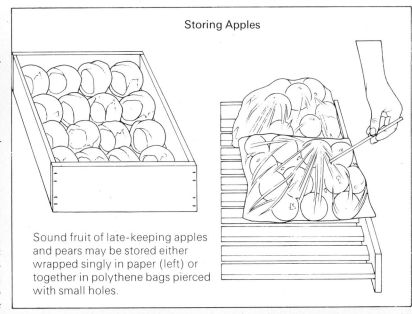

Storing Apples

Sound fruit of late-keeping apples and pears may be stored either wrapped singly in paper (left) or together in polythene bags pierced with small holes.

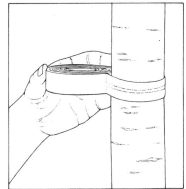

Other popular fruits which can be grown successfully on a wall, fence or trellis, or over an arch, include blackberries and the related loganberries, boysenberries and tayberries, also grapes and figs.

The soft fruits are self-fertile, but many others are not and need suitable pollinators. Good nurserymen can advise on requirements.

Pruning plays a very important part in the successful management of a fruit garden, not only to maintain plants in the desired form but to keep a balance between shoot growth and fruiting. Details are given on page 217.

Most fruits are best picked when ripe and eaten straight away. There are, however, many late-keeping apples and pears that are best after a period of storage.

Bark-ringing

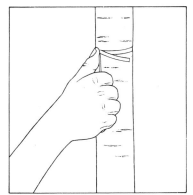

Bark-ringing apples and pears checks undue vigour. Remove a strip of bark nearly round the trunk, leaving an inch intact.

Cover the cut with adhesive tape. If done in spring, healing should be complete by autumn, when the tape may be removed.

Protected Cultivation

The term protected cultivation covers several different methods of giving plants, for all or part of their lives, a more favourable environment than they would otherwise enjoy.

There are two reasons for providing plants with protection. The first is to control humidity. Where it is necessary to keep the air moist, for example to prevent cuttings from drying out before they have developed a good root system, a simple and cheap method is to enclose them in a plastic bag fixed over the pot containing them. There are also domed covers of rigid plastic designed to fit over various sizes of pots and trays, some with small holes for ventilation and some with adjustable ventilators.

Sometimes protection is needed to prevent damage from excessively wet conditions. Several of the most desirable rock-garden plants come from mountainous regions where they experience periods of intense cold which leave them unscathed, but they do not at the same time have to face prolonged periods of rain, which may cause them to rot. Many of these plants may be brought successfully through the most severe winters with no more protection than a pane of glass held above them by a wire support during wet weather. The range of such plants successfully grown may, however, be increased with a cold frame, and extended still further in an unheated greenhouse.

The second reason for protection is to control temperature and thus provide better conditions for growth, so that the season may be extended and the range of crops grown increased.

Propagators of several different makes and designs are available, to enable seeds to be sown and seedlings raised when outdoor temperatures are unfavourable. The simplest consist of a transparent plastic cover which fits over a standard sized seed tray and is high enough to allow the seedlings room to grow before the time comes to transplant them. These simple propagating cases do not incorporate any form of artificial heating and therefore need to be placed in a sufficiently warm place for germination to take place.

A bench in a heated greenhouse provides excellent conditions. If that is not available, a windowsill will do to start with; but do not stand the propagator in direct sunlight or it may quickly become too hot inside. These simple trays with plastic covers are useful for germination and for bringing the seedlings through their early stages. The closed case provides a humid environment which after the first watering at the time of sowing may make it unnecessary to do any more until the time comes to transplant the seedlings. This should be done well before the young plants reach as far as the cover.

Larger and more elaborate propagators are available which incorporate a heating device of some kind. These are naturally more expensive to buy, but as they provide their own warmth they do not require any external source.

Most modern propagators of this type are heated by electricity and can be plugged into a socket from the mains supply, which should be installed by a qualified electrician. They are generally heated by a length of soil-warming cable, covered with a layer of sand or gravel on which seed-trays and/or pots can be stood. This provides bottom heat, which can usually be relied upon to improve the rate of germination and rooting.

The best models are thermostatically controlled. Though this adds to the initial cost it is likely to pay for itself in lower electricity bills.

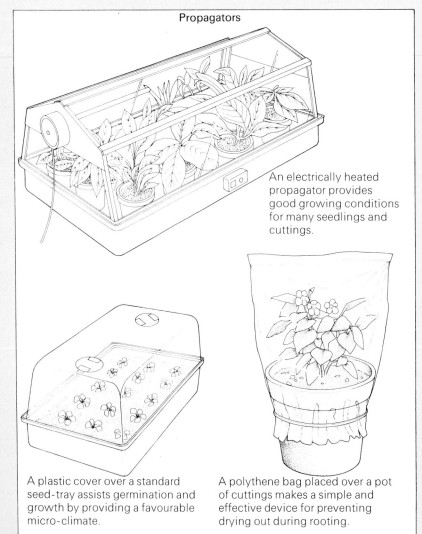

Propagators

An electrically heated propagator provides good growing conditions for many seedlings and cuttings.

A plastic cover over a standard seed-tray assists germination and growth by providing a favourable micro-climate.

A polythene bag placed over a pot of cuttings makes a simple and effective device for preventing drying out during rooting.

By the use of simple methods of protection that require no artificial heat, the growing season in the vegetable garden may be extended by several weeks, so that earlier – and in some cases later – crops may be gathered.

The essential feature of these devices is that they trap and retain heat that would otherwise be dissipated into the air, so that crops growing under them enjoy higher soil and air temperatures than those outside. As an added benefit the plants receive some shelter from driving winds and rain.

Among hardy vegetables that can be sown earlier with protection than would be otherwise possible are carrots, lettuces, radishes, peas, french and runner beans, early beetroot and turnips. These can all be left to grow to maturity where they were sown, the protection being removed as soon as it is safe to do so. In this case a low cover is enough, since it will only be needed while the plants are small.

Some other crops may be grown to full size under cover, which must therefore be higher to allow for development. These include strawberries for early fruiting, ridge cucumbers and melons.

Protection may also be given late in the year to such crops as winter lettuce, endive, leaf beets and parsley, which though hardy are likely to be of better quality if given some shelter.

The type of protection most commonly used for vegetable garden crops takes the form of a portable covering which can be assembled easily and has the property of retaining warmth while letting in light.

The cheapest are polythene tunnels, made of lightweight sheeting stretched over wire hoops pushed into the soil and usually spaced about three feet (one metre) apart. At each end the sheeting is drawn together and tied to a stake. To prevent the sides from riding up in the wind they are either buried or held down with stones or other heavy objects; it ought, however, to be possible to slip the covering up on days of bright sunshine to prevent possible overheating. Different sizes are available, the smallest for seedlings and the largest for growing to maturity such crops as lettuces.

There are many different cloches made of glass or plastic. The glass ones do not deteriorate, hold heat better and can give somewhat earlier crops; but they are usually more expensive and easily broken. Plastic ones are lighter and easier to move, so they need to be anchored firmly; they are made brittle by the action of light and when not in use should be stored in the dark; more expensive ones with an ultra-violet inhibitor may last longer. Cloches are made in several sizes, from small tent-shaped ones to the taller barn cloches.

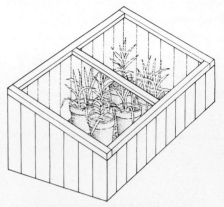

A simple and effective garden frame with wooden sides may be bought ready built or in easily assembled kit form, or can be made from available timber.

A method of protecting plants not reliably hardy in the open during icy spells is the garden frame. This consists of an enclosing wall on which is supported a glazed cover known as a light, hinged or sliding and often completely removable. A frame is useful for hardening off plants raised in heat before planting them out in the open, for early crops of lettuce, radish and carrots, and for overwintering many cuttings and seedlings. Walls of brick, concrete or wood conserve heat well; glass-sided ones provide more light.

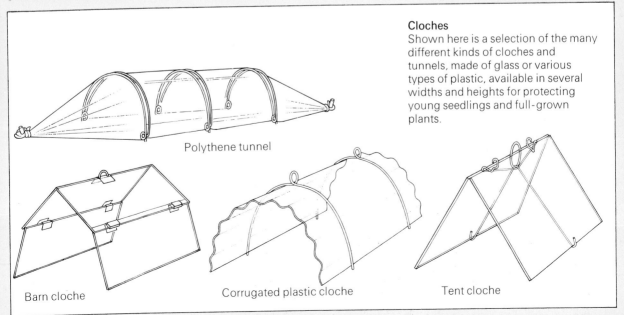

Cloches
Shown here is a selection of the many different kinds of cloches and tunnels, made of glass or various types of plastic, available in several widths and heights for protecting young seedlings and full-grown plants.

Polythene tunnel

Barn cloche

Corrugated plastic cloche

Tent cloche

Greenhouses

A greenhouse may be used for several different purposes.

A cold house (usually without any artificial heat, but sometimes given just enough warmth to prevent freezing) makes it possible to grow those plants, such as many of the choicest alpines, which though hardy are likely to be damaged, or even killed, if exposed to the wet conditions which are often experienced outside during the winter. Also given the shelter of a cold house such crops as tomatoes will be ready for gathering weeks before those grown outside. Several other vegetables and fruits can be made to produce both earlier and later crops in a cold house than would be possible in the open.

The most popular form of heated greenhouse is the cool house, with a minimum night temperature in winter between 40°F (4.5°C) and 45°F (7°C). Such a house can provide suitable conditions for a very wide range of plants, including almost all those from temperate parts of the world and many from the sub-tropics, and even the tropics. Suitable plants are basically of two kinds: those that will grow during the winter in the cool house, such as chrysanthemums and salad crops, and others, such as many bedding plants native to warm climates, which will survive the winter in a dormant state in the cool house but would die outside.

The range of plants that it is possible to grow may be increased still further if the minimum night temperature is raised to 50°F (10°C) or more, when the house is usually called an intermediate house. Against this, however, must be set the fact that every additional 5°F (2.8°C) almost exactly doubles the cost of heating. Many people nowadays limit the extra cost by partitioning off a part of the greenhouse, usually at the end opposite to the door, and keeping it warmer than the rest.

Warm houses need a minimum night temperature of between 55°F (13°C) and 60°F (15°C). Few amateurs use so much heat these days, except those who specialize in such plants as warm-growing orchids. Many tropical foliage plants that were once grown in warm greenhouses are now grown in the home, where they share the central heating at no extra cost.

There are many types of greenhouse, designed to meet different needs and pref-

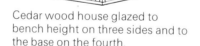

Greenhouse Types

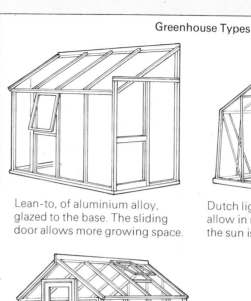

Lean-to, of aluminium alloy, glazed to the base. The sliding door allows more growing space.

Dutch light type. Sloping sides allow in more light in winter when the sun is low in the sky.

Cedar wood house glazed to bench height on three sides and to the base on the fourth.

Circular house of aluminium, a design becoming popular as a decorative garden feature.

erences. Most gardeners nowadays choose – according to how much they have to spend and what they want to grow – a ready-built model, usually sold in sections to be put together by the purchaser.

Some of the most popular designs are shown above. The first (top left) is the lean-to type, consisting of a single-span roof and three sides; the fourth side is formed by the wall against which it is erected. Though often facing south, where it can house such plants as a grape vine, grown along the underside of the roof, and perhaps a fan-trained peach on the back wall, a lean-to may face in other directions if suitable plants are grown.

The other three illustrations are of free-standing models. The most popular are the vertical-sided type and the sloping-sided dutch light pattern. So-called circular models (usually hexagonal or octagonal) are gaining popularity as garden features, forming attractive focal points.

Traditionally the structure has been of wood, but this has now been overtaken in popularity by metal. The majority of greenhouses are now made of aluminium alloy, combining strength with lightness.

For those who prefer wood there are many models available, mostly made of western red cedar, which is resistant to rot and has usually been treated with a preservative. Further painting with preservative about every five years is recommended.

Glass is by far the most widely used covering. It is stable, it does not deteriorate with time, and a good horticultural grade lets through nine-tenths of the sun's rays. On wooden structures it is still largely bedded in putty and held by glazing sprigs, but non-hardening compounds are increasingly used, and on aluminium houses clips replace sprigs. Plastic sheeting, though initially cheaper than glass, soon deteriorates and needs replacing, but research is being carried out to produce newer and better materials.

Many greenhouses are supplied with a concrete kerb made up of easily fitted sections. For a small house this kerb can stand on firm, level ground, but a larger one needs concrete foundations.

Plants grown in the greenhouse border, such as tomatoes, need glazing down to the base. For plants standing on staging, the sides can be boarded or bricked to the staging level. Many have one side glazed to the base and the rest to the staging.

The site should be unshaded, particularly in winter when the sun is low in the sky. In exposed places a windbreak will limit heat loss caused by wind striking the glass. If possible, it is generally best for the greenhouse to run east and west.

A cheap and simple heater is one of the paraffin-burning greenhouse models. At the other end of the scale are piped hot water systems, fired by solid fuel, oil or gas; though the best are excellent, they are expensive to install and mainly used for very large houses. Natural gas heaters are highly efficient; they give off water vapour and carbon dioxide, both beneficial to plant growth. Many people prefer electrical heaters, of the tubular or the fan-assisted types, with thermostatic controls that switch on the current only when needed.

To reduce heat loss in cold weather the greenhouse may be lined with clear plastic, a gap being left between it and the glass for insulation. Since this may cause condensation and growth of algae, and so reduce the amount of light, many people now line only the side facing north.

This greenhouse contains several automatic features, as listed below, to provide excellent growing conditions while needing the minimum of attention.

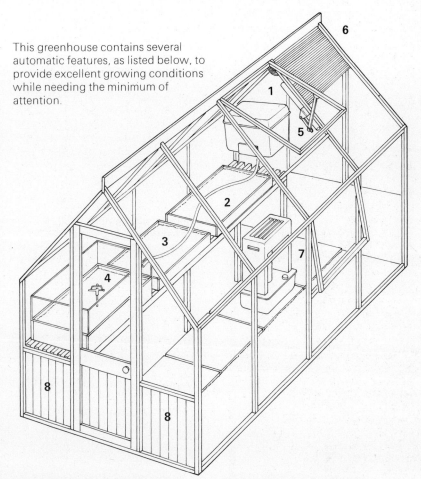

1 Header tank, supplying water to trickle irrigation system.
2 and 3 Capillary trays, for automatic watering of pot plants.
4 Mist propagation unit.
5 Automatic ventilator opener.
6 Slatted exterior blind.
7 Heater with temperature control.
8 Removable panels offering choice of light to staging or to ground.

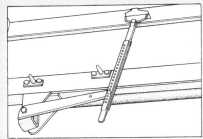

Above This automatic device opens and closes ventilators by expansion and contraction as the temperature rises and falls.

Right Roller blinds fitted inside the glass protect foliage from sun-scorch and help to reduce excessive rise in temperature.

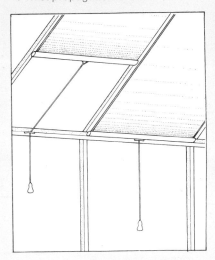

Since small greenhouses can both heat up and cool down very rapidly, it is necessary to have adequate ventilators to control the temperature. Automatic opening devices which work by expansion and contraction are good investments.

Shading may be needed on sunny days. A simple method is to paint a shading compound on the glass for the summer. Better still are blinds, used only when the sun shines; outside ones are ideal, but interior ones are considerably cheaper.

Many people are now installing automatic watering systems, with a header tank or bottle which delivers water through tubing to sand or capillary matting in trays from which plants take up moisture as needed.

Weeds and their Control

Even the most carefully looked after garden is sure to be invaded by unwanted plants, which are usually hardy natives, tough enough to overcome competition from less vigorous garden plants.

One group of weeds – most of them annual – spreads by means of vast numbers of seeds; some familiar examples are chickweed, bitter cress, and groundsel. Another group survives and spreads by means of perennial roots or underground stems; examples are couch-grass, ground-elder, dock and colt's-foot.

The most widely used ways of controlling weeds belonging to the first group are such long established cultural practices as hoeing and pulling by hand or with the help of a small fork. This is particularly appropriate among garden plants in spring; if the weeds are removed as seedlings, before they have taken firm root, the cultivated plants will soon spread their foliage and offer less opportunity for further invaders.

If cultural methods are not used or are insufficient, annual weeds may be quickly and easily eradicated with a mixture of paraquat and diquat, or propachlor may be used.

Perennial weeds are also widely dealt with by cultural methods, but these can be tedious and time-consuming. Every piece of root or stem should be dug up and destroyed; if left it is likely to grow into a new plant. For chemical control it is best to use a weedkiller that is absorbed into the plant, such as dichlobenil or glyphosate.

For areas that have to be cleared and kept clear and do not contain cultivated plants, sodium chlorate or dichlobenil can be used, followed by simazine; or a mixture of aminotriazole and simazine.

Weedkillers work in various ways. Some must be sprayed or dusted on the top growth, through which they are absorbed, to circulate in the sap to every part of the plant. Others affect the green colouring matter of the foliage to which they are applied. Some, absorbed by the roots, must be put on the soil.

Solutions, powders or granules are available. They must be used with great care, especially among cultivated plants; they do not differentiate between the wanted and the unwanted. Selective weedkillers, much used on lawns, act on broad-leaved weeds only, not on the grass.

Weedkillers

Chemical and formulation	Type and purpose	Remarks
Aminotriazole, solution	total, top growth, paths, ground clearance	available only as mixture with simazine
2,4–D, 2,4,5–T, MCPA, solution	selective hormone, top growth, lawns, scrub, general	available as mixtures
Dalapon, solution	selective hormone, couch and other grasses, top growth	
Dicamba, solution	selective top growth, difficult lawn weeds	available only in mixtures
Dichlobenil, granules	total, or selective at manufacturer's directions, roots, ground clearance, general	very light and fine, easily blown by wind
Dichlorprop, fenoprop, mecoprop, solution	selective, top growth, lawns	particularly good for small-leaved weeds; available as mixtures only
Glyphosate, solution	total, top growth, general	can be used with care amongst cultivated plants
Ioxynil, solution	selective, roots, seedling weeds in new lawns	also with mecoprop
Paraquat/diquat, solution	total, through green parts, small and annual weeds	works quickly in a few days, inactivated on reaching soil
Propachlor, granules	selective, roots, amongst vegetables and some ornamental plants	kills weed seeds as they germinate in the soil
Simazine, solution	total, roots, to keep cleared ground clear	lasts 12 months, does not move in soil, remains in top few inches
Sodium chlorate, solution	total, roots, for clearing and to keep cleared ground clear	lasts at least 6 months, moves downwards and sideways beyond point of application, should contain a fire-depressant

Plant pests, diseases and other troubles

Couch grass

Bindweed

Ground elder

Nettle

Creeping thistle

Coltsfoot

Groundsel

Chickweed

Annual meadow grass

Lesser celandine

Creeping buttercup

Horsetail

It cannot be emphasized too strongly that a plant which is given the most suitable growing conditions from the start will have the kind of vigour and constitution which either does not succumb at all to alien invasion, or which prevents and defeats its advance to any great degree. To this end it is essential that the soil should have a good structure, that is, be well-drained and aerated, and contain sufficient mineral nutrients to ensure that the plant grows and matures fully. Whether a plant is started from a seed, a rooted cutting, a division, a layer or a graft, the individual selected should be straight, strong, well-coloured, and with plenty of root; it goes without saying that it, too, should have had the best possible soil or compost in which to start life.

However, in spite of all efforts, inevitably ill-health will make itself apparent at some time in one plant or another, if only because epidemics of pests or fungus diseases occur as a result of weather conditions. Plant sickness (phytopathology) is an umbrella term for a variety of health problems; they include insect and related pests, fungus diseases, bacterial diseases, viruses, nutrient deficiencies, physiological disorders, and animal damage.

Insects and Other Pests

Insects and related pests include greenfly, caterpillars, slugs and snails, ants, earwigs, leatherjackets, eelworms and many others. Some will literally bite holes in plant tissues, leaves being the main target; but flowers, stems, buds and roots, particularly fleshy ones, will also come under attack. Other pests feed by drawing on the sap of a plant, again mainly from the leaves, for which purpose their mouth-parts have become specially adapted, so that the sap is sucked through a long, needle-like arrangement which pierces the tissue, and supplies the channel along which the sap runs.

The biting insect type of damage is the most easily recognised. If it is on soft, lush new shoots and leaves close to the ground, slugs and snails are usually the culprits, though it is not unknown for them to advance high up a plant, for instance on runner beans. Irregular large holes in leaves higher up plants are more likely to be due to caterpillars, and if so, are easily seen and dealt with. Slugs and snails feed at night.

On the whole this type of damage is of much less concern (unless there is a plague of the pest concerned) than that of the sucking type of pest.

Feeding by 'suckers' causes yellowing or other discoloration of leaves, and so prevents their efficient functioning; distortion, blistering and curling, stunting of new shoots, discoloration and malformed development of flowers, misshapen fruits, and wilting of small plants to the point of death. Leaf fall can be complete and premature, and plants may be infected with virus disease, for which there is no remedy.

Furthermore, such pests have a devastating rate of increase, and population explosions of aphids (greenfly, blackfly, American blight) can occur in a matter of days, in suitable conditions. If the weather is hot and dry, in spring or summer, and plants are allowed to run short of water, then the numbers of such pests will increase to epidemic proportions, and no amount of spraying, watering, and subsequent feeding will restore plants to their previous health. For every one greenfly you can see, assume there are twenty.

These are the insect pests which live on the top growth of plants, but there is an invisible army in the soil, mostly the caterpillar type which feeds in and on plant roots, or the aphid type. Unfortunately the first sign of their activity is a plant wilting or turning yellow, and often it is then beyond help. Again, watering in drought conditions is important, and maintaining a supply of humus within and on top of the soil, to act as a sponge and water reservoir.

Eelworms or nematodes are a class on their own. They are microscopic and cannot be seen with the naked eye, transparent, and exactly like miniature eels in shape. They feed inside leaves, stems and roots, causing discoloration, swelling, distortion and eventual decay. Control is difficult for the gardener, since the chemicals available to him or her do not help. Spread of these pests is in the soil, on plant tissue, in water, by birds, man, and such insects as beetles.

Fungus Diseases

Fungus diseases infect a plant unseen, through a healthy leaf, or through an injury, often to the stem, but also through an insect injury to leaf or flower. Fungus spores are continuously present in the atmosphere, and will grow rapidly on plants, again where weather conditions are suitable, or where a plant is already sick. Many plants have a natural inbuilt defence against fungi, but it will not be sufficient at all times, and under conditions of mono-culture, spread will again be rapid.

As with pests, fungus diseases also infect underground plant parts, the roots, and again, plants diseased in this way are often beyond revival. Clubroot of brassicas is an example; another is honey fungus.

Virus Diseases

Reference was made earlier to virus diseases, transmitted mainly by sucking insect pests. Virus particles are so small as to be invisible except with an electron microscope, and they live and multiply in the nucleus of a plant cell. Symptoms of their presence are irregular yellow, white or cream streaking, flecking, speckling and blotching of leaves (sometimes marking is circular), unnaturally slow growth, stunting, distortion, swelling and lack of flower or fruit. Such a plant can also become heavily infested with pest or fungus disease and subsequently die.

Virus diseases are spread by aphids as they suck up the particles in the sap and move from an infected to a healthy plant, and also by capsids, eelworms, and beetles. Attempts to control them chemically so far have only resulted in killing the host plant as well, since they are an integral part of the nucleus, and infected plants should be destroyed when infection is diagnosed.

Nutrient Deficiencies

These have definite symptoms, specific to each deficiency, and some are fairly obvious. Lime-induced chlorosis shows as yellow to white leaves and stems at the tip of shoots, and is due to a shortage of iron, the mineral required in the formation of chlorophyll.

In the average garden, however, very few mineral nutrients are likely to be so lacking as to weaken the plant. Their diagnosis is difficult, because discolorations of leaves can superficially resemble that caused by virus diseases or insect pests. For example, magnesium shortage can show as purple-brown tints in apple leaves, and interveinal yellowing in tomatoes. If such a deficiency is suspected, and many plants are badly affected, it is best to call in a professional adviser.

Other Troubles

Physiological disorders are those due to weather conditions, unsuitable soils or growing mediums, and poor manage-ment. Cracks in apples caused by frost, or in tomatoes by watering heavily after drought, and brown margins to leaves after salt-laden gales are some typical examples and, apart from improving one's own garden management, little can be done to offset them. But the healthier and stronger the plant is in the first place, the better it will withstand such onslaughts.

Animal damage by mice, rabbits, deer, squirrels, moles and birds is all too obvious: gnawed bark, damaged fruit and flower-buds, disturbed seed-beds and molehills in lawns are some of their depredations, but action in the form of protection or repellents can be taken.

Remedies

The gardener has a variety of weapons at his command in the treatment of all these plant malfunctions, and while the chemicals contained in insecticides are certainly effective, they are not the only methods for control. The manual one in the form of handpicking is easy and cheap, and other alternatives include: sowing or planting at times which avoid the main life-cycle of a pest; growing mixtures of plants rather than monocultures; growing plants and varieties known to be disease-resistant; obtaining plants from outside sources certified to be free of disease; providing sufficient food and water; a good soil structure and the right temperatures; avoiding injury to plants; keeping a 'clean' garden so that pests and diseases do not have a home-base such as rubbish piles, stones, wood, etc; burning or otherwise destroying diseased plants.

There are also biological controls in the form of predatory and parasitic insects, fungi and bacteria, of particular use in greenhouse cultivation, and quantities of these can be bought by mail-order from specialist companies.

Common pests and diseases and their chemical controls

There is a bewildering variety of products available for the control of plant pests and diseases, but like proprietary medicines, many contain the same chemical – only the brand name is different. Below are given the most common pests and diseases, together with the appropriate chemical control under its accepted scientific name – some are insecticides, for treating insects and related pests, some fungicides. Most are deposited on the plant surface and break down in a few days, but some – dimethoate, benomyl, thiophanatemethyl, carbendazim and propiconazole – are systemics, which means that they are absorbed into the plant's sap and they may remain viable there for several weeks.

Trees and shrubs: pests and diseases

Symptoms	Cause	Remedy
Beech hedge: curled leaves, white woolly patches on leaves, stunted growth, stickiness	beech aphid	spray under strong pressure, malathion, resmethrin, dimethoate
Birch, hornbeam, conifers: clusters of twigs in heads of trees, like birds' nests	witches' broom, due to pests, fungi virus or other causes	not necessary unless unsightly
Box: shoot tip leaves curl to form rounded tight cluster, growth checked	box sucker	cut off affected growth, spray malathion, dimethoate
Elm: yellow leaves on one branch, spreading to others, tree dies in 2 years or less	dutch elm disease, spread by elm bark beetles	none for gardener, destroy infected tree as soon as seen, strip bark off stump
Firethorn (pyracantha): black spots on leaves, brown coating on berries	scab disease	cut off affected growth, spray benomyl, captan
Hawthorn and other trees/shrubs: 1.5 cm holes low down on tree trunks, or in branches, frass present	goat or leopard moth caterpillars inside tree or shrub, up to 5 cm long	remove badly damaged branches, fill other holes with HCH (BHC), seal
Heathers: slow poor or yellow growth, some die back or complete death	phytophthora root death	destroy affected plants, improve soil drainage, do not replant in same site
Holly: leaves with pale green winding lines or pale brown blisters	leafminer	dimethoate, remove badly affected growth
Oak: small round red raised spots on underside of leaves	spangle gall caused by gall-wasps	not necessary
Privet: large holes in leaves	caterpillar or privet hawk moth, up to 7 cm long, with 'tail'	not necessary
Pyracantha and hawthorn: shoots wilt and leaves turn brown, remaining on shoot	fireblight	cut out infected shoots
Rhododendron: buds dead and brown	frost	protect if possible
Rhododendron: buds brown, with black bristles	bud blast, fungus spread by insect	remove affected buds, spray captan, mancozeb
Rhododendron: small green, red-striped insects on leaves, hopping when disturbed	rhododendron leaf-hopper, spreads bud blast	bioresmethrin, dimethoate
Willow: brown spots on leaves, black cankers on stems, dieback, defoliation	willow anthracnose	cut out where practicable and burn prunings, spray copper containing fungicide

Climbers and wall plants: pests and diseases

Symptoms	Cause	Remedy
Camellia: pale brown patches on young leaves	scald, due to hot sun	supply shade in summer and at midday; transplant to dappled shade
Ceanothus: yellow to white young leaves, veins green	lime-induced chlorosis resulting from iron deficiency	treat soil with iron sequestrene
Clematis: irregular holes in leaves and petals	earwigs	carbaryl, HCH (BHC), dimethoate, trichlorphon
Clematis: shoots wilt and die within a few days	clematis wilt, due to fungus	remove affected growth, paint wounds with fungicidal sealing compound; spray new shoots with Bordeaux mixture as they grow
Honeysuckle: yellowing of leaves, stickiness, discoloration, slow growth	greenfly	move plant to cooler site, spray resmethrin, pirimicarb, rotenone
Ivy: whitish speckling of leaves, later all yellow or cream, slow growth	spider mites (bryobia)	move to cooler site, water, or spray rotenone, malathion
Passion flower: distorted, yellow-speckled leaves, slow weak growth	mosaic virus	none, destroy plants, control greenfly on future plants
Roses, climbing and rambling, see Rose section, p. 235		

Bulbs and corms: pests and diseases

Symptoms	Cause	Remedy
Daffodil and narcissus: no flowers, narrow, twisted leaves	small grey-white maggots in bulbs, rotting, bulbs killed, narcissus fly	destroy infested bulbs; HCH (BHC) dust leaves of healthy bulbs after flowering
distorted small leaves, with small yellow bumps	stem eelworm, brown rings in transversely cut bulb, bulb soft	destroy bulbs
bulbs in store brown and soft at base	basal rot fungus disease	destroy bulbs, do not plant in same soil for 3 years
yellow or white streaks on leaves, curling, twisted stems	virus diseases	destroy bulbs
Hyacinth: poor development of flowers/leaves, bulb soft	soft rot, bad smelling and liquid, bacterial	destroy bulbs, improve soil drainage
Iris: yellow stripes turning black on leaves, death of plant	ink spot fungus disease, bulb destroyed completely, black marks on scale leaves	destroy remains, spray other plants with dichlofluanid, do not plant in same compost
Lily: red-brown spots on leaves with yellow surround, buds killed	lily disease, especially *L. candidum*, fungus	spray benomyl or dichlofluanid, destroy fallen leaves
Tulip: withered leaf tips and flowers, buds die before opening	tulip fire, fungus disease	destroy as soon as seen, spray benomyl on remaining plants

Roses: pests and diseases

Symptoms	Cause	Remedy
Rounded, tightly packed clusters of red hairs at tips of shoots	gall wasps invading buds, producing Robin's pincushion or Bedeguar	none needed; cut off if unsightly
Fringed black spots on leaves, followed by yellowing and early fall	black spot fungus	destroy affected leaves, spray regularly thiophanate-methyl or captan
Cracking, splitting of bark, dead patches, near soil level	canker fungus	pare away affected growth, apply wound sealing compound, destroy dead shoots
Pinprick holes in young leaves and stems, buds dead	capsid bug	dimethoate, HCH (BHC)
Holes in flower buds, flowers one-sided	chafer beetles	pick off beetles if practicable
Young leaves crinkled and purple, leaf edges brown	frost	occurs when mild winter weather followed by frost, not serious
Large semi-circular holes in margins of leaves	leaf-cutting bee	none needed
Light-coloured speckling of leaf surface, growth checked, premature leaf fall	leaf-hoppers on under-surface	resmethrin, malathion, rotenone
Edges of leaves tightly rolled inwards and downwards	leaf-rolling sawfly grubs	pick off and destroy affected leaves, spray dimethoate if too many to do this
White powdery patches on leaves/buds	powdery mildew	cut off affected parts, spray benomyl, propiconazole, dinocap
Purple, brown or reddish spots on leaves	soil nutrient imbalance, poor drainage	correct soil structure, improve nutrient content and balance
Raised red-brown spots on leaf underside	rust fungus	destroy leaves and spray carbendazim, mancozeb
Dead brown tip to shoot	stem-boring sawfly maggot	destroy stem, cutting back below tunnel.
Leaves skeletonized to leave veins only, patches turn brown, tiny black 'slugs' present	rose slugworm	spray resmethrin, rotenone
'Tents' of webbing, holes in leaves	lackey moth caterpillars	handpick when seen
Yellow veins on leaves, sometimes white	vein banding, virus	not serious, but feed plant well

Borders and beds: pests and diseases

Symptoms	Cause	Remedy
Antirrhinum (hollyhock, sweet pea): raised brown spots on leaf underside	rust fungus disease	remove badly infected leaves, spray carbendazim, mancozeb
Aster: wilting plants, black stem base	aster wilt, fungus disease	destroy infected plants; do not plant asters in same soil for as long as possible
Carnation: leaves tied together with webbing, holes in leaves	tortrix caterpillars, small	handpick, spray rotenone
Chrysanthemum: brown sections to leaves, yellowing, wilting	eelworm	destroy plants, also surrounding weeds
leaves brown all over, wilting from base, stems brown internally	wilt fungus disease	destroy infected plants, remove surrounding soil, do not plant up for as long as possible
Gladiolus: silvery white streaks and marks on flowers, leaves	thrips	malathion; dust corms with HCH (BHC) if attacked in summer
Peony: brown buds, brown patches on leaves, brown rot of stem bases	peony blight	cut growth to soil level autumn, remove surrounding surface soil, replace with fresh, spray benomyl, thiram
Peony: large brown marks on leaves	peony blotch	spray mancozeb, thiram
Phlox: narrow leaves with frilly edge reduced to midrib	eelworm	destroy plants, but use roots to provide cuttings
Violet: thickened leaves, curl up and inwards, growth stunted	violet leaf midge, tiny maggots	destroy infected leaves; spray dimethoate
Wallflower: tiny round holes in seedlings, leaves of young plants	flea beetle	rotenone dust or spray

Rock gardens and pools: pests and diseases

There are no particular troubles on rock garden plants in general, though they will be afflicted with the common ones, especially slugs and snails, greenfly, caterpillars and ants (see p. 241)

POOLS

Symptoms	Cause	Remedy
Holes in leaves, buds, flowers of waterlilies, leaves rot	brown-black grubs of waterlily beetle	spray leaves forcibly with water, fish will eat grubs
Brown-red concentric leaf-spots turning black on waterlily leaves	leaf spot fungus disease	remove affected leaves and destroy, do not use fungicide
Holes in leaves and stems and flowers bitten off and floating loose	Limnaea species of snail, long pointed shell	trap with whole lettuce left over night on water surface

Lawns: pests and diseases

Symptoms	Cause	Remedy
Green or black jelly-like patches	algae	improve drainage, water patches with moss-controlling chemical (dichlorophen)
Small mounds of dry soil, grass wilting in patches	ants	spray resmethrin
Small brown patches, spring, summer often on new lawns	chafer grubs, large white curved caterpillars	HCH (BHC) dust
Small heaps of soil on turf after heavy rain, from small holes	earthworms	repellant such as derris (rotenone) dust watered in; make soil acid
Rings of toadstools, dark green grass in centre or centre dead	fairy rings, fungus disease	remove turf and soil to well below white threads in soil and beyond ring, replace with new, or sterilize formaldehyde
Yellow to light brown patches, autumn-spring or any time, grass killed, white mould at edges of patches	fusarium patch (snow mould), often after prolonged snow, fungus disease	thiophanate-methyl or benomyl, improve drainage
Brown patches autumn-spring, grass dead, starlings working turf	leather jackets (Cranefly larvae) feeding on roots	flood affected areas, cover overnight, sweep up grubs, or dust HCH (BHC)
Flat, leathery, overlapping growth, grey-brown on lawn surface	dog-lichen, appears on sandy or starved soil	remove manually or use lawnsand; supply plant foods and topdress soil mixture
Small, cone-shaped mounds with hole in top, singly on turf	mining-bee making nest in soil	none needed normally; if many every year, dust HCH (BHC) spring
Hillocks of fine soil on turf	moles	Repel with smell: creosote, garlic, mothballs; trapping; kill worms
Bleached patches turning pink, red growths 6 mm long on tips of grass late summer, grass not killed	red thread (corticium), fungus disease	add plant foods; apply thiophanate-methyl or benomyl
Random toadstools on turf in autumn	fungus on decaying organic matter in soil, such as wood or tree roots	remove toadstools and destroy

Fruit: pests and diseases

Symptoms	Cause	Remedy
Apple: pinkish grub in fruit July–August which falls and is inedible	codling moth larva eating flesh, pips and core	spray fenitrothion 2nd wk June and again 3 wks later; sacking traps round trunk
ribbon scars on skin, whitish grub in fruitlets, which fall	apple sawfly larva feeds on immature fruit May–June	spray malathion 7 days after 75% petal fall
white fluffy patches on bark of tree	woolly aphid or American blight	spray malathion under strong pressure
black-brown spots on fruit, leaves, blisters on young shoots (also pears)	scab fungus disease, causes early leaf fall	spray thiophanate-methyl fortnightly from April–July; burn leaves and shoots
Blackcurrant; buds round and swollen, fail to open in spring, no fruit	big bud, due to gall mite infesting buds	remove buds and destroy in early spring, spray benomyl for partial protection
leaves pointed, nettle-like, fruit sparse or non-existent	reversion, virus disease, spread by feeding of big bud mites	destroy bushes
Cherry: tiny round holes in leaves, yellow leaves, canker on branches	bacterial canker, branches and tree can be killed	spray Bordeaux mixture 3 times at 2-weekly intervals from mid August
Gooseberry: leaves reduced to main veins, green/black caterpillars present	gooseberry sawfly larvae	handpick, may be 3 broods in season, spray rotenone if still necessary
white patches on plant, later brown felt on fruit and stems	American gooseberry mildew, fungus disease	cut out affected growth, spray thiophanate methyl; fruit is edible
Peach: leaves with red blisters, covered with grey bloom, drop early	peach leaf curl, fungus disease	destroy fallen leaves early, spray mid February, repeat 2 weeks later as buds swell
Pear: yellow, red blisters on leaves, turning black, drop early	pear leaf blister mite	destroy leaves as soon as seen, also any affected fruit
enlarged misshapen fruitlets, black, fall early	pear gall midge, white maggots feed in fruitlets	destroy infected fruitlets when seen, spray fenitrothion as blossom opens
blackened young leaves and tips of shoots spring, shoots killed	fireblight, bacterial disease, spread in moisture or by insects (bees)	notifiable disease to Ministry of Agriculture; Laxton's Superb susceptible
Plum: silvered leaf surface, later brown, branches die, plate-like growths on bark	silver leaf, fungus disease	may recover naturally; if not, remove dead growth and treat wounds with paint
fruit eaten by red maggots in summer	plum fruit moth larvae	destroy affected and fallen fruits
Raspberry; white maggots in fruit July	raspberry beetle larvae	dust rotenone immediately after flowering
Strawberry: berries rotting with grey fur	grey mould (Botrytis cinerea)	pick off infected berries and leaves, spray thiophanate-methyl fortnightly from first open flower to white fruit

Vegetables: pests and diseases

Symptoms	Cause	Remedy
Asparagus: defoliation, stems eaten	yellow/black beetle, grey larvae	rotenone, remove plant debris
Beetroot, wilting, black areas in flesh	boron deficiency	borax at 3 gm per sq metre to soil
Bean, broad, black insects on stem tips	blackfly	pinch out shoot tips when seen
Bean, broad, dark brown spots all over plant, crop reduced, plants die	chocolate spot fungus disease	improve drainage, add potassium, spray benomyl to check, destroy dead plants
Bean, runner, bud and flower drop	drought, sparrow attack, wind	water well, net, provide shelter
Brassicas, large holes in leaves green, yellow and black caterpillars	cabbage white butterfly caterpillars	handpick, spray resmethrin, rotenone
Wilting, blue-green leaves on young plants, slow growth	cabbage root fly maggots in roots, all brassicas	prevent by tar felt collar on soil round plants when planting, destroy infected plants
Wilting leaves, death or slow growth	clubroot, roots swollen, distorted	destroy infected plants, lime soil, do not replant for as long as possible
Small round holes in brassica seedlings	flea-beetles, hop when disturbed	dust or spray rotenone
Young plants' stems narrow and tough near soil	wirestem of brassicas	destroy affected plants, use sterilized compost, spray young plants with benomyl or thiophanate-methyl
Celery, pale brown blotches on leaves	celery leafminer	handpick, spray trichlorphon
Cucumber, stem rots at soil level	basal stem rot, bacterial	destroy plant, keep water off stems in future
Cucumber, young fruits shrivel from tip	wither-tip due to draught or drought, waterlogging, too-hard pruning	feed, do not water for several days, maintain even temperature
Cucumber, yellow mottling of leaves	cucumber mosaic virus	destroy plant, spray for greenfly
Lettuce, wilting for no good reason	white aphids on roots	water with malathion solution
Lettuce, wilt and die, stem eaten through	cutworm caterpillars in soil	handpick, dress soil with bromophos
Lettuce, root/stem tunnelled vertically	swift moth caterpillars	handpick, control weeds, hoe frequently
Lettuce, yellow/brown spots, white mould beneath	downy mildew fungus disease	destroy plants, spray mancozeb, do not plant in same soil for as long as possible
Marrow, yellow mottling of leaves	cucumber mosaic virus	destroy plant, spray for greenfly
Onion, yellow wilting plants, soft bulbs (and carrots)	onion fly, white maggots in bulb	destroy infested plants, interplant with parsley
Pea, holes in peas and pods	pea moth, white maggots	sow early/late, permethrin 7 days after first flowers open

(Vegetables: pests and diseases contd.)

Symptoms	Cause	Remedy
Potato, brown blotches on leaves, stems and tubers (tomato, also fruit)	potato blight, fungus disease	destroy infected plants, tubers and fruit, spray mancozeb midsummer onwards
Potato, stems blacken at soil level	black-leg, bacterial, tubers infected	do not store potatoes with brown patches at heel end, destroy infected plants
Potato, tubers with black scabby spots	common scab, fungus disease	use resistant cvs, line planting hole with green vegetation, water in drought
Potato, stunted growth, yellow leaves	potato cyst eelworm on roots	destroy infected plants/tubers, wait 6 years before growing tubers in same land
Potato, brown curved lines in tuber	spraing, due to virus, water shortage, or nutrient deficiency	none, destroy plants/tubers, control greenfly
Potato, leaves rolled or yellow mottled	virus diseases	no remedy, destroy plants/tubers, use certified seed potatoes
Tomato, brown spots on leaf upper side, growth checked, poor crop	tomato leaf-mould fungus disease	destroy badly infected leaves, spray mancozeb or benomyl, ventilate well
Tomato, brown sunken patch at base of stem and higher, leaves yellow	stem canker (*Didymella*), fungus disease	destroy badly infected plants, or scrape stem and spray captan or benomyl

Greenhouse, frame and indoor plants: pests and diseases

This group suffer all the common problems (see p. 241), especially greenfly, grey mould, leafminer (cineraria), mealy bug (vines), mildew, red spider mite (peaches, ivy), scale insect (palms, ferns), vine weevil maggots, whitefly (fuchsias, tomatoes). In addition there are some more specific problems as follows:

Symptoms	Cause	Remedy
Red to grey-white thickened leaves on azaleas, flowers discoloured	azalea gall, fungus disease	cut off infected shoots before they whiten and destroy them
Stems rot at soil level, especially *Sansevieria trifasciata* and cacti	cold or wet compost or two combined, commonly seen in winter	reduce watering in future, raise temperature a little
Brown edges and tips to leaves, thin leaves, notably palms	dry air, or acid growing medium when plant prefers limy	supply humidity; add little chalk to compost, use soft water
Flowers and buds drop, notably fuchsia, Christmas cactus, camellia	moving plant, dry air, irregular watering, dry compost, lack of light	do not move plant once buds form, increase light and moisture
Leaves fall without discolouring	dry air, dry compost, draught, cold, too much water	keep warmer and take more care with watering
Leaves at base of plant turn yellow	if many, overwatering; otherwise normal	decrease water, especially in winter
Leaves at top turn yellow	hard water or alkaline compost for plants needing acid conditions	use boiled water and acid-reacting compost or rain
Black patches on leaves already sticky	sooty mould on honeydew excreted by scale, greenfly, whitefly or mealy bug	sponge off mould and stickiness, spray resmethrin or dimethoate

Common pests and their treatment

Symptom on plant	Cause	Remedy
Curling, distortion of leaves and flowers, discoloration, stunting	aphids (greenfly, blackfly), small green, grey, black, blue, pink insects	bioresmethrin, resmethrin, malathion, pirimicarb, rotenone (derris)
Pinprick holes in young leaves, ragged tips to shoots, one-sided buds/blooms	capsid bugs, green, 3–6 mm long, fast moving, suck sap	dimethoate, HCH (BHC)
Large irregular holes in leaves/stems, hollow roots/bulbs, skeletonized leaves	caterpillars, various colours, some hairy	fenitrothion, rotenone, trichlorphon
Irregular small–medium size holes, in leaves, ragged petals	earwigs	carbaryl, HCH (BHC), dimethoate, trichlorphon
White speckling of leaf surface, white 'insects' on under-surface	leafhoppers, like greenfly but hop when disturbed, cast skins are white	bioresmethrin, resmethrin, malathion, rotenone
White winding lines on leaf surface, beige-coloured blisters ditto	leaf-miner, minute grubs feed within tissue of leaf surface	dimethoate
Discoloration of leaves, wilting, slow growth, stickiness present	mealy bug, small insects covered with white fluff, suck sap	malathion, dimethoate, rotenone, spray under strong pressure
Yellow-, grey- or brown-green leaves, withering, slow stunted growth, webbing present, premature leaf fall, wilting	red spider mite on leaf underside, tiny insects needing hand lens to be seen, suck sap	malathion, dimethoate, rotenone
yellowing of leaves, slow stunted growth, stickiness, sooty patches	scale insect, small brown or grey, round or mussel shaped, on bark, under-surface of leaves, suck sap	malathion, dimethoate, diazinon
Large holes in leaves near soil, also in stems and petals, new shoots eaten	slugs and snails	methiocarb, metaldehyde
Semi-circular holes in edges of leaves near soil, plants wilting without cause	vine weevils, small black beetles eat leaves, white larvae plant roots	HCH (BHC)
Plants wilting, mounds of soil appearing	ants, may indicate presence of green fly	bioresmethrin, resmethrin, trichlorphon, chlordane
Plants wilting, dull grey-green leaves, grey coating to leaves, stickiness	whitefly, white, moth-like, tiny, on underside of leaves, suck sap, fly off when disturbed	bioresmethrin, resmethrin, malathion

Common diseases and their treatment

Sympton on plant	Cause	Remedy
Cracking, peeling bark in patches, if affected limb encircled will die	canker, on branches, stems, tree trunks, fungus	clean away diseased bark, and paint wound with sealing compound; cut off dead growth
Fluffy grey mould on leaves, stems, petals, yellowing beneath it, decay following	grey mould (*Botrytis cinerea*), fungus	benomyl
Tips of shoots die back down the stem	die-back, caused by various fungi	cut back to healthy growth, paint large wounds
Yellow toadstools in clusters at base of trunks and stems, tree or shrub dies	honey fungus (*Armillaria mellea*), black strands in soil round plants	destroy dead plants, treat neighbours with soil sterilant
Brown, purple, reddish spots on leaves	leaf-spot, caused by various fungi	remove, and spray plant with thiram or benomyl
White powdery patches on leaves, stems, buds and flowers	powdery mildew stunts and slows growth, fungus	cut off, spray dinocap, benomyl, thiophanate-methyl, propiconazole
Foul-smelling liquid rotting of root, bulb, fruit, black or brown	soft rot, bacterial	destroy affected plant, or cut off diseased part if practicable
Small, raised red-brown blobs on leaf under-surface and stem	rust fungus	carbendazim, mancozeb, propiconazole
Distorted, discoloured leaves/stems, flowers, no insects present	virus diseases	destroy affected plant

Glossary of gardening terms

A

Adventitious Of buds and roots, developing where they would not normally appear.

Aeration Treatment to open up soil and let in air.

Aerial roots Roots from stems above ground, such as ivy.

Aerobic Needing air, as with bacteria in a well aerated compost heap.

Algae Primitive plants, some forming a green film in damp places and on pots.

Alpine Strictly, a mountain plant; loosely, any rock-garden plant.

Annual Plant whose life-cycle is completed within one growing season.

Anther Pollen-producing part of a stamen.

Apex Tip of a stem, from where extension growth proceeds.

Apical bud Bud at the end of a shoot, usually showing apical dominance by inhibiting growth of side-buds.

Axil Upper angle between leaf and stem, from which axillary buds develop.

B

Bacteria Micro-organisms, mostly beneficial, although some cause disease.

Bare-root plant One lifted from ground, not container-grown.

Base dressing Fertilizer applied to the soil before planting or sowing.

Bedding plant One used for temporary display, usually in spring or summer.

Biennial Plant whose life-cycle is completed within two growing seasons.

Blanching Excluding light, to make vegetables such as celery, leeks and chicory more tender and less bitter.

Bleeding Loss of sap from injuries or cuts, often because of late pruning.

Blindness Failure of growing point to develop or of plant to flower.

Bloom Flower. Also a white or bluish coating on fruits or leaves.

Bolting Premature running to flower, usually caused by check to growth.

Bottom heat Warmth from below, in order to encourage rooting.

Bract Modified leaf below a flower stalk or an inflorescence.

Break Growth from axillary bud, occurring naturally or resulting from pinching out the growing tip.

Broadcast Sow seed evenly over the surface instead of in rows or drills.

Bud Embryo shoot or flower(s), usually protected by scales.

Budding Form of grafting, much used for roses and fruit trees, with a single bud as scion.

Bulb Storage organ consisting of an embryo plant enclosed in fleshy leaves or leaf-bases.

Bulbil Small bulb formed on stem or flower-head.

C

Callus Tissue that grows over wounds.

Calcifuge Term applied to plants that cannot thrive in limy soils.

Cambium Actively growing tissue, constantly producing new cells.

Cane Slender stem, woody and often hollow, such as those of raspberries and blackberries, also bamboos.

Cap Hard crust on soil surface, making emergence of seedlings difficult.

Capillary action Upward movement of water through fine channels.

Catch crop Fast maturing crop grown after harvesting one crop and before the same ground is needed for another.

Clamp Store for potatoes and root vegetables, covered with straw and soil against frost.

Chitting Germination of seeds before sowing.

Chlorophyll Green substance in most plants by which carbohydrates are made.

Climber Plant that clings by various means; loosely, any plant with stems trained up or over a support.

Clove Section of a shallot or garlic bulb.

Compost, garden Organic matter processed by means of a compost heap (see page 183).

Compost, seed and potting Mixture of ingredients for raising and potting plants (see page 219).

Cordon Trained form restricted by spur pruning to a single main stem.

Corm Storage organ formed from a thickened stem-base.

Corymb More or less flat-topped inflorescence with outer flowers opening first.

Cotyledon Seed leaf, usually first to appear after germination, but sometimes remaining underground.

Crown Basal part of a herbaceous perennial from which roots and shoots develop; also main branches of a tree.

Cultivar Term – from the words cultivated variety – for plant with distinctive characteristics maintained in cultivation.

Curd Head of cauliflower or broccoli formed of massed flower-buds.

Cutting Portion removed from a plant

for propagation (see pages 192–5).

Cyme Inflorescence in which growing points end in a flower, with successive blooms borne on a succession of side stems.

D

Damping down Wetting floors and benches of greenhouses to increase humidity of the air.

Damping off Disease attacking seedlings soon after germination.

Dead-heading Removing faded blooms to stop seeding and produce more flowers.

Dibber Blunt pointed tool for making planting holes.

Disbud Remove unwanted buds to channel growth into remaining ones.

Drawn Weak and spindly through overcrowding and/or poor light.

Dressing Material applied to the soil.

Drill Shallow furrow for sowing seeds.

E

Earthing up Drawing up soil round plants to exclude light.

Espalier (Support for) trained tree with a vertical trunk and horizontal branches in tiers.

Evergreen Plant that bears foliage all the year round.

Eye Dormant growth bud.

F

Falls Outer perianth segments of an iris flower.

Fan Tree with branches trained like ribs of a fan to a support.

Fertilizer Material, organic or inorganic, that supplies plant food.

Floret Individual flower forming part of a head or cluster.

Flushes Successive production of flowers and fruit, as with some roses and strawberries.

Forcing Speeding growth by such means as giving warmth and excluding light.

Friable Crumbly and easily worked.

Fruit bud Bud producing fruit blossom.

Fungicide Substance applied to prevent or control disease caused by fungus.

G

Genus Botanical term for group of related species. (Plural *genera*.)

Germination Starting of seeds into growth.

Grafting Uniting one plant (the scion) with another (the rootstock) for propagation and/or controlling growth.

Ground cover Plants that clothe the ground and discourage weeds.

Growth bud Bud producing shoot growth.

Growing point Tip of shoot or root.

H

Half-hardy Suitable for growing outdoors during summer but unlikely to survive winter cold unprotected.

Half-standard Tree with three to four feet (90–120 cm) of clear main stem.

Hardening off Acclimatizing plants grown in warmth to colder conditions.

Hardy Able to survive winter cold outdoors without protection.

Heeling in Placing plants in a trench and covering roots with soil till weather is suitable for planting.

Herbaceous Without woody stems.

Humus Dark brown product of decomposed organic matter.

Hybrid Plant derived from crossing different species or variants.

I

Inflorescence The part of a plant bearing one or many flowers.

Inorganic Not vegetable or animal in origin; not containing carbon.

Insecticide Substance to control insects and similar pests.

Internode Part of stem between nodes.

J

June drop Natural thinning by fall of immature fruitlets.

Juvenile Of young growth, sometimes different from that of adult stage.

L

Lateral Side-shoot growing out from a main stem.

Layering Propagation by rooting stems still attached to the parent plant.

Leader Extension shoot continuing the forward growth of a branch.

Loam Soil consisting of a well balanced mixture of clay, sand and humus, rich in nutrients.

M

Maiden One year old tree or shrub.

Manure Bulky material, including animal residues, added to soil to improve structure and fertility.

Mulch Surface layer, usually of organic matter, spread around plants.

Mutant Variant plant, or part of plant, resulting from genetic change.

N

Naturalizing Establishing plants where they thrive and increase with little or no attention.

Node Stem joint where a leaf or leaf-bud appears.

O

Offset Plantlet produced around base of parent plant (see page 197).

Organic Term usually applied to matter derived from decayed animal and/or vegetable substances.

Oxygenator Aquatic plant that emits oxygen into the water.

P

Pan Hard layer in soil, natural or caused by cultivation.

Panicle Branched inflorescence, strictly one composed of racemes.

Perennial Having a possible life-span of at least three seasons.

Pesticide Substance to control pests.

pH Measure of acidity or alkalinity. Below 7 is acid, above 7 alkaline.

Pinching or **Stopping** Removal of the growing point of a shoot.

Plunge Sink container-grown plant to its rim in sand, ashes or peat, to protect against drying out and temperature fluctuations.

Pricking out First transplanting of seedlings (see page 198).

R

Raceme Unbranched inflorescence with stalked flowers.

Rhizome Horizontal, usually underground, stem that forms a storage organ producing roots and shoots.

Rootball Soil or compost around roots, especially of container-grown plants.

Root cutting Piece of root used for propagation (see page 194).

Rootstock Plant on which another is grafted or budded.

Rose Perforated attachment for a watering can or hose.

Runner Rooting stem growing along the ground (see page 197).

S

Scarifying Thorough raking of the lawn to remove debris and matted growth.

Scion Shoot or bud of one plant grafted on rootstock of another.

Seed leaf Same as **Cotyledon**.

Spike Inflorescence with stalkless flowers along an unbranched axis.

Spit One spade's depth of soil.

Sport Same as **Mutant**.

Spur Short branchlet on fruit tree bearing flower buds.

Standard Tree with between five and seven feet (1.5–2.1 m) of clear stem.

Stolon Creeping stem producing new shoot and root growth at its tip.

Stopping See **Pinching**.

Strike Of cuttings, to take root.

Sub-lateral Side-shoot growing from a lateral.

Sucker Shoot arising from underground parts of a plant.

T

Tender Liable to be killed or damaged by cold if grown in the open.

Terminal Endmost, applied mainly to a bud, shoot or flower.

Thatch Of lawns, matted surface layer, impeding growth of finer grasses.

Tilth Crumbly surface of soil, in preparation for sowing seed.

Top dressing A dressing applied to the surface of the soil or compost.

Top fruit Term used for fruit produced on trees, or for the trees themselves.

Transpiration Exhalation of water vapour through leaves and stems.

Trace elements Elements essential to plant growth but needed only in very small quantities.

Truss Term used for a cluster of flowers or fruit.

Tuber Thickened root or underground shoot forming a storage organ.

U

Umbel Inflorescence in which individual flower stalks originate at the same point.

Union Point on a grafted plant where rootstock and scion have joined.

V

Variety Naturally occurring variant of a species.

Vegetative propagation Method of producing plants by means other than from seed.

W

Weed A plant growing where it is not wanted.

X

Xeropyte Plant that can withstand dry conditions for long periods.

Index

A

Abelia × grandiflora 142
Acacia
  dealbata 34; false 81
Acantholimon glumaceum 120
Acanthus spinosus 131
Acer
  davidii 162; griseum 162; grosseri 162;
    negundo 50; opalus 50; palmatum 153;
    platanoides 65, 152
Achillea
  argentea 105; aurea 105; 'Coronation
    Gold' 12, 102; 'King Edward' 105;
    'Moonshine' 102; ptarmica 102;
    tomentosa 105; umbellata 120
Achimenes 107, 123
Acidanthera bicolor (see Gladiolus
  callianthus)
Aconite 36, 44, 148
Aconitum
  anglicum 102; × bicolor 116
Acorus calamus 21
Adam's needle 114
Adonis vernalis 68
Aechmea fasciata 136
Aesculus
  flava 152; hippocastanum 81, 98; indica
    99; parviflora 112
Aethionema 21, 86
African violet 59, 123, 165, 173
Agapanthus 12, 17, 21, 131
Ageratum 108
Agrostemma Milas 73
Ajuga reptans 105
Akebia × pentaphylla 21
Alchemilla mollis 21, 102
Alder 50
Alder buckthorn 153
Algae 109
Allium 85
  cernuum 103; karataviense 103;
    moly 103; oreophilum 103;
    schubertii 103
Allotments 26
Almond 21, 65
Alnus
  orientalis 50; serrulata 50
Alpines 21, 109, 174
Alstroemeria
  aurantiaca 116; ligtu 116
Alyssum (now Aurinia) 71, 76
  maritimum 118; saxatile 71

Amaryllis belladonna 146
Amelanchier lamarckii 65, 152
Anaphalis triplinervis 17
Anchusa azurea 21, 46, 83
Androsace 21
  primuloides 86; pyrenaica 75;
    strigillosa 75; vandellii 75
Anemone
  apennina 70; blanda 58; coronaria 70;
    de Caen 17, 47, 70; Japanese 46;
    nemorosa 58; St Brigid 47, 70
Angelica tree 128
Antennaria
  aprica 105; dioica 105
Anthemis
  biebersteinii 105; E. C. Buxton 102;
    tinctoria 102
Anthericum liliago 102
Anthurium scherzerianum 123
Aphelandra squarrosa 91
Antirrhinum 108, 149
Aponogeton distachyus 21, 88
Apple (see also Malus)
  dwarf rootstocks 28; cordon and
    espalier 203; 'May Queen' 29;
    'St Edmund's Pippin' 134; storing
    225; test of ripeness 123
Apricot 28, 65, 123
April 63–77
Aquilegia 21, 83, 101, 102
Arabis caucasica (albida) 21, 55, 71
Aralia elata 128
Arbutus 92
  andrachne 162; unedo 154;
    × andrachnoides 162
Arctostaphylos 21
Arctotis 108
Arenaria
  balearica 105; montana 105
Armeria
  juniperifolia 86; maritima 86;
    plantaginea 102
Aruncus dioicus 102
Artichoke, globe 26, 122, 123
Asclepias speciosa 131
Ash 81, 142, 152
Asparagus 26, 89, 159
Asperula
  gussonii 120; nitida 120
Asphodeline lutea 102
Asphodelus albus 102
Aster (see also Michaelmas daisy)

acris 17, 108; alpinus 134; dumosus 12;
  grandiflorus 164; novae-belgii 144;
  'Professor A. Kippenburg' 145;
  thomsonii 17, 131; × frikartii 131
Astilbe
  chinensis 120; 'Federsee' 121;
  glaberrima 120
Astrantia maxima 102
Aubergine 61, 109, 136
Aubretia deltoidea 71, 86, 109
Aucuba 162, 170
August 127–139
Aurinia (see Alyssum)
Autumn foliage 152–153, 168
Azalea, many hybrids 66, 67, 80
  pontica (see Rhododendron luteum)
Azara
  browneae 52; integrifolia 52;
    microphylla 52; 'Variegata' 52

B

Ballota pseudodictamnus 172
Bamboo 114
Baptisia 21
Bark, attractive 162, 170
Basil 136
Beans
  broad 47, 61; french 93, 109;
    runner 93, 109
Bee balm 117
Bees 95
Beetroot 25, 61, 139
Begonia 25, 39. 93, 165
  semperflorens 137
Bellis perennis 69, 83
Beloperone guttata 123
Berberidopsis corallina 130
Berberis
  'Atropurpurea Nana' 17; Bunch
    o'Grapes 171; darwinii 66, 67;
    linearifolia 50, 66, 67; lologensis 67;
    stenophylla 67; thunbergii 17, 152,
    162; wilsoniae 152
Bergamot 117, 136
Bergenia 21, 35
  'Morning Blush' (Morgenrote) 68;
    purpurascens 17
Betula pendula 152
Birch 42, 152
Bird cherry 65
Blackberry 147, 149, 175